# Outcomes of University Spanish Heritage Language Instruction in the United States

**Related Works**

*Innovative Strategies for Heritage Language Teaching*
Marta Fairclough and Sara M. Beaudrie, Editors

*The Changing Landscape of Spanish Language Curricula*
Alan V. Brown and Gregory L. Thompson

*El español y la lingüística aplicada*
Robert J. Blake y Eve C. Zyzik

*Sociolingüística y pragmática del español, segunda edición*
Carmen Silva-Corvalán y Andrés Enrique-Arias

*Spanish as a Heritage Language in the United States*
Sara M. Beaudrie and Marta Fairclough, Editors

# Outcomes of University Spanish Heritage Language Instruction in the United States

MELISSA A. BOWLES, EDITOR

GEORGETOWN UNIVERSITY PRESS / WASHINGTON, DC

Library of Congress Cataloging-in-Publication Data

Names: Bowles, Melissa A., editor.
Title: Outcomes of university Spanish heritage language instruction in the United States / Melissa A. Bowles, editor.
Other titles: Georgetown studies in Spanish linguistics.
Description: Washington, DC : Georgetown University Press, 2022. | Series: Georgetown studies in Spanish linguistics | Includes bibliographical references and index.
Identifiers: LCCN 2021018412 | ISBN 9781647122225 (hardcover) | ISBN 9781647122232 (paperback) | ISBN 9781647122249 (ebook)
Subjects: LCSH: Spanish language—Study and teaching (Higher)—United States. | Heritage language speakers.
Classification: LCC PC4068.U5 O88 2022 | DDC 468.0071/173—dc23
LC record available at https://lccn.loc.gov/2021018412

23 22 9 8 7 6 5 4 3 2 First printing

Printed in the United States of America

Cover design by Erin Kirk. Cover image courtesy of Adobe Stock/Tupungato
Interior design by BookComp, Inc.

# Contents

# Illustrations

## Figures



## Tables

# Acknowledgments

This volume is the result of the hard work of many talented people. First and foremost, I thank all of the contributors whose scholarship is included. Without you, the project could not have taken shape.

My heartfelt thanks also go to the friends and colleagues who generously reviewed chapters and whose feedback greatly improved the manuscript: Sergio Adrada-Rafael, Clara Burgo, Cecilia Colombi, Cynthia Ducar, Anne Edstrom, Rebecca Foote, Alberta Gatti, Florencia Henshaw, Ron Leow, Patricia MacGregor-Mendoza, Glenn Martínez, Kim Potowski, Rebecca Sachs, Ana Sánchez Muñoz, Kelly Torres, Paul Toth, Laura Walls, and Eve Zyzik.

At Georgetown University Press, I have been fortunate to work with Hope LeGro and Clara Totten, with whom I began discussions when this volume was just a seed of an idea at the American Association of Applied Linguistics (AAAL) Conference in 2017 in Portland. I thank them and series editor John Lipski for their thoughtful comments, feedback, and guidance throughout the publication process, as well as the anonymous reviewers.

I would be remiss if I did not acknowledge the support of the University of Illinois at Urbana-Champaign's Campus Research Board (Award RB19101), which provided subvention funds. Finally, I owe a debt of gratitude to my research assistant, Kara Yarrington, for her astute attention to detail with copyediting and the nuances of Chicago Style.

**INTRODUCTION**

# Why and How to Examine Outcomes of Heritage Language Instruction

*Melissa A. Bowles*
University of Illinois at Urbana-Champaign

Heritage languages include minority languages, which are spoken by a minority of the population, as well as minoritized languages, which are marginalized and discriminated against. In the context of the United States (US), any language other than English is considered a heritage/minority language, and there are more than 350 minority languages spoken. They therefore include Indigenous languages such as Navajo, Hawaiian, and Yupik as well as immigrant languages such as Spanish, Chinese, Russian, Arabic, and Tagalog (Cummins 1995; de Bot and Gorter 1995; Fishman 2001). Often, a language is both spoken by less than half of the population (i.e., it is a minority language) and it is minoritized, though this is not always the case.

According to the most recent American Community Survey data from 2017, 64.22 million of 301.15 million respondents, or 21.3 percent of the US population, reported speaking a language other than English at home (US Census 2017). A wide array of languages is represented, showcasing the linguistic diversity of twenty-first-century America. The overwhelming majority, 61.9 percent (39.77 million respondents) spoke Spanish, making it by far the most widely spoken heritage language in the country.[1] By way of comparison, the next most widely spoken heritage language was Chinese, with 3.27 million speakers (amounting to slightly more than 5 percent of the total). Despite being spoken by a majority of speakers in some areas of the United States, Spanish on a national level is both a minority language and a minoritized language (Potowski 2018, 2).

Many Spanish speakers in the US are immigrants who brought Spanish with them from their countries of origin, but the statistics also show that 53 percent of the Spanish speakers in the US are not immigrants but rather were born in the US. Based on current trends, US Census estimates place the US as the most populous Spanish-speaking country by the year 2050, when it is projected that there will be more than 130 million Spanish speakers.

A 2017 report from the American Academy of Arts and Sciences, commissioned by a bipartisan group of eight members of the US Congress, "examine[d] the nation's current capacity in languages and recommend[ed] actions to ensure excellence in all languages as well as international education and research" (American Academy of Arts and Sciences vii). The result was "a national strategy to improve access to as many languages as possible for people of every region, ethnicity, and socioeconomic background—that is, to value language education as a persistent national need similar to education in math or English, and to ensure that a useful level of proficiency is within every student's reach" (viii). The goal is therefore for children raised in English-speaking households to gain meaningful proficiency in at least one other language through education and study abroad opportunities and for children from households where languages other than English are spoken to build on their abilities in that language. The report documents that more than three-quarters (75.5 percent) of US adults who describe themselves as "fluent" in a language other than English learned that language in their "childhood home" (23), meaning that they are heritage speakers. Based on that finding, it is perhaps not surprising that of the five key recommendations elaborated in the report, three were related to heritage languages. These were (1) to work with local heritage language community partners to create in-school and after-school instructional opportunities, (2) to support heritage languages and encourage their transmission to future generations, and (3) to provide support for curricula and programs in Native American languages.

A testament to the explosion of interest in heritage languages can be seen in the creation of the National Heritage Language Research Center, a Title VI center funded by the US government, and the publication of the *Heritage Language Journal*, a peer-reviewed journal dedicated to the topic, which has been published three times a year since it was founded in 2002. In addition, in just the last seven years, nine books (six edited volumes [Beaudrie and Fairclough 2012; Fairclough and Beaudrie 2016; Kagan, Carreira, and Chik 2017; Pascual y Cabo 2016; Potowski 2018; Zapata and Lacorte 2018] and three single- or multiauthored manuscripts [Beaudrie, Ducar, and Potowski 2014; Montrul 2015; Polinsky 2018]) have been published by academic presses on the topic of heritage languages, and several recent special issues of peer-reviewed journals have also been dedicated to the topics of minority/heritage languages in that time period, in such high-profile venues as *Studies in Second Language Acquisition* and the *International Journal of Bilingualism.*

There has been particular growth in research on Spanish as a heritage language, which has led to the annual convening of a conference dedicated to the topic, the Symposium on Spanish as a Heritage Language, since 2014, and the founding of a peer-reviewed journal with the University of Florida Press titled *Spanish as a Heritage Language* in 2019.

Research on heritage languages to date has focused on a range of issues, including language policy and identity, descriptive studies of heritage speaker profiles, and sociocultural factors in language maintenance (Brinton, Kagan, and Bauckus 2008). Theoretical linguists have also begun to research aspects of such speakers' minority language grammars for the contributions they make to long-standing debates about necessary and sufficient conditions for language acquisition (Benmamoun, Montrul, and Polinsky 2013).

However, despite the growing amount of research from different perspectives on heritage speaker populations around the world, few studies have examined the *outcomes* of classroom teaching of minority languages (Bowles 2018; Bowles and Torres 2021; Montrul and Bowles 2017). According to Maria Carreira and Olga Kagan (2018), "That HL learners' language pedagogical needs differ from those of second language (L2) learners has been the central tenet of the field from its inception. However, the precise nature of these needs and what they mean for instruction have started to come into focus only recently" (155). I have argued elsewhere (Bowles 2018) that instructed heritage language acquisition (IHLA) should be a field in its own right and that only through systematic research will it be possible to determine what instructional methods are most effective for heritage learners.

This volume is a step in that direction, a collection of empirical studies on the outcomes of Spanish heritage language instruction at the university level in the United States. To my knowledge, there is only one other collection of data-based studies on outcomes of instruction in a heritage language (Zapata and Lacorte 2018), and it is focused on the impact of one specific pedagogical framework—the multiliteracies framework—at the university level with heritage learners of Spanish. Therefore, the current volume is the first of its kind, and its focus is Spanish, the most widely spoken (and taught) heritage language in the United States (Potowski 2018). Studies at the university level were chosen because, as with second language acquisition research (Norris and Ortega 2000), the lion's share of heritage language research so far has been conducted with university-level learners (Bowles and Torres 2021). Focusing on one heritage language being taught at the postsecondary level makes the volume more impactful than if it covered a range of languages and instructional levels, since it enables more robust generalizations to be made. In this book, the term *outcomes* is used to refer not just to the learning gains that are made as a result of heritage language instruction (chapters 1, 2, 3, and 5) but also to how instruction impacts learners' processing (chapter 4) and attitudes (chapters 6, 7, and 9), as well as unintended consequences it may have, as in the case of Latinx student retention (chapter 8).

Specifically, this volume addresses how receiving instruction in their heritage language affects Spanish speakers on multiple levels. Because bilingualism is not just a cognitive, but also a social, phenomenon, the studies in the volume encompass morphosyntactic, affective, attitudinal, social, and academic outcomes of heritage language instruction, with part I containing five empirical studies focusing mainly on morphosyntactic outcomes and part II containing four studies focusing primarily on social and educational outcomes. Admittedly, it is impossible to completely separate or dissociate linguistic form from social and educational issues and outcomes, since factors such as the sociopolitical context, attitudes, and identities are interrelated and inextricably linked to language. Nevertheless, each study is placed in either part I or part II according to its principal focus. This categorization is not intended to imply that studies in part I have no bearing on social or educational outcomes or that studies in part II have no bearing on morphosyntactic outcomes. Indeed, there are often intersections, as pointed out by the authors. For instance, the primary focus of Chomón Zamora's chapter is how heritage learners process feedback on morphosyntax that varies in explicitness. Therefore, it is in the morphosyntactic outcomes section, but in the discussion the author raises socioaffective issues that arose from learners' think-aloud comments. Similarly, Prada and Pascual y Cabo's chapter 8 is in the social and educational outcomes section because its primary focus is on how enrollment in a Spanish for heritage learners program impacts college retention. Nevertheless, it touches on some of the linguistic aspects of the course that contribute to its efficacy.

## Part I: Morphosyntactic Outcomes

In part I, all of the studies relate to the role of explicit or implicit instruction in heritage language acquisition. This distinction between explicit and implicit instruction comes from the sister field of second language acquisition, where scores of studies have been conducted to investigate whether one type is superior to the other in learning gains. A widely accepted definition of explicit instruction, from John Norris and Lourdes Ortega (2001), is that instruction is "considered to be *explicit* if rule explanation comprise[s] any part of the instruction (in this first sense, explicit designates deductive and metalinguistic) or if learners [are] directly asked to attend to particular forms and to try to arrive at metalinguistic generalizations on their own (in this second sense, explicit designates explicit induction). When neither rule presentation nor directions to attend to particular forms [are] part of a treatment, that treatment was considered *implicit*" (167). Limited prior research suggests that explicit instruction may be more beneficial for college-age heritage learners (e.g., Bowles 2018; Bowles and Torres 2021; Montrul and Bowles 2017; Potowski, Jegerski, and Morgan-Short 2009), but it remains an important empirical question whether it is uniformly true or whether implicit instruction is preferable for some language domains or for some learners, and to what extent the type of assessment being used to measure gains favors one type of instruction over another.

To this end, in chapter 1, Julio Torres investigates how learners perform on oral and written assessments before and after receiving task-based instruction on the subjunctive in adjectival clauses. It is the first study to my knowledge to examine how heritage learners' performance as a result of instruction is affected by the modality of the assessment being used. His results show that learners made clear gains as a result of instruction, which were largely maintained at the time of the delayed posttest two weeks later, but these gains were not uniform; instead, they varied by modality. Specifically, learners scored higher on oral posttests than on written ones, despite the fact that the instruction gave them practice using the structure in both speech and in writing. This finding has important implications for researchers, since it suggests that the modality of the assessment used to measure learning gains may affect the results. It also has direct relevance for the heritage language (HL) classroom, reinforcing the need for opportunities to use the language in both modalities and stressing that just because learners can produce something in speech, they do not necessarily exert that same control in writing.

In chapter 2, Sara M. Beaudrie and Bonnie C. Holmes compare the effects of three types of instruction—explicit deductive, explicit inductive, and implicit textual enhancement—to a tests-only control group on production and recognition of preterit and imperfect forms. Their study is unique in two ways: (1) it tests receptive bilinguals, a group that is so largely underresearched that it has been called "the most neglected category" of heritage learners (Carreira and Kagan 2018, 158), and (2) it does so by using computerized instructional materials that learners work through at their own pace, as they do in many hybrid/flipped language courses. Their findings partially supported their predictions that both explicit groups would outperform the implicit group and the control, though gains varied according to which structure was being tested and with which assessment. Their results add to the base of research, suggesting that explicit instructional treatments help to orient heritage learners toward form and tend to be more effective than implicit ones. They also suggest that computerized modules, like those used in hybrid/flipped classrooms with second language learners, could be beneficial in heritage classrooms, freeing in-class time for purposes other than grammar instruction.

In chapter 3, Adrián Bello-Uriarte examines the effects that a one-semester Spanish heritage writing course has on learners' writing in Spanish, as measured by pre-/posttest comparisons on metrics of accuracy. It is a follow-up to Bowles and Bello-Uriarte (2019), incorporating both a larger sample of learners and examining both global measures of accuracy (percentage of error-free t-units) and measures targeting specific structures covered in the course (the use of periphrastic 'a' and the use of gerunds and infinitives). Results of Bowles and Bello-Uriarte (2019) indicated that instruction had a positive impact on the instructed group, which improved in fluency and lexical sophistication, whereas the uninstructed control group made no significant gains in any measure. However, instruction did not lead to significant improvement in *all* measures or dimensions of writing; specifically, instructed learners' writing was not significantly different after the semester-long course than before in terms of complexity, overall accuracy, lexical density, or lexical diversity. These findings are in line with those in first language (L1) and second language (L2) writing, which have also showed gradual, modest gains as a result of instruction, and they set realistic expectations for instructors, who might otherwise want learners to improve in all dimensions simultaneously. Regarding accuracy, results showed that instruction did not contribute to a significant reduction of the total number of errors produced by the instructed group. However, Bello-Uriarte's chapter proved that the lack of change in overall error rate obscures specific accuracy gains, namely, that the instructed group significantly outperformed the control group, improving their accuracy in the use of 'a' in verbal periphrasis in their writing. Although trends indicated that instructed learners also reduced their use of the gerund in contexts in which the infinitive was required, a comparison between the pretest and posttest was not possible due to individual variation. Only a few participants used the gerund in their essays, and those who did, did not necessarily use the form in both essays, making comparisons impossible.

In chapter 4 Celia Chomón Zamora uses think-alouds to investigate how heritage learners process instruction that contains more and less explicit feedback. It is the first published study to my knowledge to examine how heritage learners process components of instruction. Rather than looking (only) at learners' pre/posttest gains, Chomón Zamora studies the intermediate step, learners' processing. Although her focus is on heritage learners, she also compares the processing strategies to those of second language learners to highlight salient differences. Specifically, she finds that heritage learners process more deeply and have higher retention of the target form when they make connections between the instruction and some prior knowledge related to their cultural background or experience (e.g., language they have seen in the Bible, the way relatives talked about Cuba). On the other hand, second language learners tended to make reference to prior grammar instruction, and this was linked to higher posttest scores for them. Chomón Zamora's results imply that grammar instruction can have a lasting impact on heritage learners, but that it is most effective if they can link it to their own lived experience.

In chapter 5, Sara Fernández Cuenca and Melissa Bowles compare a tests-only control group to groups of learners who received either explicit or implicit instruction on adjectival clauses requiring the subjunctive or indicative. They delve further into the question of how the type of assessment impacts the results that are obtained as a result of instruction and to my knowledge are the first to explore how explicit or implicit instruction affects explicit or implicit linguistic knowledge, with explicit knowledge measured through a bimodal acceptability judgment task and implicit knowledge measured through an elicited imitation task. They find that at the time of the delayed posttest, the explicitly instructed group outperformed the implicitly instructed group and the control in both the explicit and implicit knowledge tasks.

Readers may be surprised at the results from the chapters in part I, since overall they point to some advantages for explicit, over implicit, instruction for heritage learners. This conclusion would seem to run counter to the observation that explicit grammar instruction can cause frustration, consternation, and even confusion for heritage learners. However, these two findings are not necessarily contradictory at all; rather, the broad umbrella heading of *explicit instruction* is being used to refer to very different instructional practices in the two cases, as explained below.

## Explicit Instruction: What It Is (and Is Not)

It is important to note that all explicit instruction is not created equal. Indeed, the term *explicit instruction* often conjures up images of traditional pedagogies based on mechanical drills, repetition, and using language in isolation, as in discrete fill-in-the-blanks that are unrelated to any communicative goal. Such pedagogical practices would indeed be considered explicit, because they involve rule presentation, but they would also further be categorized as focus on forms (plural) because their primary emphasis is on linguistic structures. In fact, activities in focus on forms classrooms tend to have been created with the purpose of practicing a linguistic structure or set of structures, as characterized by the present, practice, produce (PPP) method of teaching. For instance, a typical focus on forms activity might consist of having students fill in blanks with future tense forms of verbs provided in parenthesis. In such activities, students do not even need to understand the meaning being conveyed (or sometimes even read the entire sentence) in order to successfully complete the task. Rather, they can blindly conjugate verbs according to a chart or paradigm that was provided to them without any regard for meaning. These are the sorts of activities the learners in chapter 6, Vergara Wilson's chapter, describe having done in their prior (non-heritage) Spanish coursework. Such focus on forms approaches can be contrasted with focus on form (singular) approaches, which consist of primarily meaning–focused interaction in which there is brief attention to linguistic forms. Focus on form assumes that acquisition occurs best when learners' attention is drawn to particular linguistic structures when they are needed for communication, and focus on form can include either attention to a structure that is planned in advance or attention that is spontaneous and occurs in reaction to a linguistic need that comes up in the course of communication (e.g., when a learner does not have the language form s/he needs to communicate the desired meaning in conversation). Input flood, input enhancement, and corrective feedback are all types of focus on form. Focus on form techniques by definition cannot be decontextualized or rote.

Extensive research has convincingly demonstrated that focus on form techniques are more effective than focus on *forms* techniques for second language learners (Loewen 2015), and all of the studies in part I of this volume involve the former, rather than the latter. Therefore, claims made regarding explicit instruction (or aspects thereof) in this volume must be understood in that light. It should be stressed that focus on form techniques are consistent with pedagogical recommendations for teaching grammar to heritage learners, and readers are referred to chapter 8 of Sara Beaudrie, Cynthia Ducar, and Kim Potowski (2014) for an excellent discussion of ways to implement focus on form in heritage classrooms. Indeed, when Maria Carreira describes top-down (macro) approaches to heritage language teaching in the afterword, she indicates they are "characterized by the use of real-world language at the onset of instruction, with grammar taking a supporting role as needed to engage with authentic language" (212). Such methods are prototypical examples of focus on form.

With this background in mind, I return to the question of how the findings in part I can be reconciled with observations that explicit instruction can confuse heritage learners. My answer is that the term *explicit instruction* is likely being used to mean two different things. In the studies in part I, *explicit instruction* refers to focus on form techniques and these are shown to be effective. Anecdotal evidence about disadvantages of explicit instruction probably refers not to brief attention to form in the context of meaningful communication but rather to focus on forms (plural) approaches that are all too common in many language classrooms, L2, and heritage alike (see also Vergara Wilson, chapter 6 in this volume).

## Part II: Social and Educational Outcomes

Whereas part I of the book focuses on how instruction affects the development of specific morphosyntactic features, part II encompasses studies that examine a range of other impacts that heritage language instruction has. Therefore, all of the studies relate to the central question of what social and educational outcomes Spanish heritage language instruction has on university-level learners, though each chapter does so in its own way.

In chapter 6, Damián Vergara Wilson investigates students' perspectives of their learning in Spanish as a heritage language courses, especially compared to prior (non-heritage) courses they have taken. Like Beaudrie and Holmes, his population of learners consists of receptive bilinguals from the US Southwest, and his qualitative study reveals that his learners, who placed into a beginning-level course, had seemingly contradictory views of their past courses, which involved extensive rote memorization and "worksheets" (which we can safely assume from the descriptions can be classified as focus on forms techniques, rather than the focus on form techniques investigated in the chapters in part I). Some participants described them with such comments as "[we] never really did anything" (136), but a significant number then referred to the past classes, rather than to their experiences in their homes and communities, as being where they had "learned the most Spanish" prior to joining the university. This perception belies, perhaps, a narrow definition on their part of what "learning" is, something formal that is done in a classroom and not at home. The participants found the heritage course to be more communicative, group-oriented, and less teacher-fronted, and they expressed that the course had forced them to use their Spanish, particularly in speaking, something they were initially apprehensive about but became more comfortable with over time.

In chapter 7, Claudia Holguín Mendoza reports on another qualitative study examining heritage learners' awareness of stigmatized Spanish language forms and attitudes toward such forms before and after either one or two semesters of Spanish as a heritage language, taught in a critical language awareness approach. This study is important because there have only been two published studies to date (Beaudrie, Amezcua, and Loza 2019; Holguín Mendoza 2018) that have examined the effects of critical language awareness pedagogy on heritage learners. Despite the approach's popularity, the lack of such studies means there is scant empirical evidence on how this approach impacts learners. Holguín Mendoza's results show that learners were largely unaware of stigmatized forms at the outset of the course and that awareness did not develop quickly, with changes being noticeable only after two semesters of instruction. She also found that learners slowly began to question notions they had held for a long time about such things as the perceived inappropriateness of code-switching and "Spanglish" and started to understand that they could use such language strategically. Results suggest that critical language awareness approaches can improve awareness of language form and stigmatization, though it may take more than one semester to see gains.

Readers may wonder how the findings in the studies in part I, which all deal with teaching morphosyntactic features of standard Spanish, dovetail with Vergara Wilson and Holguín Mendoza's chapters, which emphasize the importance of home/local varieties of Spanish in the classroom and an understanding of the power structures inherent in language. At first blush, these studies might seem to be at odds with each other, but they actually are not. Goals for heritage language instruction, as outlined by Valdés (1995), include (among others) the development of a prestige language variety and the development of positive attitudes toward the heritage language, including its dialects and its cultures. In order for heritage learners to develop or acquire a prestige variety (the first goal), it is important for them to build on the home/local variety that they bring to the classroom. In order to understand and appreciate language variation and dialects, learners benefit from exposure to sociolinguistics concepts as part of critical language awareness. They learn that although no dialect is "better" than any other, society makes judgments based on language use. Successful heritage language instruction should empower learners to have choices in their linguistic repertoire and to make informed decisions about where and with whom to use which forms. As Glenn Martínez (2003, 53) states,

> If our students walk into the class saying *haiga* and walk out saying *haya*, there has been, in my estimation, no value added. However, if they walk in saying *haiga* and walk out saying either *haya* or *haiga* **and** having the ability to defend their use of *haiga* if and when they see fit, then there has been value added. It is critical that we strive to allow students to develop this type of sociolinguistic sophistication in our endeavors as SHL educators" (italic and bold emphasis in original text).

Across all of the chapters in this volume, the authors take a sociolinguistically informed approach, which never seeks to eradicate or replace a home variety but rather to expand upon it.

In chapter 8 Josh Prada and Diego Pascual y Cabo undertake a first-of-its-kind case study, finding that Latinx students who were enrolled in one or more semesters of university heritage Spanish at their institution had substantially higher retention rates than Latinx students not enrolled in the program. Using data from open-ended interviews with a subset of students, the authors highlight features of the program that they believe (and that research has shown) are correlated with increased retention rates. Their data show that in an inclusive SHL environment that values learners' experiences, home varieties, and cultures, students feel a sense of community and support that is unavailable elsewhere on campus. They conclude by indicating that such positive, unintended consequences could help faculty in making their case for heritage language programs (and Spanish in particular) to deans and other university administrators.

Finally, in chapter 9, Florencia Henshaw examines students' attitudes toward being enrolled in mixed versus heritage-tailored courses. It is novel in that it examines the attitudes of both heritage and L2 learners in mixed courses; does so at the intermediate level, which has been understudied compared to lower- and higher-level courses; and investigates the role that prior coursework has on learner perceptions. Studies of this type are extremely important because even in universities that do have separate courses or even tracks for heritage learners of Spanish, the two types of learners are almost always together in mixed-, intermediate-, or advanced-level content courses (Beaudrie 2011, 2012; Carreira and Kagan 2018). Henshaw's results showed that experience mattered; heritage learners who had never taken a tailored course were happy with mixed courses, whereas those who had taken a tailored course preferred separate, rather than mixed, courses. Henshaw's findings therefore help to understand why some of the past research on mixed classes found seemingly contradictory results and also delve into learner perceptions not just at the curricular level but also at an individual level (in terms of their attitudes toward working with a heritage or L2 partner in paired and small-group activities). Henshaw's results call into question previous studies' positive findings regarding mixed classrooms, suggesting that in cases where heritage-tailored classes cannot be offered, differentiated instruction is particularly important. See Carreira and Claire Hitchins Chik (2018) for further information about providing differentiated instruction to heritage learners.

Both Henshaw's chapter and Vergara Wilson's chapter highlight the importance of student voice and past experience in heritage language instruction. Students in Vergara Wilson's first-level SHL class came in expecting the sort of instruction they had been exposed to in the past, the only kind of language instruction they knew. Over the course of the semester, they came to see that they could become much more confident in speaking Spanish through an approach that values the funds of knowledge they bring to the classroom. In Henshaw's chapter, both heritage and L2 learners' questionnaire responses showed that their past experiences with grades, tests, and teachers' different standards based on their linguistic background impacted their desire to work with a heritage or L2 peer. Those who had never taken a class for heritage speakers did not have expectations for such a class and were happy to enroll in mixed classes, whereas those who had taken a heritage class preferred it. Heritage learners do not come to our university classes as blank slates: they not only bring with them the linguistic knowledge they acquired in their homes and communities; they also bring with them a lifetime of experiences in social and educational settings, many of which may have caused them to have negative associations with their heritage language. We must remember that and make every effort to ensure that they have the opportunity to share their experiences and concerns with us. If we want to be successful in heritage language teaching, we cannot only think of the language in terms of linguistic features, but rather we must be aware of the rich, multifaceted nature of the heritage learning endeavor and all that it entails for learners—not just words but attitudes, identities, and emotional connections.

## Moving Forward: Future Directions

As outlined in the previous sections, this book breaks new ground, but this is just the beginning of what promises to be a very productive line of inquiry for decades to come. It is my hope that the studies in this volume will spark further research into the ways that heritage language instruction impacts learners, not just of Spanish at the university level but at elementary, middle, and high school levels, as well as in community/Saturday/weekend school contexts, where research is sorely needed (Bowles and Torres 2021). Indeed, results of a recent meta-analysis suggest that heritage language instruction may be even more effective on younger learners than on college-age heritage learners (Bowles and Torres 2021), and a body of work to inform both K–12 and university evidence-based pedagogy is essential for the goals outlined by the American Academy of Arts and Sciences to be accomplished.

I also encourage researchers and HL teachers to consider engaging in multisite collaborations, whereby the same instructional materials and assessments are used with HL learners in different places. For instance, Spanish HL teachers could examine pre- and postinstruction gains in their learners in different locations (assuming that the learners are comparable in terms of their proficiency, of course), thereby simultaneously having a larger sample size, which gives quantitative studies more statistical power, and, in the event that significant differences between the locations are found, enabling them to examine contextual differences that could have contributed to the findings.

In addition to encouraging more original research on IHLA, I reiterate a call for researchers to conduct replication studies in order to gather more data from a larger number of learners, which will make results more generalizable (Bowles and Torres 2021). Replication takes two forms—direct and conceptual—and both make valuable additions to the field. Direct replications use the same materials and procedures as the original study on a similar group of learners as the original study to determine whether the same results are obtained. Conceptual replications, on the other hand, allow for significant alterations to the original study to examine the effects of instruction in a different context (e.g., a different population of HL learners). For example, when appropriate, experimental tasks or treatments could be adapted and used with learners of a different age group to see whether results are similar or different. Open sharing of materials, through the IRIS Database (www.iris-database.org), or through the National Heritage Language Resource Center's digital repository (https://nhlrc.ucla.edu/nhlrc/research#researchproficiency), can facilitate such replication, and readers interested in replications are referred to Porte and McManus (2019) for detailed information about how to carry out a replication of either type.

Finally, although all of the studies presented here focus on Spanish, it is my hope that researchers and teachers of other heritage languages will benefit from the research as well, either through the pedagogical implications that they can take to their classrooms or because the studies here ignite an interest and lead them to create their own replication or original IHLA research study that results in evidence-based pedagogical practices for their context. Pedagogical implications are provided for practitioners in each chapter, as are suggestions for future research. Furthermore, in her afterword Maria M. Carreira makes recommendations based on each study for three groups: HL instructors, HL researchers, and HL learners themselves.

## Note

1. It is very likely that the Census numbers significantly underrepresent the true number of Spanish speakers in the US, with some estimating that the actual number is more than 50 million. Indeed, according to a report from the Instituto Cervantes, Spanish-speaking media outlets widely reported in 2015 that the US had surpassed Spain to become the country with the second-largest number of Spanish speakers in the world, with their estimate (at that time) being 52.6 million (Instituto Cervantes 2015). The most recent statistics from the 2017 report estimate that there are 58 million speakers (Instituto Cervantes 2017, 7).

## References

American Academy of Arts and Sciences. 2017. *America's Languages: Investing in Language Education for the 21st Century*. https://www.amacad.org/language.

Beaudrie, Sara M. 2011. "Spanish Heritage Language Programs: A Snapshot of Current Programs in the Southwestern United States." *Foreign Language Annals* 44(2): 321–37.

———. 2012. "Research on University-Based Spanish Heritage Language Programs in the United States: The Current State of Affairs." In *Spanish as a Heritage Language in the United States: The State of the Field*, edited by Sara M. Beaudrie and Marta Fairclough, 203–21. Washington, DC: Georgetown University Press.

Beaudrie, Sara, Angelica Amezcua, and Sergio Loza. 2019. "Critical Language Awareness for the Heritage Context: Development and Validation of a Measurement Questionnaire." *Language Testing* 36(4): 573–94.

Beaudrie, Sara M., Cynthia Ducar, and Kim Potowski. 2014. *Heritage Language Teaching: Research and Practice*. New York: McGraw Hill.

Beaudrie, Sara M., and Marta Fairclough, eds. 2012. *Spanish as a Heritage Language in the United States: The State of the Field*. Washington, DC: Georgetown University Press.

Benmamoun, Elabbas, Silvina Montrul, and Maria Polinsky. 2013. "Heritage Languages and Their Speakers: Opportunities and Challenges for Linguistics." *Theoretical Linguistics* 39(3–4): 129–81.

Bowles, Melissa A. 2018. "Outcomes of Classroom Spanish Heritage Language Instruction: State of the Field and an Agenda for the Future." In *The Routledge Handbook of Spanish as a Heritage/Minority Language*, edited by Kim Potowski, 331–44. New York: Routledge.

Bowles, Melissa A., and Adrián Bello-Uriarte. 2019. "What Impact Does Heritage Language Instruction Have on Spanish Heritage Learners' Writing?" In *Evidence-Based Second Language Pedagogy: A Collection of Instructed Second Language Acquisition Studies*, edited by Masatoshi Sato and Shawn Loewen, 219–39. New York: Routledge.

Bowles, Melissa A., and Julio Torres. 2021. "Instructed Heritage Language Acquisition." In *The Cambridge Handbook of Heritage Languages and Linguistics*, edited by Maria Polinsky and Silvina Montrul, 826–50.

Brinton, Donna M., Olga Kagan, and Susan Bauckus, eds. 2008. *Heritage Language Education: A New Field Emerging*. New York: Routledge.

Carreira, Maria, and Claire Hitchins Chik. 2018. "Differentiated Teaching: A Primer for Heritage and Mixed Classes." In *The Handbook of Spanish as a Heritage/Minority Language*, edited by Kim Potowski, 359–74. New York: Routledge.

Carreira, Maria, and Olga Kagan. 2018. "Heritage Language Education: A Proposal for the Next 50 Years." *Foreign Language Annals* 51(1): 152–68.

Cummins, Jim. 1995. "A Proposal for Action: Strategies for Recognizing Heritage Language Competence as a Learning Resource within the Mainstream Classroom." *Modern Language Journal* 89(4): 585–91.

deBot, Kees, and Durk Gorter. 1995. "A European Perspective on Heritage Languages." *Modern Language Journal* 89(4): 612–16.

Fairclough, Marta, and Sara M. Beaudrie, eds. 2016. *Innovative Strategies for Heritage Language Teaching: A Practical Guide for the Classroom*. Washington, DC: Georgetown University Press.

Fishman, Joshua. 2001. "Three Hundred Plus Years of Heritage Language Education in the United States." In *Heritage Languages in America: Preserving a National Resource*, edited by Joy K. Peyton, Donald A. Ranard, and Scott McGinnis, 81–97. McHenry, IL: Center for Applied Linguistics.

Holguín Mendoza, Claudia. 2018. "Critical Language Awareness (CLA) for Spanish Heritage Language Programs: Implementing a Complete Curriculum." *International Multilingual Research Journal* 12(2): 65–79.

Instituto Cervantes. 2015. "El español: Una lengua viva, Informe 2015." https://cvc.cervantes.es/lengua/espanol_lengua_viva/pdf/espanol_lengua_viva_2015.pdf.

———. 2017. "El español: Una lengua viva, Informe 2017." https://cvc.cervantes.es/lengua/espanol_lengua_viva/pdf/espanol_lengua_viva_2017.pdf.

Kagan, Olga E., Maria M. Carreira, and Claire Hitchins Chik, eds. 2017. *The Routledge Handbook of Heritage Language Education: From Innovation to Program Building*. New York: Taylor and Francis.

Loewen, Shawn. 2015. *Introduction to Instructed Second Language Acquisition*. New York: Routledge.

Martínez, Glenn. 2003. "Classroom Based Dialect Awareness in Heritage Language Instruction: A Critical Applied Linguistic Approach." *Heritage Language Journal* 1, no. 1 (Fall): 44–57.

Montrul, Silvina. 2015. *The Acquisition of Heritage Languages*. Cambridge: Cambridge University Press.

Montrul, Silvina, and Melissa A. Bowles. 2017. "Instructed Heritage Language Acquisition." In *The Routledge Handbook of Instructed Second Language Acquisition*, edited by Shawn Loewen and Masatoshi Sato, 488–502. New York: Routledge.

Norris, John, and Lourdes Ortega. 2000. "Effectiveness of L2 Instruction: A Research Synthesis and Quantitative Meta-analysis." *Language Learning* 50(3): 417–528.

———. 2001. "Does Type of Instruction Make a Difference? Substantive Findings from a Meta-analytic Review." *Language Learning* 51: 157–213.

Pascual y Cabo, Diego, ed. 2016. *Advances in Spanish as a Heritage Language*. Amsterdam: John Benjamins.

Polinsky, Maria. 2018. *Heritage Languages and Their Speakers*. Cambridge: Cambridge University Press.

Porte, Graeme, and Kevin McManus. 2019. *Doing Replication Research in Applied Linguistics*. New York: Routledge.

Potowski, Kim, ed. 2018. *Handbook of Spanish as a Minority/Heritage Language*. New York: Routledge.

Potowski, Kim, Jill Jegerski, and Kara Morgan-Short. 2009. "The Effects of Instruction on Linguistic Development in Spanish Heritage Language Speakers." *Language Learning* 59(3): 537–79.

US Census Bureau, American Community Survey. 2017. https://www.census.gov/programssurveys/acs/.

Valdés, Guadalupe. 1995. "The Teaching of Minority Languages as 'Foreign' Languages: Pedagogical and Theoretical Challenges." *Modern Language Journal* 79(3): 299–328.

Zapata, Gabriela, and Manel Lacorte, eds. 2018. *Multiliteracies Pedagogy and Language Learning: Teaching Spanish to Heritage Speakers*. London: Palgrave Macmillan.

# PART I

# Morphosyntactic Outcomes

ONE

# Modality Matters! A Look at Task-Based Outcomes

*Julio Torres*
University of California, Irvine

The variability exhibited within and across heritage language (HL) bilingual speakers' grammars is a salient feature of HL outcomes (e.g., Montrul 2016). While monolingual native speakers can demonstrate variable knowledge of low-frequency lexical items and complex grammatical constructions (Hulstijn 2015), HL speakers, as bilingual native speakers of the HL, exhibit greater variability since they are managing more than one language. This variability can be explained to some extent by HL speakers' differences in exposure to the HL from an early age. Adult HL speakers who received early schooling in the HL, for example, demonstrate grammatical knowledge that aligns more closely to those of monolingual natives (e.g., Kupisch et al. 2014; Torres, Estremera, and Mohamed 2019). Another factor that appears to contribute to this variable behavior is the modality of experimental tasks. Studies have documented that HL speakers' performance largely depends on the modality of the experimental task in that HL participants demonstrate superior performance on oral experimental tasks vis-à-vis written ones (e.g., Montrul, Foote, and Perpiñán 2008; Alarcón 2011; Montrul et al. 2014; Torres, Estremera and Mohamed 2019). This observation is mostly due to HL speakers' early and prolonged prior language experience using the HL in oral communication in a naturalistic environment (e.g., Sanz and Torres 2018). However, what remains unclear is whether modality can also differentially alter HL learners' performance on assessment tasks that aim to measure language development from pedagogical interventions. To further explore this issue, the goal of this chapter is to provide empirical evidence on whether assessment modality (i.e., oral vs. written) can alter university-level HL learners' access to knowledge of the Spanish subjunctive in adjectival relative clauses as a result of task-based instruction. The findings of this study will have implications for the design of pedagogical intervention studies as well as pedagogical practices with HL learners.

## Literature Review

### HL Speakers' Performance on Oral and Written Experimental Tasks

A number of empirical studies with university-level HL speakers of Spanish have documented the nature of their knowledge of the HL through experimental tasks manipulated for modality. Silvina Montrul, Rebecca Foote, and Silvia Perpiñán (2008) investigated HL and second language (L2) speakers' acquisition of Spanish gender agreement through oral and written experimental tasks. Their findings indicated that while both HL and L2 learners exhibited a pattern of gender agreement errors, the modality of the experimental tasks differentially affected the degree of those errors for each group of speakers, with HL speakers demonstrating more control of the target form in the oral production task. The authors attributed their results to the context and mode of acquisition of the HL and L2 speakers. That is, HL speakers are exposed to more oral input in a naturalistic environment, whereas L2 speakers acquire the language with a greater amount of written input in classroom contexts. Irma Alarcón (2011) also examined Spanish gender agreement, but with advanced HL and L2 speakers. Similar to Montrul and colleagues, Alarcón found that her HL participants performed at monolingual native-like levels in the oral production task, especially in comparison to L2 speakers.

Montrul and colleagues (2014) administered three aural experimental tasks to measure HL and L2 participants' explicit and implicit knowledge of Spanish gender agreement. Given that previous research had shown that HL speakers demonstrated suboptimal performance on more explicit experimental tasks (Bowles 2011a), their goal was to minimize the role of modality by administering all aural tasks to investigate HL speakers' performance on explicit tasks. Indeed, the researchers found that HL and L2 participants performed equally well on the explicit tasks and HL participants demonstrated superior performance on the implicit task. More recently, Julio Torres, Ricardo Estremera, and Sherez Mohamed (2019) investigated the predictive nature of psychosocial individual differences (e.g., motivation) and biographical variables (e.g., frequency of language use) on HL learners' access to linguistic knowledge of vulnerable structures (e.g., gender agreement, past subjunctive mood) in HL acquisition. The researchers administered an oral and a written experimental task testing the same vulnerable structures. The findings revealed that HL learners demonstrated superior performance on the oral experimental task, and, interestingly, individual differences only predicted participants' performance on the written experimental task.

These studies imply that the modality of the experimental task determines the ease or difficulty with which HL speakers access their linguistic knowledge in the HL. This is due to HL speakers' prolonged exposure to mostly oral input in the HL since childhood, whereas their exposure to written input in the HL will vary according to differences such as early schooling in the HL. Therefore, because of this context of bilingual acquisition, HL speakers develop stronger linguistic representations of the HL in an oral mode. From a usage-based theoretical account, this outcome can be explained by the high frequency and cue consistency of oral input (and not written input) during HL speakers' first language (L1) acquisition experience, which are most likely determinants of the type of form-function mappings that become entrenched linguistic representations in HL speakers' grammars (e.g., Lieven and Tomasello 2008). Thus, as Elena Lieven and Michael Tomasello argued, "the strength and nature of representations that different tasks draw on may differ" (2008, 191), which can explain how HL speakers' superior performance on oral experimental tasks is indicative of stronger linguistic representations of the HL. Due to this prior language learning experience of HL bilinguals, however, what remains unknown empirically is whether adult HL learners, who decide to (re)learn the HL in an instructed setting, will retrieve with equal ease linguistic constructions across oral and written modes as a result of instruction. That is, do adult HL learners' stronger linguistic representations in oral mode provide them a learning advantage in oral production that results from pedagogical interventions?

## Researching Assessment Modality in L2 Acquisition

The field of L2 acquisition has long been interested in the design of assessment tasks because it can determine the type of L2 linguistic knowledge that is elicited (e.g., Bialystok 1982; Sanz 1997; Ellis 2009). Researchers have claimed that the variability often observed in L2 performance can be attributed in part to the demands that an assessment task places on L2 speakers such as tapping into explicit and implicit knowledge (e.g., Ellis 2009) or into comprehension and production of the L2 (e.g., De Jong 2005). For example, Paul Malovrh (2014) found that gender agreement with Spanish direct object clitics was evident in oral and written production at the beginning stages of L2 development but not necessarily in later stages. As such, the assessment task can alter the type of linguistic knowledge elicited, as an "individual learner's retrieval procedures vary according to the demands of the situation, the information required and the fluency or automaticity of the individual's control over the information" (Bialystok 1982, 183).

For instructed L2 acquisition contexts, Cristina Sanz (1997) proposed that the mode of the assessment task ought to be considered an important variable because mode places different cognitive demands on the L2 speaker. To test this claim, Sanz (1997) administered four assessment tasks to forty-four L2 learners of Spanish, which consisted of the following: an oral sentence completion task, an oral video retelling task, a written sentence completion task, and a written video retelling task. Participants who were assigned to the experimental condition were exposed to processing instruction (e.g., VanPatten 2004) on the use of accusative clitics (e.g., Ella *la* abraza "She hugs her") in Spanish. Her results overall revealed that participants exhibited significantly superior performance in the written assessment tasks vis-à-vis the oral assessment tasks. These results imply that the oral assessment tasks placed higher cognitive demands on the L2 participants, which competed for attentional and memory resources that would have facilitated the retrieval of the target form. According to Sanz, the oral assessment task placed a greater burden on L2 learners' processor to encode the production of their messages in a quick and efficient manner. Surprisingly, to the best of my knowledge, this is the only study that has isolated the role of assessment modality in instructed L2 acquisition research.

In sum, the demands of assessment tasks can alter to different degrees the retrieval processes of target forms among adult L2 speakers. These demands can have varying effects on the cognitive resources that L2 speakers deploy during the execution of assessment tasks. Sanz's (1997) findings further demonstrated that these effects occur even immediately after pedagogical interventions. As such, the effects of pedagogical interventions can be modulated by the modality of assessment tasks. This modulation has implications for assessing L2 learners' proficiency levels in instructed settings. In this chapter, I extend this inquiry to a population of HL learners given that HL and L2 learners differ in their prior language experience. One explanation for the results in Sanz (1997) can also be related to L2 learners' prior language experience with the L2. Arguably, in foreign language instructed contexts, L2 learners receive more exposure to written than aural input, which can lead to an imbalance in the strength of retrieving L2 linguistic knowledge according to mode. Therefore, L2 learners may have an advantage when completing written assessment tasks. Conversely, as argued above, adult HL learners typically enter the learning scenario with an oral production advantage in the HL. Therefore, potentially, having more automatized knowledge of the HL in the oral mode can ease HL learners' cognitive burden, as they would be able to draw on more attentional and memory resources to retrieve form-meaning mappings. To examine this issue, I analyze data from task-based instruction with the same population of HL learners reported in a previous study (Torres 2018) but isolating here the role of assessment modality.

## Task-Based Interventions with HL Learners

The subfield of instructed HL acquisition is still emerging, as more empirical studies are needed to answer questions about how HL learners respond to pedagogical interventions (Bowles 2018). Within the few studies published in this area, researchers have examined the effects of task-based instruction on HL learners' language performance and development (e.g., Blake and Zyzik 2003; Kang 2010; Bowles 2011b; Bowles, Adams, and Toth 2014; Henshaw 2015; Torres 2018; Torres and Cung 2019). These studies have addressed the effects of task-based interaction patterns on learning opportunities (e.g., Bowles, Adams, and Toth 2014; Henshaw 2015) as well as focus on form techniques such as corrective feedback on task-based learning outcomes (e.g., Kang 2010; Torres 2018). To report on the patterns that we are observing from these task-based studies is beyond the scope of this chapter. Suffice it to say that the use of tasks has served as a window into how HL learners deploy their linguistic and cognitive resources during task-based pedagogical interventions. In this chapter, I adopt the definition of tasks as a workplan in which a communicative and purposeful context has been created that allows HL learners to make use of their linguistic resources (Ellis 2018). Following Rod Ellis and Natsuko Shintani (2014), tasks as a workplan ought to meet the following criteria: a primary focus on meaning, some kind of gap, a main reliance on learners' own linguistic and nonlinguistic resources, and a nonlinguistic communicative outcome. Moreover, the task for the current study is considered a focused task for which the HL learners are oriented toward using a particular grammatical structure (Ellis 2018). It is within this instructional context that I will examine whether modality alters HL speakers' performance on assessment tasks that measure learning gains from task-based interventions.

Therefore, the goal of this chapter is to further explore the role of assessment modality on HL learners' access to linguistic knowledge as a result of task-based pedagogical interventions. The following research question will be addressed: To what extent does assessment modality alter HL learners' performance in producing the Spanish subjunctive in adjectival relative clauses as a result of task-based instruction?

## Methods

### Participants

The current study included thirty-seven university-level HL learners of Spanish (sixteen females) whose average age at the time of the study was 20.0 (*SD* = 1.8). Their reported average age of onset for learning Spanish was 1.2 (*SD* = 1.7) and 3.9 (*SD* = 3.1) for English. Regarding classroom learning experience, none of the participants had studied in a dual language school, and their average years of formal Spanish study in secondary and postsecondary contexts was 4.1 (*SD* = 2.4). Participants self-reported their level of proficiency in Spanish and English for listening, reading, speaking, and writing skills. They self-reported native or near-native proficiency levels for all skills in English and listening skills in Spanish and advanced proficiency for Spanish for reading, speaking, and writing skills. All of the participants also completed a modified version of the Diploma de Español como Lengua Extranjera (DELE) test, which has been used in previous studies with HL speakers (e.g., Montrul 2004), as an objective measurement to estimate their proficiency in Spanish. Out of a maximum possible score of 50, the findings indicated an average score of 32.5 (*SD* = 7.1), which places most of the participants within an intermediate-level proficiency range. Finally, participants reported on their daily use (always, frequently, sometimes, rarely, never) of Spanish and English in different settings, including home, school, and work. As expected, participants reported using English more frequently (*M* = 60.1, *SD* = 7.1) than Spanish (*M* = 32.5, *SD* = 13.3) on a daily basis.

## Target Form

The instructional tasks in the current study promoted the use of the Spanish subjunctive in adjectival relative clauses. The Spanish subjunctive is a verb form that speakers use to express unknown or doubtful events (Zagona 2002). The subjunctive mood is typically expressed in the embedded clauses of a sentence, and the licensing of its use depends on the content of the main clause. In obligatory contexts, for example, if the main clause of the sentence has a verb of doubt (e.g., *Dudo que*, "I doubt that"), it will trigger the use of the subjunctive in the embedded clause for speakers who have acquired it. However, there are cases in which the licensing of the subjunctive will depend on pragmatic context and not necessarily on the selection of a certain predicate (e.g., verbs of doubt). Therefore, with such predicates, it is how the speaker evaluates the proposition in certain contexts that determines the use of the subjunctive (see Quer 2001). This is the case with the subjunctive in adjectival relative clauses. These adjectival relative clauses are found in embedded clauses to describe, qualify, or specify a referent (e.g., Campos 1993) such as in *Los estudiantes que duermen mucho* "The students who sleep a lot." The adjectival clause *que duermen mucho* serves to specify a group of students (i.e., those who sleep a lot) from a possible universal set of students. In Spanish, the subjunctive can be used in adjectival clauses when the speaker expresses some degree of uncertainty of the existence of the referent in the main clause. For example, if a school principal is looking for students who sleep in class, but she is uncertain whether such students exist, she will use the subjunctive (e.g., *Busco a estudiantes que duerman*-SUBJ *en clase*, "I am searching for students who sleep-SUBJ in class"). On the other hand, the indicative mood is preferred for a context in which the school principal is certain that these students who sleep in class exist (e.g., *Busco a estudiantes que duermen*-IND *en clase*, "I am searching for students who sleep-IND in class"). Note that both sentences used the verb *busco* in the main clause; however, the licensing of the indicative or subjunctive mood depends on the speaker's epistemic knowledge of the situation.

Sociolinguistic and formal studies have corroborated that the use of the subjunctive mood in adjectival relative clauses is a vulnerable structure in HL acquisition (e.g., Silva-Corvalán 1994; Montrul 2009; Montrul and Perpiñán 2011). In these cases of subjunctive use, which Carmen Silva-Corvalán (1994) refers to as optional contexts, HL speakers oftentimes employ the indicative even in the contexts that ought to trigger the subjunctive mood. According to Josep Quer (2001), the indicative is the default mood in these contexts, and it is the speaker's evaluation of the proposition that can determine a shift that will lead to the use of the subjunctive. Therefore, it is no surprise that HL speakers overuse the indicative in such optional contexts because it is the default mood. This is because HL speakers have not acquired the knowledge to map the use of the subjunctive mood for contexts in which a shift in evaluating a proposition has occurred. As such, this is an appropriate target form to test in instructional contexts. Notably, participants in the current study lacked knowledge of the Spanish subjunctive in adjectival relative clauses, as demonstrated by oral and written production pretests.

## Task-Based Pedagogical Interventions

HL participants who were assigned to two experimental conditions completed monologic computerized tasks that delivered written recasts as a form of corrective feedback but differed according to their cognitive demands (i.e., task complexity) (see Torres 2018 for the results on the effects of task complexity). Participants were instructed that they were going to play the role of a resident director at a university dormitory hall at the University of Puerto Rico. The communicative outcome of the task was to explain to the dean of student life the misbehavior among the residents of their dormitory hall. Participants were exposed to thirty different situations of student misbehavior and saw three slides that provided them with context about each situation, including whether they knew the reason for the misbehavior. On the fourth slide, participants needed to orally produce the reason for the misbehavior based on the information from the previous slides and on either one or a selection of four photos, which depended on the experimental condition. Participants were provided with a main clause, and they needed to complete the sentence with an adjectival embedded clause, as in the following: *Las estudiantes tocan música alta que . . .* , "Students play loud music that . . . " Since this was a focused task, along with the photo(s), students had an option of two verb forms (i.e., indicative and subjunctive) to guide them in providing the reason for the students' misbehavior. In the example above, participants had to provide a reason for students playing loud music in the dormitory. It was expected that students would use the indicative mood for the scenarios that they knew the reason for the misbehavior and the subjunctive for those that they did not. Once participants submitted their verb form selection along with their oral response, they would get feedback. When participants selected the correct verb form, they saw a message with the word *Sí*, "Yes." However, for incorrect verb forms, they received a written recast with the correct verb form, and they were instructed to repeat their response with the correct verb form. It is important to note that the presentation of the situations was delivered in oral and written mode. That is, participants both read and heard the stimuli before selecting the verb, producing their oral response, and getting feedback.

## Oral and Written Production Assessment Tasks

To measure the development of the Spanish subjunctive in adjectival relative clauses as a result of the above task-based interventions, participants completed three distinct oral and written production assessment tasks (pretest, immediate posttest, and delayed posttest) that were counterbalanced across the three sessions. The assessment tasks were piloted to ensure that all versions were fairly reliable and comparable as far as level of difficulty (see Torres 2013). For each assessment task, participants were instructed to complete twenty-four sentences based on an available picture and a sentence with contextual information to guide their response. Of the twenty-four items, twelve were experimental and another twelve were distractors. Out of the twelve experimental items, half of the items required the use of the subjunctive in adjectival relative clauses and the other half required the indicative. For the experimental items, participants needed to rely on the sentence with contextual information (e.g., *No sé si hay estas obras de arte*, "I don't know if there are these works of art"), which should have triggered the use of the subjunctive for instances in which the antecedent of the main clause was nonexistent (see figure 1.1). On the distractor items, students were prompted to complete sentences using the past or future tense based on the sentence with contextual information. The oral and written production assessment tasks differed in that the oral version followed the format of the task-based interventions, which presented the stimuli in oral and written modes and participants provided an oral response. The written production assessment task, on the other hand, required participants to read the stimuli and write out their responses. That is, unlike the oral version, participants did not listen to the items or produce an oral response.

To score the data, the experimental items were assigned one point if the correct verb form was produced (i.e., subjunctive or indicative mood) and "zero" points if the correct verb form was not produced. No point was granted for incorrect verb mood, a nonfinite verb form, or no verb in the embedded clause. Since there were twelve experimental items, participants could get a maximum possible score of twelve points. The researcher coded 100 percent of

**No sé si hay estas obras de arte**

**Preferimos ir a museos que...**

Submit

**FIGURE 1.1.** Experimental item on assessment production task. English translation: No sé si hay estas obras de arte (I don't know if they have these works of art); Preferimos ir a museos que . . . (We prefer to go to museums that . . . ).

the data, and an independent coder, who was a graduate student in Spanish linguistics, coded 20 percent of the data. An inter-rater reliability analysis yielded $K$ = .80 before rater socialization, which resulted in consensus being reached.

## Procedure

Upon consenting to participate in the study, participants were randomly assigned to experimental conditions ($n$ = 26) or a control group ($n$ = 11). Participants completed the modified DELE proficiency test and a version of the oral and written production assessment task during the first session. During the second session, participants in the experimental conditions completed their corresponding treatment task and a second version of the oral and written production assessment task. The control group only completed the assessment tasks. After a period of one to two weeks, all participants completed a third version of the oral and written production assessment task as well as language background and debriefing questionnaires. Participants were compensated with extra credit for their participation in the study.

## Results

The current study posited to what extent does modality alter HL learners' performance on assessment tasks that aimed to measure their development of the Spanish subjunctive in adjectival relative clauses. To address this question, only data from the experimental groups were analyzed, as the control group performed at floor on both oral and written assessment tasks, as detailed in Julio Torres (2018). Two repeated measures Analyses of Variance (ANOVAs) were first conducted comparing the scores of the oral and written production assessment tasks during the pretest, immediate, and delayed posttest phases of the experiment. The data were submitted to the testing of assumptions for this parametric measure. Further, effect sizes were calculated with Cohen's *d* to ascertain the magnitude of improvement from pretest to immediate posttest and pretest to delayed posttest. Table 1.1 summarizes the descriptive results, and figure 1.2 shows the distribution of the data. For oral production, the results of the repeated measures ANOVA yielded a significant finding for Time, $F(29, 18.15) = 2.00$, $p < .001$, *partial* $\eta^2 = .59$. Post hoc comparisons using the Bonferroni test revealed that the scores in the oral immediate and delayed posttests were significantly greater ($p < .001$) than the pretest scores. However, no differences were found between the immediate and delayed posttests, indicating that the gains from instruction were durable at the time of the delayed posttest one to two weeks later. Another repeated measures ANOVA was conducted to examine participants' performance on the written assessment tasks, and a significant effect for time was also found, $F(17.54, 37.62) = 2.00$, $p < .001$, *partial* $\eta^2 = .41$. A Bonferroni post hoc analysis also revealed that the scores on the immediate and delayed posttests were significantly greater than the pretest scores. A marginally significant ($p = .07$) difference was found for differences between the immediate and delayed posttests.

To determine effect sizes, Cohen's *d* was calculated based on the scores from pretest to immediate posttest and pretest to delayed posttest as shown below.

| Assessment production test | Effect size (Cohen's *d*) |
|---|---|
| Immediate oral | 1.98 |
| Immediate written | 1.67 |
| Delayed oral | 1.95 |
| Delayed written | 0.85 |

Based on effect size benchmarks for the field of L2 acquisition (Plonsky and Oswald 2014), participants demonstrated large gains from pretest to immediate posttest and pretest to delayed posttest in the oral production assessment tasks (immediate oral = 1.98, delayed oral = 1.95). Likewise, a large effect was found for pretest to immediate posttest for the written production assessment task ($d = 1.67$), though the effect sizes for the oral assessment tasks were larger. However, a medium effect size was obtained for pretest to delayed written production assessment task ($d = 0.85$). Therefore, based on these results, the

**TABLE 1.1.** Descriptive Statistics for Experimental Groups

| Assessment production task | Mean | SD | Max. | Min. |
|---|---|---|---|---|
| Pretest oral | 5.95 | 0.21 | 6 | 5 |
| Pretest written | 5.69 | 0.54 | 6 | 4 |
| Immediate oral | 7.18 | 0.85 | 9 | 6 |
| Immediate written | 7.11 | 1.07 | 10 | 5 |
| Delayed oral | 7.36 | 1.00 | 9 | 6 |
| Delayed written | 6.46 | 1.14 | 9 | 5 |

*Note:* SD = standard deviation; Max. = maximum score; Min. = minimum score.

**FIGURE 1.2.** Boxplots of assessment task scores.

modality of the assessment tasks altered HL learners' performance in the production of the Spanish subjunctive in adjectival relative clauses, and this was particularly noticeable one to two weeks after receiving task-based instruction in the written mode.

## Discussion

Previous research has revealed that the variability often observed in adult HL speakers' performance on experimental tasks is in part due to the modality of the task, with superior performance on oral tasks (e.g., Montrul, Foote, and Perpiñán 2008). This observation can be attributed to HL speakers' early bilingual experience that entails a major exposure to oral input in a naturalistic environment. These findings imply that HL speakers can access their linguistic knowledge more easily in oral mode due to encoding usage events that occur to a greater extent during oral communication. However, what remains unknown is whether assessment modality can also alter HL learners' performance in retrieving linguistic forms as a result of pedagogical interventions, especially as this seems to be the case in instructed L2 acquisition (e.g., Sanz 1997). This information is relevant for the research design of instructed HL acquisition studies in light of calls for the need to examine the effects of pedagogical interventions on adult HL learners' performance and development (e.g., Bowles 2018; Sanz and Torres 2018). Therefore, the goal of the current study was to further investigate the effects of modality on adult HL learners' performance on assessment tasks after task-based instruction.

The results of the study revealed that learners overall scored higher on the oral assessment tests, and the asymmetry between oral and written tests was particularly apparent one to two weeks after task-based instruction. Further, the effect sizes showed that task-based instruction had a greater impact on HL learners' oral production of the Spanish subjunctive in adjectival clauses. Examination of individual variation on the immediate posttest showed that 40 percent of the participants scored lower on the written test in comparison to the oral test; whereas 15 percent of participants scored higher on the written test. The remaining 45 percent of participants scored the same on both the oral and written tests. On the delayed posttest, 68 percent of the participants scored lower on the written test than on the oral test, and no participant scored lower on the oral test than on the written one. In fact, the participants who had higher scores on the written test during the immediate posttest scored lower on the written test than on the oral one at the time of the delayed posttest. Overall, the distribution of the individual data in figure 1.2 shows that the participants' scores on the immediate and delayed oral assessment test were rather comparable. In stark comparison, the written assessment scores were more unevenly distributed across immediate and delayed posttests.

Therefore, these findings indicate that modality did alter to a certain extent HL learners' performance on the written assessment task that elicited the production of the Spanish subjunctive in adjectival clauses. The findings align with those of Sanz (1997) with adult L2 learners; that is, assessment modality can place processing demands that can affect learners' retrieval of linguistic forms. The current study differed from Sanz's study in that her L2 learners demonstrated suboptimal performance in the oral mode, which is not surprising given the differences in prior language experiences between L2 and HL learners. Another difference is that the assessment mode had immediate effects on L2 learners' performance in Sanz's study, but in the current study those effects were more pronounced in the delayed posttests.

One possible explanation for the results of the current study is that HL learners enter the learning scenario with an advantage for oral production, as studies have documented their superior performance on oral experimental tasks. Arguably, then, HL learners have developed automatized linguistic knowledge of the HL in the oral mode. This permits HL learners to engage more easily in parallel processing of conceptualizing and formulating verbal messages during speech production (e.g., Kormos 2006). As bilingual native speakers, HL learners typically acquire basic language cognition knowledge, which is characterized by oral knowledge of frequent lexical items and grammatical constructions (Hulstijn 2015; Zyzik 2016). Since this knowledge is implicit and automatized, HL learners can easily activate this knowledge into working memory. As such, an oral assessment task will not place heavy cognitive demands on the HL learner, which, in turn, makes attentional resources more available to retrieve grammatical structures that are still under HL learners' controlled processing. Conversely, this retrieval process will be more difficult in the written mode given that the HL learners in the current study most likely lacked extended language cognition knowledge, which entails written discourse in the HL (Hulstijn 2015). This is supported by the fact that our HL learners did not attend any type of early bilingual education program (e.g., dual language schools), and the average years of formal Spanish study was about four years in secondary and postsecondary contexts. The HL learners here were educated primarily in mainstream English-only programs since elementary school. Therefore, to echo Sanz (1997), the written production assessment task demanded more of HL learners' processors, which affected the retrieval process of the target form in written mode, especially during the delayed posttest. Future research ought to investigate this issue with HL speakers who have been exposed to some early schooling, as research has revealed that early schooling in the HL is a significant predictor of written knowledge in the HL among adult learners (Torres, Estremera, and Mohamed 2019). It is reasonable to posit that the written modality of an assessment task may not have the same effect for HL learners with some early schooling in the HL. As such, in addition to the assessment modality, researchers ought to consider HL learners' early exposure to written input through schooling, as these factors may be at play during their performance on written assessment tasks.

A second possible explanation for these results could be due to the match between the format of the task-based interventions and the oral production assessment tasks. That is, while the stimuli were presented in both modes during the interventions, participants only provided their answers orally during instruction. According to the Transfer Appropriate Processing (TAP) hypothesis, learners activate their memory resources better if the activation process mirrors that of the learning process (Lightbown 2008). In other words, for best results, the context of the retrieval process needs to match the encoding process of the linguistic data. TAP also endorses that attention is limiting and that learners, in general, are unable to encode every event that they are exposed to in a particular environment. However, the retrieval process is optimized when the retrieval conditions are similar to the learning conditions. In the current study, then, HL learners may have also enjoyed a slight advantage in the oral production assessment task given that it matched the learning condition. While the participants did receive written input through the presentation of the scenarios and written recasts for incorrect verb choices, output practice in the oral mode may have granted HL learners more opportunities to consolidate stronger associations of the target form into long-term memory, especially in light of the important benefits of the role of output in adult L2 development, which can be extended to adult HL learners as well (Swain 1998). Furthermore, during the oral assessment task, participants read and listened to the prompts before submitting their oral response. This was not the case for the written assessment task, in which participants only read the prompts, another difference with the intervention tasks. Therefore, being able to only read the prompts during the written production assessment tasks could have placed an additional cognitive burden on the participants.

In sum, Melissa Bowles (2018) argued for a research agenda that would examine the outcomes of instruction on HL development to address fundamental questions such as whether instruction is beneficial for HL development, and, if so, what features make instruction most effective. Sanz and Torres (2018) also called for the inclusion of online methodologies (e.g., eye-tracking) to better understand how HL learners process linguistic data through pedagogical interventions to explain their learning outcomes. To further understand the role of pedagogical interventions on HL development, the evidence from the current study suggests that HL researchers ought to consider carefully assessment modality as part of their study designs. (See also Fernández Cuenca and Bowles, chapter 5 this volume). It is critical to understand exactly how HL learners are benefiting from pedagogical interventions across modes. That is, due to their prior language experience, which entails an imbalance of linguistic knowledge across the two modes, how does modality have an effect on how they are processing, storing, and retrieving form-meaning mappings they are developing as a result of pedagogical interventions? Therefore, careful attention needs to be paid to assessment modality as well as how the learning conditions match assessment tasks according to mode.

## Research Implications

The field of instructed HL acquisition can benefit from future studies on isolating assessment modality to better understand its effects on how HL learners retrieve linguistic structures to inform the design of effective pedagogical conditions. One of the issues that could not be disentangled from the current study was to what extent effects of assessment modality were due to HL learners' advantage with oral production or the match between the task-based conditions and the oral assessment production tasks. Additionally, we need to examine whether HL learners with more exposure to written input through early formal schooling or attending community/Saturday classes in the HL can differentially improve their ability to retrieve target forms in writing. Even if the priority of instructed HL acquisition studies may not be on isolating the effects of assessment modality, this study offered empirical evidence that, at minimum, future studies need to consider assessment modality as part of the study design.

Another issue for future research is how the role of HL learners' individual differences (e.g., motivation, working memory) can further contribute to the variability we observe in written assessment outcomes. For instance, Torres, Estremera, and Mohamed (2019) found that motivation was a significant predictor in HL learners' ability to detect ungrammatical items in a written untimed grammaticality judgment task, which was not the case with the findings of a spoken elicited imitation task. Also, surprisingly, years of formal Spanish study was not a significant contributor to the performance on either task. Potentially, then, just studying the HL in an instructed setting may not be sufficient, as HL learners' motivation driven by a desire to bridge the gap between their current and ideal selves as Spanish speakers can have larger implications in their learning process in a written mode. Therefore, more research is needed to carefully examine the dynamic relationship among pedagogical interventions, assessment task modality, and individual differences to understand how HL learners adapt their linguistic resources to meet communicative task goals.

## Pedagogical Implications

Teachers need to consider modality when they are evaluating students' knowledge after a lesson or unit on a particular grammatical structure. It is important to evaluate both modalities in the classroom to understand what types of scaffolding HL learners will need. This certainly will have an impact on the design of curriculum and classroom activities and tasks. Of importance, more classroom time may need to be devoted to recycling information in the written mode to promote HL students' automatization of learned knowledge in the written mode.

With regards to a task-based teaching approach, researchers recommend sequencing tasks from easy to more difficult in a syllabus design, which is known as task complexity (e.g., Long 2015). Given the results of this study, in deciding the sequencing of tasks for a particular course such as business Spanish that involves HL learners, for instance (see Torres and Serafini 2016), course designers ought to include modality as a potential design feature to determine task complexity for HL learners. That is, it may be useful to begin task-based curriculum building with oral tasks and assessments to tap into learners' existing linguistic resources and build their confidence. Then, instructors can help HL learners make a transition to written modes of communication through tasks and assessments with adequate support during the task cycle phase, which includes pretask and posttask activities that help learners make the necessary form-meaning connections from the task phase. See Torres and Baralt (2022) for more detail about designing task-based instruction for HL learners and Carreira's discussion of From-to Principles in heritage language teaching in the afterword to this volume.

## Conclusion

Given the important role that the mode of experimental tasks has played in eliciting HL speakers' linguistic knowledge, the current study sought to investigate whether the effects of assessment modality can also be extended to HL learners' performance in retrieving linguistic knowledge (i.e., the Spanish subjunctive in adjectival relative clauses) as a result of task-based pedagogical interventions. While HL participants demonstrated learning gains, the findings revealed that modality altered the extent to which participants were able to retrieve their linguistic knowledge in the written mode, especially at the time of the delayed posttest approximately two weeks after instruction. These results are attributed to HL learners' early bilingual experience with the HL, which consists mostly of exposure to oral input in the HL, that may have conferred on them an advantage for oral production of the target form. Furthermore, the match between the task-based conditions and the oral production assessment tasks most likely added an additional advantage to their retrieval of the target form.

## References

Alarcón, Irma V. 2011. "Spanish Gender Agreement under Complete and Incomplete Acquisition: Early and Late Bilinguals' Linguistic Behavior within the Noun Phrase." *Bilingualism: Language and Cognition* 14, no. 3 (July): 332–50.

Bialystok, Ellen. 1982. "On the Relationship between Knowing and Using Linguistic Forms." *Applied Linguistics* 3, no. 3 (October): 181–206.

Blake, Robert, and Eve Zyzik. 2003. "Who's Helping Whom? Learner/Heritage Speakers' Networked Discussions in Spanish." *Applied Linguistics* 24, no. 4 (December): 519–44.

Bowles, Melissa A. 2011a. "Measuring Implicit and Explicit Knowledge." *Studies in Second Language Acquisition* 33, no. 2 (June): 247–71.

———. 2011b. "Exploring the Role of Modality: L2-Heritage Learner Interactions in the Spanish Language Classroom." *Heritage Language Journal* 8, no. 1 (Spring): 30–65.

———. 2018. "Outcomes of Classroom Spanish Heritage Language Instruction." In *The Routledge Handbook of Spanish as a Heritage Language*, edited by Kim Potowski, 311–44. New York: Routledge Press.

Bowles, Melissa A., Rebecca Adams, and Paul Toth. 2014. "A Comparison of L2–L2 and L2–Heritage Learner Interactions in Spanish Language Classroom." *Modern Language Journal* 98, no. 2 (October): 497–517.

Campos, Héctor. 1993. *De la oración simple a la oración compuesta: Curso superior de gramática española*. Washington, DC: Georgetown University Press.

De Jong, Nel. 2005. "Can Second Language Grammar Be Learned through Listening? An Experimental Study." *Studies in Second Language Acquisition* 27, no. 2 (June): 205–34.

Ellis, Rod. 2009. *Implicit and Explicit Knowledge in Second Language Learning, Testing and Teaching*. Bristol, UK: Multilingualism Matters.

———. 2018. *Reflections on Task-Based Language Teaching*. Bristol, UK: Multilingual Matters.

Ellis, Rod, and Natsuko Shintani. 2014. *Exploring Language Pedagogy through Second Language Acquisition*. London: Routledge Press.

Henshaw, Florencia. 2015. "Learning Outcomes of L2–Heritage Learner Interaction: The Proof Is in the Posttests." *Heritage Language Journal* 12, no. 3 (December): 245–70.

Hulstijn, Jan H. 2015. *Language Proficiency in Native and Non-native Speakers: Theory and Research*. Amsterdam: John Benjamins.

Kang, Hyun-Sook. 2010. "Negative Evidence and Its Explicitness and Positioning in the Learning of Korean as a Heritage Language." *Modern Language Journal* 94, no. 4 (Winter): 582–99.

Kormos, Judit. 2006. *Speech Production and Second Language Acquisition*. Mahwah, NJ: Lawrence Erlbaum Associates.

Kupisch, Tanja, Tatjana Lein, Dagmar Barton, Dawn J. Schröder, Ilse Stangen, and Antje Stoehr. 2014. "Acquisition Outcomes across Domains in Adult Simultaneous Bilinguals with French as Weaker and Stronger Language." *French Language Studies* 24, no. 3 (November): 347–76.

Lieven, Elena, and Michael Tomasello. 2008. "Children's First Language Acquisition from a Usage-Based Perspective." In *Handbook of Cognitive Linguistics and Second Language Acquisition*, edited by Peter Robinson and Nick C. Ellis, 168–96. New York: Routledge Press.

Lightbown, Patsy M. 2008. "Transfer Appropriate Processing as a Model for Classroom Second Language Acquisition. In *Understanding Second Language Processes*, edited by ZhaoHong Han, 27–44. Clevedon, UK: Multilingual Matters.

Long, Mike. 2015. *Second Language Acquisition and Task-Based Language Teaching.* Chichester, UK: Wiley.

Malovrh, Paul. 2014. "Variability and Systematicity in Interlanguage Development: An Analysis of Mode and Its Effects on L2 Spanish Morphology." *Studies in Hispanic and Lusophone Linguistics* 7, no. 1 (November): 43–78.

Montrul, Silvina. 2009. "Knowledge of Tense-Aspect and Mood in Spanish Heritage Speakers." *International Journal of Bilingualism* 13, no. 2 (June): 239–69.

———. 2004. "Subject and Object Expression in Spanish Heritage Speakers: A Case of Morphosyntactic Convergence." *Bilingualism: Language and Cognition* 7, no. 2 (July): 125–42.

———. 2016. *The Acquisition of Heritage Languages.* Cambridge: Cambridge University Press.

Montrul, Silvina, Justin Davidson, Israel de la Fuente, and Rebecca Foote. 2014. "Early Language Experience Facilitates the Processing of Gender Agreement in Spanish Heritage Speakers." *Bilingualism: Language and Cognition* 17, no. 1 (January): 118–38.

Montrul, Silvina, Rebecca Foote, and Silvia Perpiñán. 2008. "Gender Agreement in Adult Second Language Learners and Spanish Heritage Speakers: The Effects of Age and Context of Acquisition." *Language Learning* 58, no. 3 (September): 503–33.

Montrul, Silvina, and Silvia Perpiñán. 2011. "Assessing Differences and Similarities between Instructed Heritage Language Learners and L2 Learners in Their Knowledge of Spanish Tense-Aspect and Mood (TAM) Morphology." *Heritage Language Journal* 8, no. 1 (Spring): 90–133.

Plonsky, Luke, and Frederick L. Oswald. 2014. "How Big Is 'Big'? Interpreting Effect Sizes in Research." *Language Learning* 64, no. 4 (October): 878–912.

Quer, Josep. 2001. "Interpreting Mood." *Probus* 13, no. 1 (March): 81–111.

Sanz, Cristina. 1997. "Experimental Tasks in SLA Research: Amount of Production, Modality, Memory, and Production Processes." In *Contemporary Perspectives on the Acquisition of Spanish*, edited by Ana Pérez Leroux and William R. Glass, 2:41–56. Somerville: Cascadilla Press.

Sanz, Cristina, and Julio Torres. 2018. "The Prior Language Experience of Heritage Bilinguals." In *The Handbook of Advanced Proficiency in Second Language Acquisition*, edited by Paul A. Malovrh and Alessandro G. Benati, 179–98. Hoboken, NJ: John Wiley.

Silva-Corvalán, Carmen. 1994. *Language Contact and Change: Spanish in Los Angeles.* Oxford: Oxford University Press.

Swain, Merrill. 1998. "Focus on Form through Conscious Reflection." In *Focus on Form in Classroom Second Language Acquisition*, edited by Catherine Doughty and Jessica Williams, 64–82. Cambridge: Cambridge University Press.

Torres, Julio. 2013. "Heritage and Second Language Learners of Spanish: The Roles of Task Complexity and Inhibitory Control." PhD diss., Georgetown University, Washington, DC.

———. 2018. "The Effects of Task Complexity on Heritage and L2 Spanish Development." *Canadian Modern Language Review* 74, no. 1 (February): 128–52.

Torres, Julio, and Melissa Baralt. 2022. "El enfoque por tareas en el aprendizaje del español como lengua de herencia." In *El español como lengua de herencia*, edited by D. Pascual y Cabo and J. Torres, 81–96. New York: Routledge Press.

Torres, Julio, and Bianca Cung. 2019. "A Comparison of Advanced Heritage Language Learners' Peer Interaction across Modes and Pair Types." *Modern Language Journal* 103, no. 4 (December): 815–30.

Torres, Julio, Ricardo Estremera, and Sherez Mohamed. 2019. "The Contribution of Psychosocial and Biographical Variables to Heritage Learners' Linguistic Knowledge of Spanish." *Studies in Second Language Acquisition* online ed. (May): 1–25. https://doi.org/10.1017/S0272263119000184.

Torres, Julio, and Ellen J. Serafini. 2016. "Micro-evaluating Learners' Task-Specific Motivation in a Task-Based Business Spanish Course." *Hispania* 99, no. 2 (June): 289–304.

VanPatten, Bill. 2004. *Processing Instruction: Theory, Research and Commentary.* New York: Routledge Press.

Zagona, Karen. 2002. *The Syntax of Spanish.* Cambridge: Cambridge University Press.

Zyzik, Eve. 2016. "Toward a Prototype Model of the Heritage Language Learner: Understanding Strengths and Needs." In *Innovative Strategies for Heritage Language Teaching: A Practical Guide for the Classroom,* edited by Marta Fairclough and Sara M. Beaudrie, 19–38. Washington, DC: Georgetown University Press.

**TWO**

# The Differential Effects of Three Types of Form-Focused, Computer-Based Grammar Instruction: The Case of Receptive Heritage Learners

*Sara M. Beaudrie*
Arizona State University

*Bonnie C. Holmes*
Southern Oregon University

As growing numbers of Spanish heritage language learners (HLLs)[1] enroll in university Spanish-language courses and researchers home in on aspects of their grammatical knowledge that may benefit from instructional support, two questions that emerge are whether grammar should be expressly taught and, if so, using what methods? Much progress has been made in the last two decades in our understanding of the profiles, abilities, and learning needs of Spanish HLLs in the United States (Beaudrie, Ducar, and Potowski 2014; Pascual y Cabo 2016; Potowski 2018; among many others), and one finding is that HLLs often experience difficulties with inflectional morphology due to its vulnerability to divergent development. This vulnerability is understood to derive from variable input and opportunities for Spanish language use in childhood, which often result in production and interpretation difficulties that are measurable in adulthood (e.g., Cuza et al. 2013; Montrul 2011; Montrul and Perpiñán 2011). Morphological variability is not exclusive to HLLs; it is also present in second language (L2) learners who have acquired their L2 postadolescence and primarily in classroom settings. However, while comparative studies of L2 and HLL grammars have shown that both groups make similar types of morphological errors (omitting morphemes and/or producing ungrammatical affixes), these errors manifest themselves differently depending on the type of language task in which the learners are engaged (Bowles 2011; Montrul 2009; Montrul and Bowles 2008, 2009). HLLs are typically more accurate in oral production tasks, while L2 learners make fewer errors on written tasks and those that tap explicit grammatical knowledge (see also Torres, chapter 1 in this volume; Fernández Cuenca and Bowles, chapter 5 in this volume).

These task effects are likely rooted in the distinct language-learning experiences of each learner population and the way grammatical knowledge (implicit and explicit) develops and is subsequently stored and accessed (Bowles 2011; Montrul 2011). Implicit knowledge is the automated, intuitive awareness about what is possible in one's language that can be accessed quickly but not verbalized: for example, the type of knowledge children develop while learning to speak but before starting school and studying structural aspects of the language (Bowles 2011; Ellis 2005). In contrast, explicit knowledge is conscious knowledge about language that can be at least partially described. Metalinguistic awareness, for example, encompasses explicit, abstract knowledge about the language itself that governs learners' ability to do things such as describe why a given form is grammatical or not. This awareness requires conscious retrieval of rules and is often the result of classroom learning (Bowles 2011; Roehr and Gánem-Gutiérrez 2009). While implicit knowledge underlies spontaneous oral production, explicit knowledge facilitates performance on tasks that require a conscious awareness of language structures and rules, such as written production/interpretation or grammaticality judgment tasks (Ellis 2005). Since HLLs grow up hearing and speaking their heritage language in naturalistic settings but do not necessarily formally study it in school, it therefore follows that they are typically more accurate in oral production and comprehension tasks than they are in written exercises requiring explicit structural knowledge. Conversely, L2 learners are frequently exposed to written registers and explicit grammar-based learning activities in the classroom while opportunities for oral production may be less frequent in comparison to those of HLLs. L2 learners therefore understandably make fewer errors in written tasks than they do in oral tasks that draw on implicit knowledge in real time. These task effects help shed light on the differences between HLL and L2 grammars, and also suggest that L2 teaching methods could serve as effective tools to help build the explicit grammatical knowledge of HLLs.

Despite the evidence that supports targeted instruction to address grammatical difficulties in L2 learner populations, only a few studies to date have examined whether instructional interventions developed for L2 grammatical learning will also be effective for HLLs (Montrul and Bowles 2008, 2010; Potowski, Jegerski, and Morgan-Short 2009; Torres 2018). While the results of these studies have been promising, the degree of grammatical gains made by HLLs has not always matched those of L2 learners. This is particularly true for written acceptability and grammaticality judgment tasks (see Bowles 2018). The task effects and variable results between the two learner populations once again underscore how differences in past language experiences are reflected in particular patterns of performance. That said, each of these studies targeted different grammatical structures and utilized distinct experimental methods. For this reason, further inquiry is needed to determine which specific instructional techniques will be most effective in developing HLL knowledge, given the particular grammatical structures and language tasks in question.

As in the L2 learning literature, the role of explicit grammar learning and instruction in HLL pedagogy has not gone undebated. This is particularly true as the recommendations for HLL teaching have evolved. At the heart of the matter are questions about the purpose and essential goals of heritage language education. Current HLL pedagogical models favor a macro-based approach to teaching the heritage language, which is similar to a language arts approach for monolingual learners (Beaudrie, Ducar, and Potowski 2014; Carreira 2016; Carreira and Kagan 2018). This approach addresses higher-order and functional skills at the outset of instruction via the use of authentic texts while balancing the other linguistic, cultural, and affective needs and abilities that HLLs bring to the classroom. Grammatical instruction is to be selective and target those forms that are most difficult for HLLs specifically. Overall, these recommendations represent a distancing from instructional techniques that privilege metalinguistic knowledge over communication and a shift toward those that engage learners in top-down, meaning-based communicative activities to help build students' multiliteracy skills (Colombi 2009; Carreira and Kagan 2018; Kagan, Carreira, and Hitchens Chik 2017; among others). However, this approach does not preclude the inclusion of grammatical instruction in HLL teaching, and there have indeed been calls for form-focused instruction to support HLL grammatical learning, particularly for populations of lower-proficiency learners (Carreira 2004; Carreira and Potowski 2011; Montrul and Bowles 2009; Potowski, Jegerski, and Morgan-Short 2009), such as the learners in this study. One practical consideration that emerges, then, is how to balance HLLs' grammatical learning needs with the other pedagogical recommendations for HLL classroom instruction. For example, considering class time limitations, how might effective grammatical instruction be designed so that the amount of instructional time available for building other higher-order skills is also maximized? Two recent studies (Cerezo, Caras, and Leow 2016; Zhuang 2019) suggest that the use of Computer Assisted Language Learning (CALL) technology might present one solution. In these studies, the authors demonstrate how computer-mediated technology can be harnessed to provide tutorial-based instruction that results in significant grammatical gains for L2 learners without necessitating an instructor's presence. The implication of these results is that certain aspects of grammar learning could be shifted to outside of the classroom, thereby freeing class time for other activities. These studies also point to the promising role of CALL in increasing explicit knowledge of target grammatical forms. While the role that explicit knowledge plays in L2 language acquisition has also been contested, it is precisely this sort of grammatical awareness that HLLs do not typically develop as a result of their past language experiences. In this case, its absence likely contributes to production or perception errors in tasks that are facilitated by a conscious knowledge of what is grammatical and what is not. Evidence for this can be found in the modest gains shown by HLLs in studies testing the effectiveness of explicit L2 methodologies on HLL grammatical learning, which are discussed later in the literature review. Subsequent studies must therefore determine what methods will produce the greatest grammatical gains for HLLs and in which specific language domains and tasks.

The focus of the current study is how to best support the grammatical learning needs of a particular subset of HLLs, namely, Spanish-English receptive HLLs. Receptive HLLs report the ability to understand their heritage language when spoken to but comparative difficulty speaking, reading, and writing it. The considerable asymmetry between their receptive and productive skills is the primary characteristic that sets them apart from other HLLs (Beaudrie 2009; Beaudrie and Ducar 2005; Sherkina-Lieber, Perez-Leroux, and Johns 2011). While only a handful of studies to date on HLL grammars have focused on receptive bilinguals as a distinct subgroup, their results have nevertheless revealed patterns in receptive HLL grammatical knowledge that pattern with those of more proficient HLLs and L2 learners. More specifically, receptive HLLs experience difficulties identifying and producing grammatical verbal agreement morphology (Beaudrie 2009), with knowledge of later-acquired forms and tense/aspect inflectional morphemes being particularly affected (Holmes 2017). Heritage bilinguals in the US are generally found in situations of subtractive bilingualism (Montrul 2018), which is characterized by a gradual weakening of the minority heritage language that can occur intergenerationally, and sometimes even within the same generation (e.g., Anderson 2012; Polinsky 2011). Due to these patterns in language loss, receptive HLLs may be the last in their families to have functional knowledge of Spanish (Beaudrie 2006). Examining effective teaching methodologies for receptive bilinguals is therefore particularly important for Spanish language maintenance in the US. To this end, the aim of the current study is to support the grammatical learning of a population of HLLs for whom language maintenance and (re)acquisition efforts are especially vital.

## Literature Review

### CALL and Grammatical Learning

CALL subsumes a wide range of sophisticated technologies that can be utilized to mediate and support language learning and use in a variety of ways. From computer and web-based programs to multimedia resources, social networking, and virtual worlds, these tools make it possible to target and support the acquisition of a wide range of language skills such as pronunciation, vocabulary, grammar/syntax, pragmatics, listening, reading, writing, intercultural competence, and multiliteracies, among others. The efficacy of CALL is promising though not clear cut and depends on a multitude of factors including learner type, the nature of the technology, the language task, learning goals, etc. (See Levy and Stockwell 2013 for an overview of CALL and language learning.) This study concerns itself specifically with tutorial CALL to enhance learners' grammatical development. Although recent studies in this area are limited, findings have shown promising results for improved grammatical abilities. For example, Luis Cerezo, Allison Caras, and Ronald P. Leow (2016) and Jingyuan Zhuang (2019) find superior results in grammatical gains by using a video game and guided induction to teach L2 grammar in comparison to classroom-based deductive instruction. The implications of these results will be discussed in more detail in the section dedicated to form-focused instruction below.

### Spanish Preterit/Imperfect Tense/Aspect Morphology

In Spanish, the temporal reference of a given situation is denoted by perfective and imperfective aspect, which is expressed via bound morphemes affixed to the verb. Although the discussion of tense/aspect distinctions has been simplified here for brevity (and examples adapted from Montrul 2009), the preterit generally emphasizes the beginning or completion of an event in the past ("El año pasado *visité* Europa") while the imperfect indicates certain unboundedness. This unboundedness or incompleteness in the past can denote actions that were in progress ("Marisa *caminaba* por el pasillo cuando saludó a Marcos"), actions that occurred habitually ("Cuando *era* niña me *gustaba* jugar con muñecas"), or generic events that are otherwise not temporally restricted ("Los dinosaurios *ponían* huevos").

### Spanish-English HLL Language Skills and Knowledge of Verbal Morphology

Studies of Spanish L2 learners' and HLLs' grammatical knowledge converge in that verbal morphology, and especially tense/aspect morphology, is especially susceptible to variable development during the acquisition process in comparison to other grammatical structures. Thereafter, learners may not have access to the full range of aspectual distinctions that are expressed grammatically via verbal morphology, or the ability to consistently identify and produce grammatical morphemes (see Montrul 2018 for a review of studies on heritage bilingual grammatical abilities). Little is known about the morphological abilities of Spanish-English receptive HLLs, however, who are the learners at the center of this study. Like more proficient heritage bilinguals, receptive HLLs are exposed to naturalistic Spanish input during childhood, generally through conversation with a parent or grandparents, but are formally educated in English (Beaudrie 2006; Beaudrie and Ducar 2005). Since these learners are typically exposed to reduced rates of Spanish input that is primarily aural and many times passive in nature, they often report later that they are able to understand Spanish but have more difficulty speaking it. Productively and typically, they are able to perform at a novice high level in familiar communicative contexts, and receptively they comprehend at an intermediate low to mid level according to the American Council on the Teaching of Foreign Languages (ACTFL) standards for L2 learners (Beaudrie 2009). Generally, their literacy skills (reading and writing) in Spanish are largely undeveloped (Beaudrie 2009; Beaudrie and Ducar 2005). In regard to their morphological knowledge, previous studies have found patterns of production errors in subject/verb agreement (Beaudrie 2009) and difficulty distinguishing grammatical from ungrammatical tense/aspect morphemes in aural input (Holmes 2017). These early indications suggest that tense/aspect morphology is an area of receptive HLLs' grammatical system that would benefit from support in the Spanish language classroom, though which types of support would be most effective are still undetermined. In the following section, we review recent studies that have examined the effects of instructional methods typically used in L2 populations to instruct heritage learners on specific grammatical forms.

## Form-Focused Instruction and the Role of Explicitness in Grammatical Gains

While the role for form-focused instruction in language-learning programs is well justified in the L2 literature, research about its efficacy in HLL populations and the ways it should be employed is still in its early stages. In one of the first studies of form-focused grammatical instruction on the language development of HLLs, Silvina Montrul and Melissa Bowles (2009), administered an explicit, grammatical explanation of the *a* indirect object marker with *gustar*-type verbs using computer-based instruction. While pretest results showed that HLLs' use of the indirect object marker was irregular and unsystematic, posttest results revealed significant gains in both production and grammatical intuitions.

This study highlights the promising role of computer-mediated technology in imparting form-focused instruction in the absence of an instructor and also supports the role of explicit instruction in HLL grammatical development.

Kim Potowski, Jill Jegerski, and Kara Morgan-Short (2009) compared the effects of two L2 instructional techniques—processing instruction and traditional output-based instruction—on HLL development of the past subjunctive. HLL improvement showed task-based effects; while HLLs exhibited modest linguistic improvement on production and interpretation tasks, that improvement was not seen in a grammaticality judgment task, unlike in the L2 comparison group. While still offering support for form-focused grammatical instruction, this study also highlights the ways in which differences in language-learning context and experience manifest themselves as task effects.

Julio Torres (2018) also examined the gains in subjunctive knowledge in both HLL and L2 learner populations via a CALL task manipulated differentially by intentional reasoning demands. Participants were assigned to either a simple condition, a complex condition, or a control group, and they completed three versions of an oral and written production task (pretest, immediate, and delayed posttests) to measure learning outcomes. Results showed that participants in both experimental conditions performed similarly in the oral production task. However, the L2 learners showed greater gains in the delayed posttest for the written production task compared to HL learners. Exit questionnaires indicated that HL learners seemed to assign more importance to the communicative purpose of the task, whereas L2 learners were more cognizant of the grammatical form being tested. These results again show how past language experience can affect the performance on different tasks.

Another question that researchers have grappled with is which particular types of form-focused grammatical instruction most positively affect grammar learning outcomes. Empirical studies of L2 acquisition have shown a clear advantage of explicit, form-focused methods over implicit learning. However, the results of studies comparing the relative effectiveness of particular types of form-focused methods, such as explicit deductive techniques (in which rules are provided to learners), versus explicit inductive techniques (in which rules are elicited from learners), or implicit textual enhancement (visually drawing learners' attention to relevant forms in the text of an otherwise content-focused activity) have been mixed (Ayoun 2001; Erlam 2003; LaBrozzi 2016; Lee and Huang 2008; Rosa and O'Neill 1999; Vogel et al. 2011). From a theoretical standpoint, deductive metalinguistic instruction provides the learner with declarative (conscious) knowledge about L1-L2 contrasts. Declarative knowledge is thought to be converted to implicit knowledge over time through practice (Carroll 2001; Cerezo, Caras, and Leow 2016; DeKeyser 1995). Inductive instruction, on the other hand, in which learners are asked to attend to patterns and to form metalinguistic rules on their own, is believed to stimulate deeper processing due to the problem-solving nature of the instruction (Cerezo, Caras, and Leow 2016; Oded and Walters 2001; Zhuang 2019). Input enhancement techniques, such as textual enhancement, which make target forms visually more salient, are designed to aid the "noticing" of target forms. This noticing is believed to promote the conversion of the input to intake, which eventually results in the learner acquiring and being able to use the form (LaBrozzi 2016; Sharwood Smith 1993).

Two recent studies (Cerezo, Caras, and Leow 2016; Zhuang 2019) combine both CALL technology and a guided induction approach with promising results. Guided induction is a particular type of inductive approach in which learners receive help co-constructing rules. This is done by directing their attention to relevant aspects in the input while asking guiding questions along the way.

Cerezo, Caras, and Leow (2016) examined the comparative effect of deductive versus guided-inductive instructional methods on grammatical accuracy in a population of Spanish L2 learners. This study also looked simultaneously at the comparative effectiveness of CALL-based versus traditional classroom instruction. The results showed superior gains for CALL-based guided induction over deductive methods on the acquisition of Spanish *gustar* structures. These gains were observed in oral and written production tasks, though no comparative advantage was found for a receptive task. The experimental design was replicated in Jingyuan Zhuang (2019) to test the effectiveness of deductive instruction versus guided induction on complex Chinese *ba* structures. The guided induction group experienced greater learning gains on production tasks that were more durable over time than did the deductive instruction group. The authors of both these studies interpret these results as evidence that guided induction can best affect deeper processing, which is then reflected in grammatical gains. The results also lend further support to the promising role of CALL technology in grammatical instruction and learning. We now turn to the current study, which examines the comparative effectiveness of three types of form-focused, computer-based grammar instruction on the grammatical gains in preterit and imperfect inflectional morphology in a population of receptive, Spanish-English HLLs: textual enhancement, inductive instruction, and deductive instruction.

## Present Study

### Purpose and Research Questions

The present study set out to examine the effectiveness of computer-mediated grammar instruction and the role of instructional explicitness on the accuracy gains in Spanish past tense verbal agreement morphology (preterit and imperfect) in a group of receptive HLLs. The study comprised two experiments that measured knowledge of the (1) preterit and (2) imperfect individually, each of which followed a pre/posttest design. The first examined the effect of the instructional treatment on the accuracy of preterit agreement morphology, and the second measured the effect of the instructional treatment on the accuracy of imperfect agreement morphology. The primary research questions posed in the study were (1) whether a computer-mediated grammar intervention would produce measurable gains in verbal morphology agreement accuracy, and (2) whether that accuracy would vary as a function of the type of form-focused instruction provided in comparison to a control group. Based on prior research, we hypothesize that participants in all instructional conditions (deductive, inductive, and textual enhancement) will outperform those in the control group and that the explicit (deductive and inductive) groups will outperform the implicit textual enhancement group.

## Method

### Subjects

The final subject pool comprised sixty-one students who were concurrently enrolled in and recruited from four sections of an elementary Spanish heritage course for receptive bilinguals at a large university in the US Southwest. Students initially enrolled in the course based on the results of a heritage language placement exam that places learners into one of three levels of heritage language courses depending on the specific language profile of each student. In addition, instructors conduct written and oral diagnostic tests at the beginning of the semester to ensure that students have been placed in the appropriate language track and level. In the event that students' language skills exceed those of a receptive bilingual, they may be encouraged to switch to the next in the series of Spanish heritage courses. Conversely, students who do not have a discernible degree of productive or receptive proficiency in Spanish may be advised to enroll in an L2 course. All students who participated in the study were receptive bilinguals as determined by both the placement exam and follow-up instructor assessments.

Of the 61 subjects, 45 were female (74 percent) and 16 male (26 percent). Their age range spanned from 18 to 22, with a mean of 18.32. None of these students had previously taken a Spanish course at the university level, though all participants had taken at least one Spanish course in high school. All but two students were born in the United States; one participant was born in Guatemala and the other in Panama City; however, both were raised and educated in the US. Students were also asked to report their language dominance

(English-Spanish). All but two students indicated that English was the language they felt most comfortable using.

## Design

Participants were randomly assigned to one of four experimental treatment conditions. These included 3 instructional conditions (2 explicit, 1 implicit), and a control group. The initial sample consisted of 91 heritage learners, who were randomly assigned to one of the experimental groups (textual enhancement, *n* = 23, explicit induction, *n* = 23, explicit deduction, *n* = 23, or to a control group, *n* = 22). Participants who were absent or late to class during the experiment period or who did not complete all sessions were eliminated from the final sample, which resulted in the groups being uneven (textual enhancement, *n* = 16, explicit induction, *n* = 9, explicit deduction, *n* = 21, control, *n* = 15). Per Robert DeKeyser (1995), in the two explicit conditions participants were instructed to attend to form, and grammatical rules were either provided or elicited. In the implicit condition rules were not provided or elicited, and no instructions were given to attend to form. The experimental groups and the instructional treatment they received in each of the four conditions are explained below.

### Implicit Textual Enhancement

In this condition, sixteen students read a contextualized story divided into three, eighty-to-one-hundred-word paragraphs/readings, each of which contained one of the following three sets of target forms embedded in the text: ten *-ar* verbs (reading 1), ten *-er* verbs (reading 2), or ten *-ir* verbs (reading 3). All verbs were regular and were bolded and highlighted in a different color from the rest of the text to make the target forms salient. After each reading, students were asked to complete a comprehension question to ensure that they were attending to meaning.

### Explicit Induction

In this condition, nine students read the same three eighty-to-one-hundred-word paragraphs containing ten *-ar* (reading 1), ten *-er* (reading 2), and ten *-ir* (reading 3) regular verbs and answered a comprehension question after each text. They were then presented with a list of the ten verbs from each paragraph in the infinitive form and were asked to copy the corresponding inflected forms from the experimental treatment text next to the infinitive forms. Next, participants were presented with a list of personal pronouns and verb stems from an exemplary verb pertaining to each verb class (e.g., "yo tom__" for *-ar* verbs) and were then asked to complete the corresponding forms of the verbs by inferring the correct inflectional bound morphemes from the input in the instructional treatment.

### Explicit Deduction

In this condition, twenty-one students read the same three eighty-to-one-hundred-word paragraphs containing ten *-ar* (reading 1), ten *-er* (reading 2), and ten *-ir* (reading 3) regular verbs and answered a comprehension question after each text. They were then provided with explicit rules that explained preterit and imperfect morphology from a metalinguistic perspective. For example, for preterit tense formation, subjects were presented with one contextual example per pronoun (e.g., "Tú bailaste → -aste, for example: ¿Bailaste salsa?").

### Control Group

In this condition, fifteen students read the same three eighty-to-one-hundred-word paragraphs containing ten *-ar* (reading 1), ten *-er* (reading 2), and ten *-ir* (reading 3) regular verbs and answered a comprehension question after each text. The control group was not instructed to attend to nor was their attention drawn to form in any way.

### Study Instruments

The effect of the instructional treatment on the accuracy gains for preterit and imperfect agreement morphology accuracy was measured by comparing results of pretest and posttest instruments designed by the investigators.[2] The instruments consisted of two distinct tasks: Task 1, a recognition task, measured participants' ability to recognize target preterit and imperfect forms. Task 2, a controlled written production task, evaluated how accurately participants could produce the target forms in contextualized sentences. Both of these tasks measured explicit knowledge, given their controlled nature (Cerezo, Caras, and Leow 2016; Spada and Tomita 2010).

Task 1 was designed so that sentences containing target, contextualized forms (preterit in Experiment 1 and imperfect in Experiment 2) were intermixed with sentences containing verbs from nontarget tense/aspect categories. Participants were instructed to circle the items containing the target forms, as would be the case for number 2 below in the posttest for Experiment 1.

Instructions: Can you recognize verbs in the preterit? Circle all the sentences that contain verbs that refer to the past and have past tense verb forms in the preterit.

1. No viven aquí.
2. Abrí la ventana.

Task 2 was designed so that participants were required to attend to tense/aspect agreement morphological markers in the instrument and in their written responses in order to produce the correct agreement morphology and inflected verb in a written cloze activity. The activity consisted of twenty-five sentences in which verbs with target bound morphemes had been omitted and replaced with a blank space. Participants were instructed to write the correct form of the missing inflected verb (provided to participants in its infinitive form) in the blank space. The following example illustrates the structure of items in this testing instrument:

3. El mes pasado mis primos ___________ (viajar) a Europa.

### Procedure

Students completed each of the two experiments in separate fifty-minute intact classroom sessions spaced two weeks apart, and they were administered prior to students' receiving any classroom grammatical instruction on preterit and imperfect morphology. The delay between experimental sessions was scheduled to prevent task repetition effects and to reduce the risk that participant fatigue would affect the results. Students completed both experiments while seated at a computer in a computer lab, and the instructional treatment was administered via a text-based PowerPoint presentation through which participants advanced at their own rate.

### Scoring Procedure

Possible scores for each of the individual tasks (recognition and written production) ranged from 0 to 25, for a potential overall total score of 50, representing one point per accurate item. No partial credit was given on any items, and spelling errors were not considered.

## Results

### Experiment 1: Preterit

Descriptive statistics, shown in table 2.1 and figure 2.1, were calculated for both pre- and posttests, and raw scores were submitted to a repeated measures Analysis of Variance (ANOVA) to determine if there was an effect of instructional treatment on accuracy. The ANOVA results for both tasks combined yielded a significant main effect for time, $F(1, 54) = 19.83$, $p < 0.000$, $\eta p^2 = .26$, and a significant interaction of time by condition, $F(3, 54) = 3.49$, $p < 0.05$, $\eta p^2 = .16$, with small effect sizes. These results indicate that, overall, subjects were more accurate after the intervention, but the interaction effect indicates a differential improvement between the treatment conditions. A paired samples t-test conducted to further examine the main effect of time within each condition showed that only the deductive group (change = 11.29) made significant gains [$t\,(21) = 4.13$, $p < 0.01$, $\eta p^2 = 1.12$] after the intervention.

**TABLE 2.1.** Descriptive Statistics for Experiment 1

| Type of test | Time of test | Condition 1: Implicit textual enhancement ($n$ = 17) Mean | SD | Condition 2: Explicit inductive ($n$ = 10) Mean | SD | Condition 3: Explicit deductive ($n$ = 18) Mean | SD | Control ($n$ = 13) Mean | SD |
|---|---|---|---|---|---|---|---|---|---|
| Recognition task | Pretest | 16.75 | 3.71 | 17.89 | 4.70 | 17.71 | 2.45 | 17.87 | 3.40 |
| | Posttest | 16.75 | 2.82 | 19.78 | 4.84 | 18.95 | 3.99 | 17.33 | 4.30 |
| | Change | 0.00 | | 1.89 | | 1.24 | | –0.54 | |
| Production task | Pretest | 14.63 | 12.44 | 16.56 | 12.98 | 13.48 | 8.55 | 14.77 | 10.90 |
| | Posttest | 16.90 | 9.30 | 21.72 | 10.74 | 23.52 | 7.68 | 17.90 | 10.55 |
| | Change | 2.27 | | 5.16 | | 10.04 | | 3.13 | |
| Total | Pretest | 31.37 | 14.85 | 34.44 | 16.82 | 31.19 | 9.37 | 32.63 | 12.50 |
| | Posttest | 33.66 | 11.24 | 41.50 | 13.74 | 42.48 | 10.66 | 35.23 | 13.44 |
| | Change | 2.29 | | 7.06 | | 11.29 | | 2.60 | |

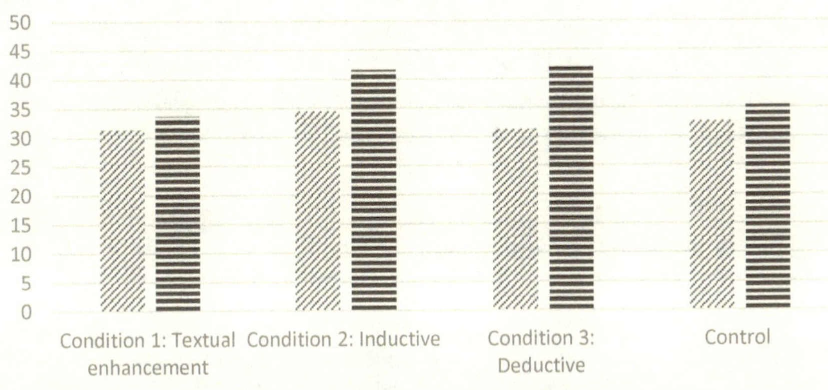


**FIGURE 2.1.** Accuracy gains for Experiment 1.

The ANOVA results for tasks showed that there was a significant interaction for time by task and by time by task by condition, $F(3, 57) = 3.06, p < 0.05$, $\eta p^2 = .14$, with a small effect size. These results indicate that gains were different for each treatment group and also for each experimental task. Thus, further analysis was conducted for each task separately. For Task 1 (the recognition task), there was no significant interaction of time by treatment condition, $F(3, 57) = 1.42, p > 0.05$. For Task 2 (the written production task), there was a significant interaction of time by condition, $F(3, 54) = 3.69, p < 0.05, \eta p^2 = .16$.

A paired samples t-test conducted to further examine the main effect of time within each condition showed that only the deductive group made significant gains [$t(21) = 4.47, p < 0.001, \eta p^2 = 1.24$].

## Experiment 2: Imperfect

Descriptive statistics, shown in table 2.2 and figure 2.2 below, were calculated for both pretests and posttests, and raw scores were submitted to a repeated measures ANOVA to determine if there was an effect for treatment (textual enhancement, inductive, deductive, and control). The ANOVA yielded a significant main effect of time. Subjects were more accurate after the intervention, $F(1, 54) = 29.64, p < 0.000, \eta p^2 = .35$. All effect sizes were small. Results of the ANOVA also revealed a significant interaction of time by condition, $F(3, 54) = 8.03, p < 0.000, \eta p^2 = .31$, indicative of a significant treatment effect. Tukey post hoc analyses revealed that the deductive group outperformed both the control group, $p < 0.000$, and the textual enhancement condition, $p < 0.05$, while the inductive condition was marginally significantly better than the control group, $p = 0.051$. In addition, a paired samples t-test was performed to further examine the main effect of time within each condition. Two treatment groups made significant gains: the textual enhancement group [$t(16) = 2.19, p < 0.05, \eta p^2 = .36$] and the deductive group [$t(17) = 6.24, p < 0.01, \eta p^2 = 1.48$], whereas the inductive group made marginally significant gains, [$t(9) = 2.16, p = 0.059, \eta p^2 = .99$]. The control group made no significant gains [$t(12) = .043, p > 0.05$].

**TABLE 2.2.** Descriptive Statistics for Experiment 2

| Type of test | Time of test | Condition 1: Implicit textual enhancement (*n* = 17) Mean | SD | Condition 2: Explicit inductive (*n* = 10) Mean | SD | Condition 3: Explicit deductive (*n* = 18) Mean | SD | Control (*n* = 13) Mean | SD |
|---|---|---|---|---|---|---|---|---|---|
| Recognition task | Pretest | 17.47 | 3.30 | 17.40 | 4.95 | 17.11 | 4.24 | 17.54 | 3.84 |
| | Posttest | 17.06 | 5.76 | 20.90 | 3.48 | 20.72 | 4.61 | 15.00 | 6.87 |
| | Change | 0.41 | | 3.50 | | 3.61 | | −2.54 | |
| Production task | Pretest | 8.44 | 10.58 | 6.05 | 6.11 | 7.14 | 10.98 | 10.58 | 13.76 |
| | Posttest | 14.35 | 13.47 | 17.15 | 16.93 | 25.64 | 12.43 | 12.12 | 15.38 |
| | Change | 5.91 | | 11.10 | | 18.50 | | 1.54 | |
| Total | Pretest | 25.91 | 12.55 | 23.45 | 9.83 | 24.25 | 14.29 | 28.12 | 19.34 |
| | Posttest | 31.41 | 17.86 | 38.05 | 18.40 | 46.36 | 15.59 | 27.12 | 16.59 |
| | Change | 5.50 | | 14.60 | | 22.11 | | −1.00 | |

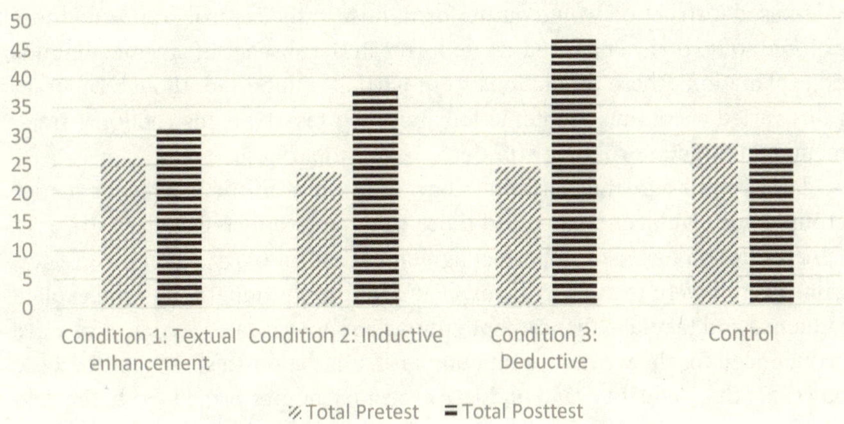


**FIGURE 2.2.** Accuracy gains for Experiment 2.

For the experimental tasks, there was a significant interaction of time by task and of time by task by condition, $F(3, 54) = 8.03$, $p < 0.000$, $\eta p^2 = .16$, with a small effect size. Further analysis was conducted for each task separately. For Task 1 (the recognition task), there was a significant interaction of time by condition, $F(3, 54) = 3.31$, $p < 0.05$, $\eta p^2 = .16$. As seen in Table 2.2, the only two groups that made significant gains after the intervention are inductive and deductive groups (change = 3.50 and 3.61 respectively). For Task 2 (the written production task), there was a significant interaction of time by condition, $F(3, 54) = 6.37$, $p < 0.05$, $\eta p^2 = .26$. As seen in Table 2.1, all three treatment groups outperformed the control group (change = 5.91, 11.10, and 18.50, respectively).

## Discussion

The present study set out to examine the effects of different form-focused instructional methods varying in explicitness and delivered by computer-mediated technology on the grammatical accuracy gains in a population of receptive HLLs. Our first research question asked whether a computer-mediated pedagogical intervention would produce measurable gains in accuracy in tense/aspect verbal agreement morphology for these particular learners. According to the results, the answer to that question is affirmative. Overall, learners were significantly more accurate on posttest instruments measuring grammatical accuracy after the experimental treatment. Our second research question asked whether grammatical gains would vary as a function of explicitness and the type of form-focused instruction that participants received. We hypothesized that participants who received explicit, deductive, and inductive rule-based instruction would outperform those in the control group and those exposed to textually enhanced target forms in the absence of any metalinguistic explanation. These predictions were partially supported, though accuracy gains varied according to interactions between task type, instructional treatment, and target morphology (preterit versus imperfect).

For preterit agreement morphology, only those in the explicit deductive group made significant gains, and those gains were only reflected in the written production task. For imperfect agreement morphology, again the greatest gains overall were found for the explicit deductive group, though the explicit inductive and textual enhancement group also showed gains, which were most pronounced for the written production task. On the posttest recognition task, however, the deductive and inductive groups outperformed both the text enhancement and control group. As a whole, the greatest gains were made by subjects in the deductive group across the tasks and verbal forms.

These findings are in line with previous studies in both L2 and HL contexts that found superior gains for explicit grammar instruction in comparison to other types of grammar presentation (Montrul and Bowles 2010) when learning outcomes are assessed through tasks that favor use of explicit grammatical knowledge. Deductive approaches in particular seem to be more effective for this type of computer-based instruction targeting certain language modalities. These results corroborate previous findings in the L2 context that also support the role of deductive instruction in accelerating language development (Carroll 2001) and suggest that instruction featuring explicit focus on form may be especially effective for learners who struggle with accuracy on tasks facilitated by explicit, metalinguistic knowledge.

Although the descriptive statistics presented in table 2.1 show trends that also point to beneficial effects for the inductive condition both in terms of gains made from the pre- to posttests and also in terms of overall accuracy percentage achieved at the time of the posttests, these gains, importantly, are not significant.[3] In this sense, results of the current study both overlap with and diverge from those reported in Cerezo, Caras, and Leow (2016). Both studies show the promising role of CALL in grammatical learning and provide empirical support for explicit, form-focused grammatical instruction as part of building explicit grammatical knowledge within a language program. In addition, both studies show that the instructional treatment was more effective for accuracy in written production tasks than on tasks measuring receptive knowledge. Cerezo, Caras, and Leow (2016) suggest that the greater benefit for form-focused, computer mediated grammar instruction on production rather than receptive tasks is due to the fact that receptive tasks are less challenging for learners in the first place. This is also the case for receptive HLLs, though it is also likely that the results of the current study are explained by the fact that the instructional treatment provided the metalinguistic knowledge that HLLs often lack but need in order to perform accurately on certain types of tasks.

Where our study differs from that of Cerezo, Caras, and Leow (2016) is in the comparative effectiveness of explicit deductive versus inductive methods. While the results of the two studies are not directly comparable due to differences in experimental design, nevertheless Cerezo, Caras, and Leow found that guided inductive methods were more effective, while the current study provides support for deductive methods. One important difference in experimental design, however, is that Cerezo, Caras, and Leow's inductive approach included a guided element, in which students received feedback along the way. Future research with Spanish-English receptive HLLs should also explore a guided inductive approach to gauge its benefits in this particular population of learners.

Differences between the explicit inductive and deductive conditions, and marginally significant gains for the inductive condition for some experimental tasks in this study, suggest that a computer-based inductive approach to morphology instruction may also be effective practice. Past research in the L2 context suggests that inductive instruction may be slow, requiring extensive exposure to L2 input (Ellis 1993). It is therefore possible that given additional exposure, a computer-based inductive approach might promote even greater learning. In addition, recent research suggests that a guided inductive approach may be comparatively more beneficial for the production of complex and cognitively taxing structures (Cerezo, Caras, and Leow 2016), providing grounds for future research that examines guided induction as an additional condition in studies of grammatical learning.

## Conclusions, Pedagogical Implications, and Future Research

This study contributes to the growing body of knowledge about the efficacy of certain classroom instruction and grammar learning methods in the heritage language-learning context and provides support for the role of explicit methods in developing morphosyntactic knowledge in writing, and to a lesser degree in receptive tasks.

The results support the view that computer-based, explicit teaching of grammatical rules produces superior results in accuracy gains for receptive learners on certain tasks, such as written production tasks, compared to other explicit methods. However, the current study only measured participants' production and recognition of morphological markers and did not delve into the semantic/syntactic distinctions between the two past tense forms. Also, because there are fewer imperfect morphological markers than there are preterit, it is possible that more generalized increases in accuracy for the imperfect are due simply to the fact that there were fewer forms to learn. In the same vein, future research should continue this line of investigation to determine if explicit grammar presentations are also more effective in introducing semantic distinctions between the preterit and imperfect, and if this type of computer-based instruction is equally effective for other grammatical forms and when assigned as homework. In addition, future studies should also examine the long-term effects of these gains. Last, given the potential of computer-based grammar instruction to supplant in-class grammatical instruction, the potential benefits for heritage learners of all proficiency levels should be explored. By delegating grammar instruction to computer technology, which can be widely accessed, more class time could therefore be devoted to higher-order tasks and literacy development.

The study has limitations that are important to keep in mind. Primarily, due to the short duration of the study accuracy gains may not be indicative of true mastery of the linguistic features under study and may only represent the recall of a pattern stored in short-term memory. Future studies with long-term designs should confirm the benefits of explicit computer-based grammar instruction for acquisition in receptive heritage learners.

Before turning to specific pedagogical implications, how do we first reconcile these results with recommendations for HLL pedagogy that emphasize a language arts approach, or with concerns that teaching grammar explicitly to HLLs may be confusing, distressing, or even inappropriate (see Holguín, chapter 7 in this volume)? First, we would like to make it clear that the implications and recommendations that follow are meant to delineate the role that grammar instruction might take as one small element of a larger language arts curriculum, not as a replacement for such a curriculum.

Crucially, we echo the recommendations previously mentioned that grammar instruction be selective and needs based and that it target specific structures and tasks that are difficult for particular populations of HLLs. In addition, grammar instruction for learners who are still developing their own variety of the heritage language should not be equated with imposing "standardized" grammar structures on speakers of what some would consider "non-standard varieties" (see Holguín, chapter 7 in this volume). The receptive bilingual population that participants were drawn from in the current study is known to exhibit difficulty producing and identifying even frequent grammatical tense/aspect morphology in written tasks and recognition tasks, and the pedagogical interventions were designed to address specific morphology in those particular language tasks. Caution should be taken against generalizing across language modes, and more studies are needed to determine the transferability of the learning gains to different tasks.

Rather than confuse or linguistically disenfranchise learners, we view grammatical learning as a tool that, in tandem with other pedagogical practices for heritage learners, may actually empower students by bridging their access to broader repertoires of language use and by helping them develop explicit knowledge about their heritage language. Interestingly, the results in our study contradict previous results (Beaudrie 2006) in which receptive bilinguals reported teacher-led grammar explanations as confusing, especially those enrolled in an L2 classroom. It is possible that participants in the current study were aided by the computer medium and nature of the grammatical explanations, which were presented gradually and allowed participants to progress at their own rate and go back to check their answers, thereby resulting in decreased levels of confusion and frustration for students.

Keeping these parameters in mind, this study has several pedagogical implications for the language classroom. First, more computer-based materials should be designed and tested for heritage learners. Unlike L2 textbooks, books for HLLs typically have no computer-based support in the form of a web-based platform for language-learning activities. Second, teachers should examine materials designed for L2 learners to see whether they might benefit heritage learners, bearing in mind that careful reading is necessary to ensure that the vocabulary and grammar focus match the needs of the students as well as the linguistic varieties that are relevant to them. Third, the results of this study show support for explicit grammatical instruction and, more specifically, a flipped model in which students complete grammar-based activities outside of class time so that they enter the classroom with knowledge that can be utilized during class activities, allowing class time to be structured around macro-based approaches and interactive activities.

This study was the first of its kind to examine the role of CALL in language instruction for heritage receptive bilinguals, and our hope is that it will pave the way for further inquiry into how computer-mediated grammar instruction can serve as a tool inside (or outside of) the heritage language classroom.

## Notes

1. In this chapter, the term "heritage language learners" refers to those heritage bilinguals who have chosen to formally study their heritage language in a classroom setting. The term "heritage language bilinguals" is used to refer to individuals who share the same type of bilingualism but who have not necessarily undertaken formal study of their heritage language. Heritage language learners are by definition heritage language bilinguals, though the inverse is not always true.
2. This study used an intact class in which the curriculum focuses extensively on preterit and imperfect tenses. The study treatments were conducted prior to the beginning of classroom instruction on those topics, so it was not possible to administer delayed posttests due to these restrictions.
3. As pointed out by one of the reviewers, the smaller sample size of this group may have influenced these results.

## References

Anderson, Raquel. 2012. "First Language Loss in Spanish-speaking Children." In *Bilingual Language Development and Disorders in Spanish-English Speakers*, edited by Brian A. Goldstein, 193–212. Baltimore: Brookes Publishing.

Ayoun, Dalila. 2001. "The Role of Negative and Positive Feedback in the Second Language Acquisition of the *passé composé* and *imparfait*." *Modern Language Journal* 85(2): 226–43.

Beaudrie, Sara M. 2006. "Spanish Heritage Language Development: A Causal-Comparative Study Exploring the Differential Effects of Heritage versus Foreign Language Curriculum." PhD diss., University of Arizona, Tucson.

———. 2009. "Spanish Receptive Bilinguals: Understanding the Cultural and Linguistic Profile of Learners from Three Different Generations." *Spanish in Context* 6(1): 85–104.

Beaudrie, Sara M., and Cynthia Ducar. 2005. "Beginning Level University Heritage Programs: Creating a Space for All Heritage Language Learners." *Heritage Language Journal* 3(1): 1–26.

Beaudrie, Sara M., Cynthia Ducar, and Kim Potowski. 2014. *Heritage Language Teaching: Research and Practice*. New York: McGraw-Hill Education Create.

Bowles, Melissa A. 2011. "Measuring Implicit and Explicit Linguistic Knowledge: What Can Heritage Language Learners Contribute?" *Studies in Second Language Acquisition* 33(2): 247–71.

———. 2018. "Outcomes of Classroom Spanish Heritage Language Instruction." In *The Routledge Handbook of Spanish as a Heritage/Minority Language*, edited by Kim Potowski, 331–44. New York: Routledge.

Carreira, Maria. 2004. "Seeking Explanatory Adequacy: A Dual Approach to Understanding the Term Heritage Language Learner." *Heritage Language Journal* 2(1): 1–25.

———. 2016. "A General Framework and Supporting Strategies for Teaching Mixed Classes." In *Advances in Spanish as a Heritage Language*, edited by Diego Pascual y Cabo, 159–76. Amsterdam: John Benjamins.

Carreira, Maria, and Olga Kagan. 2018. "Heritage Language Education: A Proposal for the Next 50 Years." *Foreign Language Annals* 51(1): 152–68.

Carreira, Maria, and Kim Potowski. 2011. "Commentary: Pedagogical Implications of Experimental SNS Research." *Heritage Language Journal* 8(1): 134–51.

Carroll, Susanne Elizabeth. 2001. *Input and Evidence: The Raw Material of Second Language Acquisition*. Amsterdam: John Benjamins.

Cerezo, Luis, Allison Caras, and Ronald P. Leow. 2016. "The Effectiveness of Guided Induction versus Deductive Instruction on the Development of Complex Spanish *gustar* Structures: An Analysis of Learning Outcomes and Processes." *Studies in Second Language Acquisition* 38(2): 265–91.

Colombi, M. Cecilia. 2009. "A Systemic Functional Approach to Teaching Spanish for Heritage Speakers in the United States." *Linguistics and Education* 20(1): 39–49.

Cuza, Alejandro, Rocío Pérez-Tattam, Elizabeth Barajas, Lauren Miller, and Claudia Sadowski. 2013. "The Development of Tense and Aspect Morphology in Child and Adult Heritage Speakers." In *Innovative Research and Practices in Second Language Acquisition and Bilingualism*, edited by John W. Schwieter, 193–220. Amsterdam: John Benjamins.

DeKeyser, Robert M. 1995. "Learning Second Language Grammar Rules: An Experiment with a Miniature Linguistic System." *Studies in Second Language Acquisition* 17(3): 379–410.

Ellis, Rod. 1993. "Interpretation-Based Grammar Teaching." *System* 21(1): 69–78.

———. 2005. "Measuring Implicit and Explicit Knowledge of a Second Language: A Psychometric Study." *Studies in Second Language Acquisition* 27(2): 141–72.

Erlam, Rosemary. 2003. "The Effects of Deductive and Inductive Instruction on the Acquisition of Direct Object Pronouns in French as a Second Language." *Modern Language Journal* 87(2): 242–60.

Holmes, Bonnie C. 2017. "I Understand Everything You Say, I Just Don't Speak It: The Role of Morphology in the Comprehension of Spanish by Receptive Heritage Bilinguals." PhD diss., University of Arizona, Tucson.

Kagan, Olga E., Maria M. Carreira, and Claire Hitchens Chik, eds. 2017. *The Routledge Handbook of Heritage Language Education: From Innovation to Program Building.* New York: Routledge.

LaBrozzi, Ryan M. 2016. "The Effects of Textual Enhancement Type on L2 Form Recognition and Reading Comprehension in Spanish." *Language Teaching Research* 20(1): 75–91.

Lee, Sang-Ki, and Hung-Tzu Huang. 2008. "Visual Input Enhancement and Grammar Learning: A Meta-analytic Review." *Studies in Second Language Acquisition* 30(3): 307–31.

Levy, Mike, and Glenn Stockwell. 2013. *CALL Dimensions: Options and Issues in Computer-Assisted Language Learning.* New York: Routledge.

Montrul, Silvina. 2009. "Knowledge of Tense-Aspect and Mood in Spanish Heritage Speakers." *International Journal of Bilingualism* 13(2): 239–69.

———. 2011. "Morphological Errors in Spanish Second Language Learners and Heritage Speakers." *Studies in Second Language Acquisition* 33(2): 163–92.

———. 2018 "Heritage Language Development: Connecting the Dots." *International Journal of Bilingualism* 22(5): 530–46.

Montrul, Silvina, and Melissa Bowles. 2008. "Negative Evidence in Instructed Heritage Language Acquisition: A Preliminary Study of Differential Object Marking." In *Selected Proceedings of the 2007 Second Language Research Forum*, edited by Melissa Bowles, Rebecca Foote, Silvia Perpiñán, and Rakesh Bhatt, 252–62. Somerville, MA: Cascadilla Proceedings Project.

———. 2009. "Back to Basics: Differential Object Marking under Incomplete Acquisition in Spanish Heritage Speakers." *Bilingualism* 12(3): 363–83.

———. 2010. "Is Grammar Instruction Beneficial for Heritage Language Learners? Dative Case Marking in Spanish." *Heritage Language Journal* 7(1): 47–73.

Montrul, Silvina, and Silvia Perpiñán. 2011. "Assessing Differences and Similarities between Instructed Heritage Language Learners and L2 Learners in Their Knowledge of Spanish Tense-Aspect and Mood (TAM) Morphology." *Heritage Language Journal* 8(1): 90–133.

Oded, Brenda, and Joel Walters. 2001. "Deeper Processing for Better EFL Reading Comprehension." *System* 29(3): 357–70.

Pascual y Cabo, Diego, ed. 2016. *Advances in Spanish as a Heritage Language.* Amsterdam: John Benjamins.

Polinsky, Maria. 2011. "Reanalysis in Adult Heritage Language: New Evidence in Support of Attrition." *Studies in Second Language Acquisition* 33(2): 305–28.

Potowski, Kim, ed. 2018. *The Routledge Handbook of Spanish as a Heritage/Minority Language*. New York: Routledge.

Potowski, Kim, Jill Jegerski, and Kara Morgan-Short. 2009. "The Effects of Instruction on Linguistic Development in Spanish Heritage Language Speakers." *Language Learning* 59(3): 537–79.

Roehr, Karen, and Gabriela Adela Gánem-Gutiérrez. 2009. "Metalinguistic Knowledge: A Stepping Stone towards L2 Proficiency?" In *Issues in Second Language Proficiency*, edited by Alessandro G. Benati, 79–94. London: Continuum.

Rosa, Elena, and Michael D. O'Neill. 1999. "Explicitness, Intake, and the Issue of Awareness: Another Piece to the Puzzle." *Studies in Second Language Acquisition* 21(4): 511–56.

Sharwood Smith, Michael. 1993. "Input Enhancement in Instructed SLA: Theoretical Bases." *Studies in Second Language Acquisition* 15(2): 165–79.

Sherkina-Lieber, Marina, Ana T. Pérez-Leroux, and Alana Johns. 2011. "Grammar without Speech Production: The Case of Labrador Inuttitut Heritage Receptive Bilinguals." *Bilingualism: Language and Cognition* 14(3): 301–17.

Spada, Nina, and Yasuyo Tomita. 2010. "Interactions between Type of Instruction and Type of Language Feature: A Meta-analysis." *Language Learning* 60(2): 263–308.

Torres, Julio. 2018. "The Effects of Task Complexity on Heritage and L2 Spanish Development." *Canadian Modern Language Review* 74(1): 128–52.

Vogel, Séverine, Carol Herron, Steven P. Cole, and Holly York. 2011. "Effectiveness of a Guided Inductive versus a Deductive Approach on the Learning of Grammar in the Intermediate-Level College French Classroom." *Foreign Language Annals* 44(2): 353–80.

Zhuang, Jingyuan. 2019. "Computer-Assisted Guided Induction and Deductive Instruction on the Development of Complex Chinese *ba* Structures: Extending Cerezo et al. (2016)." In *The Routledge Handbook of Second Language Research in Classroom Learning*, edited by Ronald P. Leow, 391–406. New York: Routledge.

THREE

# Effects of Instruction on Specific Measures of Accuracy in Spanish Heritage Learners' Writing

*Adrián Bello-Uriarte*
Butler University

Although heritage language learners (HLLs) and their instructors rate writing as the HL skill that is most in need of further development (e.g., Carreira and Kagan 2011), there is comparatively little research on HL writing compared to L1 and L2 writing. The existing research can be categorized into three groups: (1) surveys of HL students' perceptions of their writing ability, experiences, and need to write in the HL (Valdés et al. 2006; Callahan 2010); (2) descriptions of the processes and products of HL writing (Schwartz 2003; Bermel and Kagan 2000; Colombi 1997, 2000; Martínez 2007; Gatti and O'Neill 2017); and (3) examinations of HL writers' growth over time as a result of instruction (Jegerski and Ponti 2014; Pérez-Núñez 2015; Bowles and Bello-Uriarte 2019). Due to space constraints, the focus here will be this third category.

## Literature Review

### Previous Research on Effects of Instruction on HL Writing

Writing improvement has been measured at the lexical, syntactic, and discursive levels using a variety of measurements of complexity, accuracy, and fluency in monolinguals and bilinguals (e.g., Polio 2001; Wolfe-Quintero, Inagaki, and Kim 1998), but very few studies have used these measures with HLLs. Jill Jegerski and Estefanía Ponti (2014) examined the effect of peer feedback on the revisions made by sixteen Spanish HLLs in a university-level course over the span of two weeks. Perhaps owing in part to the short duration of the study, no significant change in lexical density (calculated as a type/token ratio), or in syntactic complexity (measured as mean sentence length), was found. There was, however, a significant increase in the total word count across drafts, which the authors considered evidence of improved fluency. Antonio Pérez-Núñez (2015) studied the effects of written corrective feedback (WCF) on the written production of twenty-four learners of Spanish as a second language (SLL) and twelve HLLs of Spanish. He analyzed 385 texts written over a period of four weeks by students who were divided into two groups: one group received WCF, and the other group received only content feedback. He then analyzed the errors made in the use of four grammatical structures: gender assignment, gender agreement, omission of definite articles, and use of present subjunctive. The author found that the group with WCF made more revisions of errors with the four target structures, but only improved in the accurate use of definite articles in new pieces of writing, whereas the group without WCF made only superficial corrections such as changes to spelling and orthography. In sum, this study provided evidence that feedback, as a component of writing instruction, may have positive effects on the improvement of at least some problematic grammar structures in writing.

The present study is a follow-up to Melissa Bowles and Adrián Bello-Uriarte (2019), which investigated the effects of genre-based heritage language instruction on writing improvement of two groups of university HLLs of Spanish. The instructed group ($n$ = 25) received instruction in their intact classroom for one semester, and the control group ($n$ = 25) carefully matched for demographic and proficiency variables, did not receive any writing instruction over the same period of time. Both groups produced two writing samples, one at the outset of the study and the second at the end of the semester (twelve to thirteen weeks later) to assess writing improvement in terms of changes in fluency, syntactic complexity, accuracy, lexical density, lexical diversity, and lexical sophistication. The results indicated that instruction had a positive impact on the instructed group—which improved in fluency, complexity, and lexical sophistication—while the control group made no significant gains in any measure. That is, after receiving writing instruction in the heritage language, the students improved their fluency, expressing their ideas in writing more easily and quickly. They also wrote with greater syntactic complexity, using more clauses per T-unit and moving from compound sentences with coordinating conjunctions such as *y* ('and') to a greater number of subordinate clauses, which is an attribute of formal writing. They also used more sophisticated vocabulary, incorporating a greater proportion of lower-frequency words.

On the other hand, instruction did not have a significant impact on overall accuracy, lexical density, or lexical diversity from the pretest to the posttest. Given that the instructed group made gains in fluency and complexity, it would have been uncommon to find significant gains in accuracy, as previous studies have found that trade-off effects are the norm, whereby one aspect of writing improves at the expense of another (Skehan 2009; Hartshorn et al. 2010). For instance, in a large-scale study Charlene Polio and Mark Shea (2014) found that over one semester English as a second language (ESL) learners significantly improved on holistic measures of language and vocabulary but not on accuracy (measured as error-free T-units). However, Polio and Shea found significant improvement in one error type (preposition errors), so they suggested that a more detailed analysis of specific errors might uncover areas of specific improvement that cannot be detected by global accuracy measures. This chapter sets out to do just that.

## Target Structures

There were three target structures investigated: two that were explicitly taught in the course (use of 'a' in verbal periphrasis and use of gerunds vs. infinitives) and one that was not explicitly taught (gender assignment and agreement). Each structure is briefly described below.

### *Use of 'a' in Verbal Periphrasis*

A verbal periphrasis is a grammatical construction consisting of a combination of verbal forms that make up one predication (Garachana 2017, 49). For instance, *ponerse a leer* ('to start reading') is a verbal periphrasis as this construction forms only one predication that indicates the beginning of a new action, and the meaning does not come from the sum of its parts, whereas *me gustó hablar contigo ayer* ('I liked speaking with you yesterday') is not a periphrasis as this expression contains two predications, one represented by the verb *gustar* and the other represented by the verb *hablar*. Kim Potowski (2011) observed that HLLs have difficulties with instances of verbal periphrasis that contain the nexus 'a' (i.e., they omit the "a" in writing, especially in cases where the "a" is elided in normal speech because it precedes or follows an adjacent "a").

Elision is a common phenomenon in spoken Spanish within and across word boundaries when two unstressed identical vowels are adjacent (e.g., *campana azul* 'blue bell' is realized as [kam.pá.na.súl] and *vamos a hacer* 'we are going to do' is realized as [bá.mo.sa.séɾ]). Because HLLs' primary input is auditory, elision is likely to cause them to think a periphrasis like the one above is written *vamos hacer*, rather than *vamos a hacer*, since the two are indistinguishable in speech (Montrul 2013).

### *Use of Gerund versus Infinitive*

Potowski and Prieto-Mendoza (in progress, cited in Escobar and Potowski 2015) investigated the degree to which Spanish HLLs accepted the use of gerund and infinitive in six different contexts: (1) subject of the main clause without an object

(*Correr/*Corriendo* una milla diaria es excelente para bajar de peso); (2) subject of the main clause with an object (*Comer/*Comiendo* pescado es saludable); (3) subject of the subordinate clause with a direct object (Mis amigos creen que *estudiar/*estudiando* otro idioma agiliza la mente); (4) subject of the subordinate clause without a direct object (Mi hermano prefiere *comer/*comiendo* con cuchara); (5) object of preposition (Necesito patines nuevos para *patinar/*patinando*); and (6) attribute (Su objetivo es *llegar/*llegando*). Potowski and Prieto-Mendoza presented four sentences with gerunds and four sentences with infinitives from each of the six contexts to 130 high school English-Spanish bilingual students. They indicated their level of preference for each sentence, where 1 = totally incorrect and 5 = totally correct. HLLs were more accepting of the use of the gerund in the contexts where it functioned as either the subject of a main clause (1 and 2) or of a subordinate clause (3). On the other hand, HLLs were more accepting of the use of the infinitive when it functioned as the subject of a subordinate clause without an object (4), as an object of a preposition (5), or as an attribute (6). The authors concluded that more studies with oral and written data were needed to confirm the uses of these two forms. They found that HLLs differed from monolinguals most in functions 1, 2, and 3, preferring the gerund rather than infinitive, so the activities provided in Potowski's (2011) textbook targeted the use of the gerund as the subject of a main or subordinate clause in English and use of the infinitive in Spanish, as described below.

#### *Gender Assignment and Agreement*

In Spanish, all nouns and adjectives bear gender marking, which can be either canonical or noncanonical (Harris 1991). Canonical nouns are masculine nouns ending in 'o' (e.g., *el libro*) or feminine nouns ending in 'a' (e.g., *la silla*), whereas noncanonical nouns end in the opposite vowel, in 'e', or in a consonant (e.g., *el problema*, *el puente*, and *el corazón*, but *la fuente* and *la canción*). Montrul and colleagues (2012) distinguished three possible types of errors related to gender marking: gender assignment, gender agreement, and ambiguous errors. Given the target noun phrase *la casa blanca*, an assignment error would be indicated by the article of the wrong gender and its matching adjective of the wrong gender, as in *el casa blanco*. An agreement error would be indicated by the article of the correct gender but the adjective of the incorrect gender, as in *la casa blanco*. Finally, an ambiguous error would be indicated by *el casa blanca*.

### The Present Study

The present study conducts a more detailed accuracy analysis of the writing produced by the fifty participants in Bowles and Bello-Uriarte's (2019) quasi-experimental longitudinal study, with the addition of fifteen more participants whose data had not been analyzed at the time the original study was published. It therefore fills the aforementioned gap in the literature by comparing instructed HLLs' accuracy on two particular structures covered in the course (verbal periphrasis with 'a' and the use of gerunds and infinitives) and one structure not explicitly taught in the course (gender assignment and agreement) to those of an uninstructed control group.

The research questions that guided this study were the following:

RQ1. Are there any significant differences in the use of 'a' in verbal periphrasis between the control and the instructed groups over a semester?
RQ2. Are there any significant differences in the use of infinitive versus gerund between the control and the instructed groups over a semester?
RQ3. Are there any significant differences in the use of gender assignment and agreement between the control and the instructed groups over a semester?

If instruction affected HLLs' accuracy, the prediction would be that gains in accuracy would occur for the instructed group but not for the control in the features that were explicitly taught and that neither the instructed nor the uninstructed group would make gains in the feature that was not a target of instruction.

## Method

### Participants

A total of sixty-five second-generation Spanish HLLs participated. There were thirty-three participants in the instructed group (16M, 17F), all between eighteen and twenty-three years of age ($M$ = 20, $SD$ = 1.44) enrolled in two sections of Spanish for Bilinguals I (the first of two consecutive writing courses) taught by the same instructor at a large public university in Illinois. There were thirty-two participants in the control group (13M, 19F), also between eighteen and twenty-three years of age ($M$ = 20, $SD$ = 1.0), who were not enrolled in any Spanish courses. An independent-samples t-test revealed that there was no significant age difference between the two groups $t(63) = 1.13$, $p = .13$.

As shown in table 3.1, the participants self-rated their language proficiency overall and by skill in both English and Spanish on a four-point Likert scale: Low (1), Intermediate (2), Advanced (3), and Native-like (4).

Participants' mean self-ratings in English and Spanish (overall and by skill) at the outset of the study were then examined to ensure comparability, and a

**TABLE 3.1.** Mean Self-Ratings in English and Spanish by Skill

| | Spanish | | English | |
|---|---|---|---|---|
| | Instructed ($n = 33$) | Control ($n = 32$) | Instructed ($n = 33$) | Control ($n = 32$) |
| Writing | 1.79 (0.60) | 1.72 (0.68) | 3.55 (0.62) | 3.50 (0.72) |
| Reading | 2.21 (0.78) | 2.16 (0.72) | 3.67 (0.48) | 3.59 (0.66) |
| Listening | 2.85 (0.75) | 3.16 (0.68) | 3.76 (0.43) | 3.72 (0.47) |
| Speaking | 2.12 (0.70) | 2.47 (0.72) | 3.67 (0.54) | 3.47 (0.67) |
| Overall | 2.25 (0.53) | 2.37 (0.52) | 3.66 (0.44) | 3.57 (0.59) |

*Note*: SDs are in parentheses.

multivariate analysis of variance (MANOVA) revealed that there were no significant differences between the groups, $V = .825$, $F(9,55) = 1.298$, $p = .259$, $\eta_p^2 = .175$. Paired-samples t-tests indicated that both groups evaluated their English proficiency significantly higher, both overall and in each subskill, than their Spanish proficiency [overall, $t(64) = 13.93$, $p < 0.0001$, $d = 1.72$; writing, $t(64) = 15.04$, $p < 0.0001$, $d = 1.87$; reading, $t(64) = 11.8$, $p < 0.0001$, $d = 1.47$; listening, $t(64) = 7.3$, $p < 0.0001$, $d = 0.9$; speaking, $t(64) = 10.72$, $p < 0.0001$, $d = 1.33$]. Effect sizes indicated a large difference in the self-rated ability between the two languages, with English being rated higher. The difference was highest in writing and overall language ability, followed in descending order of effect sizes by reading, speaking, and listening. This finding is not surprising since HLLs are expected to exhibit strong speaking and listening skills but weaker reading and writing skills in their heritage language, since reading and writing are less frequently developed in the home or at school.

## Procedure

All the participants provided informed consent to participate in the research and then completed a language background questionnaire. Two timed letters were written by hand in Spanish following two similarly framed prompts. The first letter was written near the beginning of the course and the second at the end of the semester, twelve to thirteen weeks later. The letters were written in class (instructed group) or individually in a quiet office (control group) in order to ensure that the work was independent and represented the students' own production (Price and Jackson 2015). All participants were asked to produce argumentative essays because this is the genre used in the course. The letters were directed to a specific reader (a fictitious president) in order to encourage students to select the rhetorical forms for addressing a formal audience (Scott 2010) and explaining a particular situation. The first prompt elicited a letter to a new Latin American president who was looking for information and needed some suggestions to elaborate a plan to slow down emigration from his country to the United States. The second prompt elicited a letter to a new Spanish-speaking president of the United States who was looking for information about benefits immigrants provide to the country and the ways in which the US government could provide assistance to them (see Bello-Uriarte 2019 for samples). The instructed participants wrote many letters as a part of the course and did not know which specific letters would be collected for analysis, in order to minimize any potential Hawthorne effects.

All students were given the prompt written on lined paper and were given five minutes for planning because previous research has shown that planning time can help writers improve fluency and complexity (Ellis and Yuan 2004). Then they were given thirty minutes to write in Spanish. Despite the fact that counterbalancing is highly recommended to control for topic and practice effects in a repeated-measures design, it was not possible due to the curricular constraints of the class. Nevertheless, the inclusion of a control group should allow topic or practice effects to be teased out.

Because the goal of this study was to see how instruction would affect HLLs' writing, the data consisted of argumentative letters students wrote. Students had flexibility to express their ideas as they chose, unlike in a controlled production task, which could have pushed them to produce particular structures, such as gerunds and infinitives, in predetermined contexts. Although data from a controlled task would have provided information on *all* learners' knowledge of the structures, it would not have provided any information about the extent to which the instruction led students to use the structures in their own new pieces of writing, which was the focus of interest.

## Pedagogical Intervention

### Instructional Approach

The instructed group was enrolled in Spanish for Bilinguals I, which is the first of a consecutive two-course sequence that provides an introduction to formal written Spanish, grammar, and reading, with an emphasis on writing and vocabulary building, for students who already possess basic to intermediate communicative skills in the language. Since this course is focused on writing, one objective is to enable students to distinguish between informal and formal uses of the language and be aware of the distinctions between spoken and written language (Valdés-Fallis 1978). The curriculum of the course follows a genre-based approach (Atkinson 2003; Hyland 2003), requiring students to write argumentative texts (letters) addressing a real audience. The students covered the first four of eight units in the textbook *Conversaciones escritas* (Potowski 2011); the other four were covered in the following semester. Specifically, the activities included practice with accents and common problematic grammar structures ('a' vs. 'ha', 'a' in verbal periphrasis, formal language use, definite articles, and infinitive vs. gerund). Grammar instruction targeted only a few features by providing explanations of the forms, presenting incorrect and correct forms side by side for students to identify the differences and providing additional activities to practice with the correct form. In terms of language use, the course adopts a sociolinguistically informed perspective and uses contrastive analysis for students to compare two forms—formal and informal—followed by activities that exemplify the differences between them. The objective is not to replace one form with the other but rather to make students aware of their differences and to help them be able to integrate a wider variety of formal structures into their language use in the appropriate situations (Beaudrie et al. 2014). Further details on the activities for the target structures analyzed in the texts are provided in the following sections.

### *Instruction on Use of Verbal Periphrasis with 'a'*

Instruction on verbal periphrasis with 'a' (Potowski 2011, 67–68) consisted of a brief explanation of the form with some examples. After the explanation, students completed two activities. In the first activity, they were provided with sentences such as (1a) and (1b), from Potowski (2011, 68).

(1a) Mi hermano va Ø ver una película. / Mi hermano va **a** ver una película.
'My brother is going to see a movie'.

(1b) Los actores iban Ø hablar con el director / Los actores iban **a** hablar con el director.
'The actors were going to speak with the director'.

The students had to identify possible reasons for forgetting to use the nexus 'a' by circling either the last letter of the finite verb or the first sound of the infinitive (wherever elision would occur). In the second activity, they were provided with some sentences containing the target structure to translate from English into Spanish.

### *Instruction on Gerund versus Infinitive*

Instruction on the use of the gerund vs. the infinitive in English and in Spanish (Potowski 2011, 149–50) consisted of a three-step explanation. First, students were provided with a chart with examples of verbs in the gerund and infinitive forms to observe and compare how the gerund is formed in both English and in Spanish. Students were asked to provide two more examples to add to the chart. Second, they were provided with a second chart to observe that in some cases, the gerund is used in the same circumstances in Spanish as in English.

Then, students were asked to select which element comes immediately before the gerund (a noun, an auxiliary verb, a preposition) to deduce the rule for gerund use in both English and in Spanish and to notice their similarities. Then, in order to help students notice how the gerund differs from the infinitive in English and in Spanish, they were provided with contrastive analysis, including cases where English uses a gerund (e.g., She felt that *joining* a union was her only option) but Spanish uses an infinitive (e.g., Sintió que *unirse* al sindicato era su única opción) and a gerund could not be substituted (e.g., *Sintió que *uniéndose* al sindicato era su única opción).

Then, students were given a rule to test whether the infinitive form works as a subject in Spanish. This rule basically consisted of adding the article 'el' before the infinitive. For instance, the article can be added before the verb in a sentence such as *(El) trabajar 14 horas diarias le dañó los pulmones* 'Working 14 hours a day damaged her/his lungs' so this indicates that the infinitive can be the subject of the sentence.

After the explanation, the students completed two activities. In the first activity, the students were provided with sentences that required them to select either the gerund or the infinitive, and in the second activity, the students were provided with English sentences containing a verb in the gerund form, and they were asked to translate them into Spanish, using the gerund or infinitive as appropriate (e.g., It is difficult *living* in the United States and *trying* to maintain Spanish.)

## Data Analysis and Coding

Obligatory uses of the targeted forms were identified by the researcher, and a second rater, a near-native Spanish speaker with experience teaching heritage and second language learners, separately rated twelve randomly selected letters (9.2 percent of the total sample) for purposes of inter-rater agreement. Accuracy was calculated as a percentage of the correct uses as a ratio of the total number of obligatory instances (Bitchener 2008), and inter-rater agreement was 100 percent.

## Results

### The 'a' in Verbal Periphrasis

Accuracy was reported as the percentage of correct usage in relation to the total obligatory instances per group on the pretest and posttest. Therefore, participants who did not use verbal periphrasis in both essays could not be included in the statistical analysis, leaving twelve participants in the control group and fifteen participants in the instructed group. Group means and

**TABLE 3.2.** Mean Accuracy on Verbal Periphrasis by Group

| | Control ($n = 12$) | | Instructed ($n = 15$) | |
|---|---|---|---|---|
| | **Pretest** | **Posttest** | **Pretest** | **Posttest** |
| Accuracy | 63.9 (41.3) | 36.1 (44.5) | 51.5 (42.1) | 75.9 (36.0) |

*Note*: SDs are in parentheses.

standard deviations were calculated for each group on the pretest and posttest and included in table 3.2.

On the pretest, the control group produced more instances of correct verbal periphrasis (65.8 percent) than of incorrect use (34.1 percent). The instructed group followed a similar pattern, with correct use in 60 percent of instances and incorrect use in 40 percent of instances. This result indicates that both groups had a similar degree of partial knowledge of the use of 'a' in verbal periphrasis at the onset of the study.

The data in table 3.2 show a clear trend. The instructed group increased in accuracy, moving from a mean percentage of 51.5 percent on the pretest to 75.9 percent on the posttest, while the control group decreased in accuracy from 63.9 percent to 36.1 percent. In most cases, uninstructed control groups are relatively stable over time, but the decrease shown here suggests that this structure is quite variable in HLLs' grammars. Because they are unsure when to write the 'a', sometimes they do it and sometimes they do not, and the lack of systematicity is probably what is reflected in the pretest-posttest change for that group.

Inferential statistics were then performed to determine whether the accuracy difference between groups on the pretest was statistically significant. Because the data were not normally distributed, as indicated by a Shapiro-Wilks test, an independent-samples Mann-Whitney U Test was performed on the pretest accuracy scores and showed that the control group (*Mean Rank* = 15.33, $n = 12$) was not statistically different from the instructed group (*Mean Rank* = 12.93, $n = 15$), $U = 74$, $z = -.81$, $p = .416$ in terms of accuracy on this feature at the onset of the study.

In order to determine whether there was a significant difference in accuracy at the end of the study, a gain score was calculated for each participant by subtracting the pretest score from the posttest score. Another independent-samples Mann-Whitney U Test was performed, revealing that the control group's pretest/posttest accuracy difference (*Mean Rank* = 10.63, $n = 12$) was statistically different from that of the instructed group (*Mean Rank* = 16.7, $n = 15$), $U = 49.5$, $z = -2.05$, $p = .04$, with a large effect size, $r = 1.14$. That is, the members of the instructed group, which received explicit instruction on the use of the nexus 'a' in verbal periphrasis, improved their accuracy after one

**TABLE 3.3.** Individual Results from Pretest to Posttest for Verbal Periphrasis

| Group | Result | Number | Percentage |
|---|---|---|---|
| Control ($n$ = 12) | Improved | 2 | 16.7 |
| | Became less accurate | 6 | 50.0 |
| | Did not change | 4 | 33.3 |
| Instructed ($n$ = 15) | Improved | 5 | 33.3 |
| | Became less accurate | 3 | 20.0 |
| | Did not change | 7 | 46.7 |

semester compared to their peers in the control group, who did not. An individual analysis was also performed to determine the number and percentage of students who either improved, became less accurate, or did not change from essay 1 to essay 2.

As shown in table 3.3, a higher percentage of participants in the instructed group (33.3 percent) improved their accuracy in the use of 'a' in verbal periphrasis than in the control group (16.7 percent). In addition, a smaller percentage of participants in the instructed group decreased in accuracy (20 percent) than in the control group (50 percent).

## Use of Gerund versus Infinitive

In total, participants wrote 500 instances of gerunds and infinitives in the first essay, with the vast majority (480 instances) being the infinitive and just 20 instances gerunds. Of the 480 times that HLLs used the infinitive, they made only 3 errors (.62 percent) compared to 15 errors (3.1 percent) with the gerund. This confirms Potowski and Prieto-Mendoza's claim that the use of the infinitive is not problematic for HLLs, whereas the gerund is.

The learners used the infinitive in all six contexts identified by Potowski and Prieto-Mendoza, using it correctly in 281 instances (58.5 percent). The examples are reproduced unchanged from the originals. When it functioned as the object of a preposition (e.g., los inmigrantes llegan a los EEUU *para robar* los trabajos); 98 instances (20.4 percent) when it served as the subject of the subordinate clause with a direct object (e.g., se necesita *hacer* una sugerencia); 70 instances (14.6 percent) when it was the subject of the subordinate clause without a direct object (e.g., los inmigrantes latinoamericanos no quieren *trabajar*); 16 instances (3.3 percent) when it was an attribute (e.g., el primer cosa que el gobierno de los estados [*sic*] Unidos debe que hacer es *no deportar* (a) nadie); 7 instances (1.4 percent) when it served as the subject of the main clause with an object (e.g., *Mejorar* la educacion a lo largo ayudara con los trabajos), and 5 instances (1 percent) when it functioned as the subject of the main clause without an object (e.g., *Emigrar* a los Estados Unidos suena ideal).

Because HLLs in both the control and instructed groups were at ceiling, with over 99 percent accuracy in the use of the infinitive on the first essay, there is no reason to examine pretest/posttest changes for either group in detail, since there was no room for growth. Mann-Whitney U tests confirmed that control and instructed groups were statistically similar at the pretest and also that they maintained their ceiling levels of accuracy at the time of the posttest.

The gerund was not only used far less often than the infinitive, but it was also used in just four contexts. On the pretest, the participants used the gerund correctly in 5 of 20 cases (25 percent): 4 cases (20 percent) as subject of the main clause with a direct object (e.g., *Usando estas sugerencias va a ayudar a los inmigrantes mas [sic]*); and in 1 case (5 percent) functioning as the subject of the main clause without an object (e.g., *pero* odiando *somos los mismos*). Additionally, the participants used the gerund incorrectly in 15 cases (75 percent): 8 cases (40 percent) as the subject of the main clause with an object; 4 cases (20 percent) as the subject of the subordinate clause with a direct object (e.g., *los inmigrantes florezcan a la economía (en)* abriendo *sus negocios*); 2 cases (10 percent) as the subject of the main clause without an object; and 1 case (5 percent) as an attribute.

For the gerund, it was not possible to analyze accuracy improvement at the group level because only 3 participants in the control group and 5 in the instructed group used gerunds in both essays. Results of individual analyses did not show a clear pattern, with 2 of 3 students in the control having a higher number of accurate uses of the gerund in essay 2 than in essay 1, and 3 of 5 students in the instructed group having a higher number of accurate uses in essay 2 than in essay 1. Given the small number of uses in each essay for such a limited number of students, it is not possible to make further claims.

## Gender Marking

The participants in the control group produced a total of 969 instances of gender assignment with an average of 30.3 instances per text (SD = 10.7), whereas the participants in the instructed group produced a total of 1,150 instances of gender assignment with an average of 34.8 instances per text (SD = 14.4). In addition, the participants in the control group produced a total of 177 instances of gender agreement with an average of 5.5 instances per text (SD = 3.7), compared to the participants in the instructed group who produced a total of 162 instances of gender agreement with an average of 4.9 instances per text (SD = 2.6).

Regarding errors in gender marking on the first letter, participants in the control group produced a total of 56 gender assignment errors (5.3 percent), ranging from 0 to 13, with an average of 1.7 errors per text (SD = 2.9); whereas participants in the instructed group produced a total of 66 gender assignment errors (4.5 percent), ranging from 0 to 10, with an average of 2 errors per text (SD = 2.5). Additionally, the participants in the control group produced a total of 7 gender agreement errors (0.5 percent), ranging from 0 to 2, with an average of 0.2 errors per text (SD = 0.5), while the participants in the instructed group produced a total of 20 gender agreement errors (1.3 percent), ranging from 0 to 3, with an average of 0.6 errors per text (SD = 0.8). These numbers indicate that learners were at ceiling with gender agreement but not with assignment. Therefore, pre/posttest comparisons will focus only on gender assignment because it is the feature where there was room for growth.

In order to determine whether the two groups were similar at the pretest in terms of the percentage of gender assignment errors, a Shapiro-Wilks test showed that the data were not normally distributed ($p = .000$) and independent-samples Mann-Whitney U Tests were performed, indicating no significant difference in the percentage of gender assignment errors by the control group (*Mean Rank* = 32.36, $n = 32$) and the instructed group (*Mean Rank* = 33.62, $n = 33$), $U = 507.5$, $z = -.280$, $p = .779$. The two groups were also statistically similar at the time of the second essay (*Mean Rank* = 34.02, $n = 32$), $z = -.433$, $p = .665$). This result shows that instructed HLLs did not make significant gains in a feature that is highly present in input but was not a specific focus of grammar instruction, and neither did uninstructed control group participants. This outcome provides evidence to strengthen our claim that the gains in verbal periphrasis with 'a' for the instructed group are indeed due to explicit instruction rather than to mere classroom exposure.

## Discussion

The present study investigated whether one semester of genre-based writing instruction incorporating focused grammar instruction on a limited set of target structures resulted in improved accuracy on three features (verbal periphrasis, RQ1; infinitive vs. gerunds, RQ2; and gender marking, RQ3).

RQ1: Results revealed that the instructed group significantly outperformed the control group, improving their accuracy in the use of 'a' in verbal periphrasis in their writing. This improvement consisted of including the preposition 'a,' which was frequently omitted at the beginning of the study. On the other hand, the uninstructed control group significantly decreased in accurate use of this feature from essay 1 to essay 2. Significant change for the control group was not expected, but this decrease suggests that prior to instruction, HLLs are not systematic in their use of 'a' in verbal periphrasis. Accuracy improvement for the instructed group can be attributed to instruction, which was shown to be effective in making students aware that the elided "a" sound in speech is required in writing.

RQ2: The results showed that both groups used the infinitive accurately most of the time in the six contexts analyzed, with few errors. The gerund proved to be more problematic, as learners sometimes used it in contexts where the infinitive was required. As in Potowski and Prieto-Mendoza's study, HLLs in the present study used the gerund as the subject of a main clause with or without a direct object, as the subject of a subordinate clause with a direct object, and in one instance, as an attribute. However, it was not possible to conduct inferential statistical analyses on the pre-posttest comparisons because few participants used the gerund in both of their essays.

RQ3: The results showed that both groups of learners had an error rate of about 5 percent with gender assignment, and this level of accuracy remained consistent across the essays. Unlike the other two target features examined, there was no explicit instructional focus on gender assignment in the course the instructed learners were enrolled in. Therefore, these results add credence to claims that the focused instruction is what led to instructed learners' gains with verbal periphrasis.

After one semester, although the instructed learners in this study did not show significant improvements in global accuracy, measured as percent of error-free T-units (as reported in Bowles and Bello-Uriarte 2019), significant changes in a specific feature that had been targeted in the course were found. This result confirms findings in L2 writing that accuracy improvement is often better investigated by analyzing a small number of features (Lalande 1982; Polio and Shea 2014) and that analysis of all errors may mask incremental improvements in particular targets of instruction (Bitchener 2008).

Along these lines, this study's findings with HL learners suggest that it is not realistic to expect significant overall improvement in accuracy in just one semester (as Polio 2017 demonstrates for L2 writing). This indication is particularly true given that the course that the instructed learners were enrolled in focused primarily on guiding students in the production of argumentative essays with an additional focus on just a few problematic grammatical forms, which Sara Beaudrie, Cynthia Ducar, and Kim Potowski (2014) describe as "treatable" errors. Although the focus of this chapter was accuracy, it is important to remember that writing is a complex, multifaceted process of which accuracy is a small component. In the context of a genre-based writing course in which grammar played a minor role, HLLs were able to make significant improvements in the fluency, complexity, and lexical sophistication of their writing, while also becoming significantly more accurate with one of the two targeted linguistic features examined, with a large effect size (verbal periphrasis). Conclusive results regarding the second feature—use of gerunds versus infinitives—were not found because learners were at ceiling from the outset on infinitives and many learners did not use gerunds in both essays.

## Pedagogical Implications

These findings demonstrate that the approach adopted in *Conversaciones escritas* (Potowski 2011), which follows the guiding principles in chapter 8 of Beaudrie, Ducar, and Potowski (2014) for HL writing instruction, is effective. In other words, as compared to uninstructed Spanish HLLs who were using Spanish in their homes and communities but were not taking formal classes, genre-based instruction with a focus on a limited number of problematic grammatical features helps Spanish HLLs improve their writing in the heritage language on a number of dimensions. Explicit instruction was used in small doses in this course and was shown to be beneficial, as demonstrated by accuracy gains in the target structure for which there was sufficient data for statistical analysis. The results should be understood in the context of the broader curriculum, which promotes reading skills, provides models of good writing, and draws on learners' knowledge base to move from spoken to written language. The results here suggest that explicit instruction on a few features is warranted and pays dividends. Furthermore, the large effect size gain in the accurate use of verbal periphrasis suggests that a more extensive focus on explicit grammar instruction is not warranted.

Perhaps the most important pedagogical implication to be drawn is to have realistic expectations for HL learners. Teachers should not expect learners to improve in all areas, and they should recognize that some learners will likely progress more quickly in some aspects of writing than in others, based on their background experiences and their particular focus. For instance, even within the same classroom, some learners may strive more to "get their thoughts on paper" and will become more fluent, whereas others may strive to be more accurate.

Given the heterogeneous nature of HLLs and the multilevel nature of many HL classrooms, individual differences may be particularly relevant. Students come to class with different strengths and weaknesses, and not all students improve at the same pace. They need instruction that does not assume that one student's roadmap for learning is identical to another's (Tomlinson 2003) and that considers their individual differences in linguistic and affective needs. Differentiated instruction that focuses on individual differences can, according to Carol Tomlinson (1995), "shake up" what goes on in the classroom so that students have multiple options for taking in information, making sense of ideas, and expressing what they learn" (3). It is important for teachers to use formative assessment to understand students' strengths, weaknesses, and goals and be able to differentiate instruction accordingly. In a writing course such as the one in this study, grammar instruction is limited and directed at specific features, but individual learners may show variation in their knowledge, requiring more or less practice with each. In responding to learners' writing, teachers also have the opportunity to differentiate instruction through the feedback they give. See María Carreira and Claire Chik (2018) for examples of differentiated instruction techniques for HLLs.

## Limitations and Future Research

The fact that the instructed group in this study was in an intact classroom is both a benefit and a limitation. On the one hand, it is essential to conduct such studies for reasons of ecological validity in order to determine to what extent HLLs benefit from classroom instruction (Bowles 2018), but on the other, research in intact classes does not allow for the same degree of control as a laboratory setting. For instance, this design did not allow the counterbalancing of the writing prompts, though having similar prompts allowed for topic effects to be controlled for. Another limitation is that although the students were tracked longitudinally over the course of one semester, longer than most past HL writing studies (Jegerski and Ponti 2014; Pérez Núñez 2015), it would have been even better to have followed the same students over the entire two-course consecutive sequence. There is always increased attrition the longer a longitudinal study continues, but such a study would provide data on which to base further conclusions on the trajectory of writing improvement and durability of the gains. For instance, it is not known whether HL learners would continue to improve in all of the areas in which they made gains during the first semester or whether there would be evidence of U-shaped learning or trade-off effects. In L1 and L2 writing research, the process of learning to write has been shown to be nonlinear (Larsen-Freeman 2006), so it is likely that some evidence of this trait would be found across the second semester course, but this theory would need to be empirically verified.

Given the relatively small number of participants, results should be replicated with larger samples in order to make stronger generalizations. In order to replicate this study, recruiting a large pool of HLLs is suggested to account for participant attrition, which is common in a longitudinal study, as well as matching instructed and uninstructed students for proficiency, language use, and relevant demographic variables. Since all the participants were second-generation HLLs from the Chicago area, it is unclear to what extent the results can be generalized to other populations of HLLs in the US who have different backgrounds in terms of generation, variety of Spanish spoken, and degree of Spanish proficiency. Further research in this regard is needed.

Since this is the first study to analyze whether classroom instruction specially designed for Spanish HLLs has a positive effect on the improvement of written accuracy in particular structures, much more research is needed. Other future studies are needed, for example, to compare outcomes of different instructional approaches, in different geographical zones in the US, at different educational levels such as high school—which has been largely understudied—across generations, and using other genres. Although it is known that writing ability is to some extent transferable across languages, it is unclear whether improvements in HLLs' writing in the heritage language would also have an impact on their writing in the majority language, English.

It also remains to be seen whether courses such as the one reported on in this study impact HLLs' language development in areas other than writing (i.e., whether gains achieved through instruction are transferred into oral production, which could help HLLs to reach higher levels of oral proficiency on the ACTFL scale [Swender et al. 2014]). For instance, it is unknown whether increased practice writing and supporting arguments, dealing with abstract topics and using more sophisticated vocabulary, as in this course, could transfer to oral language skills in the heritage language.

As alluded to above, writing is a complex process that should not be reduced to accuracy. When researchers do include measures of accuracy in HL writing studies, however, the present study's results suggest that global measures should not be the only measures used; rather, they should be complemented by measures focusing on a select number of target features. In addition, as language improvement may not occur linearly (Larsen-Freeman 2006), it is necessary to take measurements at various points in time to track developmental trajectories. Finally, further studies are needed to track students over longer periods of instruction, since "the longer we follow students, the more we learn. Learning to write is a very long process" (Polio and Park 2016, 298).

Considering Joan Chevalier's (2005) observation that producing argumentative texts is challenging as they require "the most complex written form lexically and syntactically," and that students should "begin with simpler, less formal conversational discourse and then progress, gradually mastering increasingly sophisticated and formal genres" (33), it is also important to investigate whether other genres, which might be more appropriate for lower proficiency learners than the ones in this study, produce similar outcomes in courses for HLLs.

## Note

My deepest thanks go to Kim Potowski and the instructors and students in SPAN 113, without whom this research would not have been possible.

## References

Atkinson, Dwight. 2003. "L2 Writing in the Post-process Era: Introduction." *Journal of Second Language Writing* 12(1): 3–15.

Beaudrie, Sara, Cynthia Ducar, and Kim Potowski. 2014. *Heritage Language Teaching: Research and Practice*. Columbus, OH: McGraw Hill.

Bello-Uriarte, Adrián. 2019. "Effects of Instruction on Writing Improvement of University Heritage Learners of Spanish: A Longitudinal Study." PhD diss., University of Illinois at Urbana-Champaign.

Bermel, Neil, and Olga Kagan. 2000. "The Maintenance of Written Russian in Heritage Speakers." In *The Learning and Teaching of Slavic Languages and Cultures*, edited by Olga Kagan and Benjamin Rifkin, 405–36. Bloomington, IN: Slavica.

Bitchener, John. 2008. "Evidence in Support of Written Corrective Feedback." *Journal of Second Language Writing* 17(2): 102–18.

Bowles, Melissa A. 2018. "Outcomes of Classroom Heritage Language Instruction: State of the Field and an Agenda for the Future." In *The Routledge Handbook of Spanish as a Heritage/Minority Language*, edited by Kim Potowski, 331–44. New York: Routledge.

Bowles, Melissa A., and Adrián Bello-Uriarte. 2019. "What Impact Does Heritage Language Instruction Have on Spanish Heritage Learners' Writing?" In *Evidence-Based Second Language Pedagogy: A Collection of Instructed Second Language Acquisition Studies*, edited by Masatoshi Sato and Shawn Loewen, 219–39. New York: Routledge.

Callahan, Laura. 2010. "U.S. Latinos' Use of Written Spanish: Realities and Aspirations." *Heritage Language Journal* 7(1): 1–27.

Carreira, María, and Claire Chik. 2018. "Differentiated Teaching: A Primer for Heritage and Mixed Classes." In *The Routledge Handbook of Spanish as a Heritage Language*, edited by Kim Potowski, 359–74. New York: Routledge.

Carreira, María, and Olga Kagan. 2011. "Results of the National Heritage Language Survey: Implications for Teaching, Curriculum Design, and Professional Development." *Foreign Language Annals* 44(1): 40–64.

Chevalier, Joan. 2005. "Heritage Language Literacy: Theory and Practice." *Heritage Language Journal* 2(1): 26–44.

Colombi, María C. 1997. "Perfil del discurso escrito en textos de hispanohablantes: Teoría y práctica." In *La enseñanza del español a hispanohablantes: Praxis y teoría*, edited by María C. Colombi and Francisco X. Alarcón, 175–89. Boston: Houghton Mifflin.

———. 2000. "En vías del desarrollo del lenguaje académico en español en hablantes nativos de español en los Estados Unidos." In *Research on Spanish in the United States: Linguistic Issues and Challenges*, edited by Ana Roca, 296–309. Somerville, MA: Cascadilla Press.

Ellis, Rod, and Fangyuan Yuan. 2004. "The Effects of Planning on Fluency, Complexity and Accuracy in Second Language Narrative Writing." *Studies in Second Language Acquisition* 26(1): 59–84.

Escobar, Anna M., and Kim Potowski. 2015. *El español de los Estados Unidos*. Cambridge: Cambridge University Press.

Garachana, Mar. 2017. "Los límites de una categoría híbrida: Las perífrasis verbales." In *La gramática en la diacronía: La evolución de las perífrasis verbales modales en español*, edited by Mar Garachana, 35–80. Madrid: Iberoamericana Vervuert.

Gatti, Alberta, and Teresa O'Neill. 2017. "Who Are Heritage Writers? Language Experiences and Writing Proficiency." *Foreign Language Annals* 50(4): 734–53.

Harris, James W. 1991. "The Exponence of Gender in Spanish." *Linguistic Inquiry* 22(1): 27–62.

Hartshorn, K. James, Norman Evans, Paul F. Merrill, Richard R. Sudweeks, Diane Strong-Krause, and Neil J. Anderson. 2010. "Effects of Dynamic Corrective Feedback on ESL Writing Accuracy." *TESOL Quarterly* 44(1): 84–109.

Hyland, Ken. 2003. Genre-Based Pedagogies: A Social Response to Process. *Journal of Second Language Writing* 12(1): 17–29.

Jegerski, Jill, and Estefanía Ponti. 2014. "Peer Review among Students of Spanish as a Heritage Language: The Effectiveness of a Metalinguistic Literacy Task." *Linguistics and Education* 26 (June): 70–82.

Lalande, John. 1982. "Reducing Composition Errors: An Experiment." *Foreign Language Annals* 17(2): 109–17.

Larsen-Freeman, Diane. 2006. "The Emergence of Complexity, Fluency, and Accuracy in the Oral and Written Production of Five Chinese Learners of English." *Applied Linguistics* 27(4): 590–619.

Martínez, Glenn. 2007. "Writing Back and Forth: The Interplay of Form and Situation in Heritage Language Composition." *Language Teaching Research* 11(1): 31–41.

Montrul, Silvina. 2013. *El bilingüismo en el mundo hispanohablante*. Chichester, UK: Wiley-Blackwell.

Montrul, Silvina, Israel de la Fuente, Justin Davidson, and Rebecca Foote. 2012. "The Role of Experience in the Acquisition and Production of Diminutives and Gender in Spanish: Evidence from L2 Learners and Heritage Speakers." *Second Language Research* 29(1): 87–118.

Pérez-Núñez, Antonio. 2015. "The Effects of Comprehensive Written Corrective Feedback on the Revision and Acquisition of Specific L2 Forms." PhD diss., University of Illinois at Urbana-Champaign.

Polio, Charlene. 2001. "Research Methodology in Second Language Writing Research: The Case of Text-Based Studies." In *On Second Language Writing*, edited by Tony Silva and Paul K. Matsuda, 91–116. Mahwah, NJ: Erlbaum.

———. 2017. "Second Language Writing Development: A Research Agenda." *Language Teaching* 50(2): 261–75.

Polio, Charlene, and Mark Shea. 2014. "An Investigation into Current Measures of Linguistic Accuracy in Second Language Writing Research." *Journal of Second Language Writing* 26(December): 10–27.

Polio, Charlene, and Ji-Hyun Park. 2016. "Language Development in Second Language Writing." In *Handbook of Second and Foreign Language Writing*, edited by Rosa M. Manchón and Paul K. Matsuda, 287–306. Boston: Walter de Gruyter.

Potowski, Kim. 2011. *Conversaciones escritas*. Hoboken, NJ: Wiley.

Price, Johanna, and Sandra Jackson. 2015. "Procedures for Obtaining and Analyzing Writing Samples of School-Age Children and Adolescents." *Language, Speech, and Hearing Services in Schools* 46(4): 277–93.

Schwartz, Ana María. 2003. "¡No me suena! Heritage-Spanish Speakers' Writing Strategies." In *Mi Lengua: Spanish as a Heritage Language in the United States*, edited by Ana Roca and María C. Colombi, 235–56. Washington, DC: Georgetown University Press.

Scott, Cheryl. 2010. "Assessing Expository Texts Produced by School-Age Children and Adolescents." In *Expository Discourse in Children, Adolescents, and Adults: Development and Disorders*, edited by Marilyn A. Nippold and Cheryl Scott, 191–213. New York: Psychology Press / Taylor & Francis.

Skehan, Peter. 2009. "Modelling Second Language Performance: Integrating Complexity, Accuracy, Fluency, and Lexis." *Applied Linguistics* 30(4): 510–32.

Swender, Elvira, Cynthia L. Martin, Mildred Rivera-Martinez, and Olga Kagan. 2014. "Exploring Oral Proficiency Profiles of Heritage Speakers of Russian and Spanish." *Foreign Language Annals* 47(3): 423–46.

Tomlinson, Carol A. 1995. *How to Differentiate Instruction in Mixed-Ability Classrooms*. Alexandria, VA: Association for Supervision and Curriculum Development.

———. 2003. *Fulfilling the Promise of the Differentiated Classroom: Strategies and Tools for Responsive Teaching*. Alexandria, VA: Association for Supervision and Curriculum Development.

Valdés, Guadalupe, Joshua Fishman, Rebecca Chávez, and William Pérez. 2006. *Developing Minority Language Resources: The Case of Spanish in California*. Clevedon, UK: Multilingual Matters.

Valdés-Fallis, Guadalupe. 1978. "A Comprehensive Approach to the Teaching of Spanish to Bilingual Spanish-Speaking Students." *Modern Language Journal* 62(3): 102–10.

Wolfe-Quintero, Kate, Shunji Inagaki, and Hae-Young Kim. 1998. *Second Language Development in Writing: Measures of Fluency, Accuracy and Complexity*. Technical report 17. Manoa: University of Hawai'i Press.

FOUR

# The Secret Is in the Processing: Categorizing How Heritage Learners of Spanish Process

*Celia Chomón Zamora*
ACTFL

Although various empirical studies have described the characteristics of heritage learners (HLs) and their profiles in comparison to their second language (L2) learner counterparts, a paucity of studies have analyzed them from a psycholinguistic perspective, providing information, for example, about *how* HL learners process input in their heritage language, and whether that processing differs substantially from that of monolingually raised native speakers and/or L2 learners. As Silvina Montrul (2010) has pointed out, "we need more psycholinguistically-oriented studies of adult HS [heritage speakers] to find out how they process input in the HL and in different skills" (19).

Investigating how heritage language speakers process input, such as a target grammatical structure, or different types of feedback, holds important pedagogical implications. It should be noted that although HL instructors have anecdotal evidence of how learners respond to instruction of different kinds, this is the first study to have HLs think aloud while engaging in instruction with or without explicit feedback. It therefore contributes introspective data to provide insight into how HL learners process components of instruction.

## Literature Review

### Feedback

Feedback is defined as "any indication to the learners that their use of the target language is incorrect" (Lightbown and Spada 1999, 171). Previous studies have stated that feedback could be provided either explicitly, where it is overtly stated that there is an error (i.e., giving the learner specific corrections relevant to an error), or implicitly, where the learner has to infer the existence of an error (i.e., through indirect discourse strategies, such as clarification requests or recasts) (e.g., Carroll and Swain 1993). However, rather than creating a dichotomous label for these terms, authors such as Susanne Carroll (2001) have discussed degrees of explicitness and have claimed that these degrees can be determined based on how they aid the learner in (1) detecting the purpose of the feedback, (2) spotting the location of the error, and (3) recognizing the nature of the error (i.e., lexical, syntactic, phonetic, etc.).

A number of computer-based empirical studies have surfaced recently, examining the role of the different types of feedback, particularly regarding their degree of explicitness (e.g., Yilmaz 2012). While several such studies investigating computerized feedback have yielded positive results for groups exposed to explicit feedback over implicit feedback (e.g., Rosa and Leow 2004), others found no difference between implicit and explicit feedback groups from pretests to posttests (e.g., Sanz 2004; Sanz and Morgan-Short 2004).

Of particular interest to the present study is Rosa and Leow (2004). One hundred fifth-semester L2 advanced Spanish college students completed a multiple-choice jigsaw problem-solving task in order to investigate the effects of different task conditions on participants' recognition and production of the Spanish contrary-to-fact past conditional constructions. The study compared six conditions that varied in their degree of explicitness: (1) EPEFE (explicit pretask, +explicit feedback), (2) EPIFE (explicit pretask, +implicit feedback), (3) EFE (explicit feedback), (4) EP (explicit pretask); (5) IFE (implicit feedback); and (6) CO (control). The computerized jigsaw puzzle contained eighteen critical items and ten distractors. Participants had to select one out of four options that best presented the contrary-to-fact meaning in the past in the subordinate clause of conditional sentences. Task-essentialness was part of every group condition, whereas the type of feedback changed based on the experimental group (i.e., the explicit feedback group received a metalinguistic explanation as to why the answer provided was correct or incorrect; the implicit feedback group was only informed of the correctness of the response). Learning was measured by recognition and production of old and new items in the posttest (which took place immediately after the experiment) and delayed posttest (which took place three weeks after the treatment).

The results were mixed. The data revealed that the explicit feedback group (EFE) significantly outperformed the implicit feedback group (IFE) in the recognition of new items and the production of old items on the immediate and delayed posttest. However, no difference was found between groups in any of the assessments over time for the recognition of old items or the production of new items. An important limitation that affects the results of this study, as noted by Cristina Sanz and Kara Morgan-Short (2004), is that the implicit feedback condition only received exposure to the target linguistic form in the eighteen items in the task, which may have not been enough to adequately grasp the structure, since implicit learning is known to be slower than explicit learning (Ellis 1993, 2006). Moreover, all of the experimental groups, in one manner or another (i.e., in the form of explicit/implicit feedback or through the pretask), received some kind of input containing the target structure, with the exception of the control group, which could help explain why all of the experimental groups outperformed the control group.

## Think-Aloud Protocols

Think-aloud (TA) protocols are a primary methodological tool used to study cognitive processing (cf. Leow et al. 2014), and they consist of participants speaking their thoughts aloud either while they perform a task (in the case of concurrent think-alouds) or sometime after completing the task (in the case of retrospective think-alouds). By utilizing TAs, the researcher is not only able to glean insights on how the participants interact with the input in the target language but also able to garner insights on the levels of awareness, types of processing (data driven vs. conceptually driven), depth of processing, and levels of cognitive effort. According to Leow et al. (2014, 114), data gathered from TAs allow researchers to operationalize and measure the roles of cognitive processes postulated to impact the learning process and provide data that can be used to determine how representative participants in each experimental condition were (i.e., to what extent they were following instructions as intended).

The utility of TAs notwithstanding, both concurrent and retrospective TAs have limitations. Because concurrent TAs are collected during task completion, they are not "constrained by memory" (Leow 2015, 141), unlike retrospective TAs, which can be subject to memory decay, especially if the delay between task completion and thinking aloud is sizable. On the other hand, there is concern that concurrent TAs will impose a dual task on participants and affect their task performance (an issue known as reactivity). Research in both cognitive psychology (Ericsson and Simon 1993) and in SLA (Bowles 2010; Cohen 2000) suggests that in order for the verbalizations to be an accurate reflection of learners' processing, they should be concurrent, if at all possible, and should not require the learners to provide additional reasoning or justification to explain their thoughts (Cohen 2000; Ericsson Simon 1993). It is just this sort of TA that was used in the present study.

A large body of first language (L1) and L2 research has relied on TAs to gain insight into learners' cognitive processing, ranging from studies investigating L1 and L2 reading and writing to those exploring the development of interlanguage pragmatics and the validation of large-scale language tests. Readers are referred to chapter 1 of Melissa Bowles (2010) for further information and references on the use of TAs in various research paradigms.

### Think-Aloud Protocols in HL Research

Although TAs have been used extensively in both L1 and L2 research, there are only a couple of studies to date that have employed TAs to understand HL learners' processing (Schwartz 2003; Yanguas and Lado 2012). Both of these studies asked university Spanish HL learners to think aloud while composing text in their HL because the authors wanted to gain insight into the processes HL learners go through while writing, as opposed to just examining the final product (the written essay). Ana Schwartz's (2003) study revealed that learners drew on their funds of knowledge in both English and Spanish to compose the text and that this led them to "process the material much more deeply, to further elaborate the ideas, and to make substantive changes as [they] rewrote the paragraphs" (250). Iñigo Yanguas and Beatriz Lado's (2012) focus was more methodological, as they sought to determine whether thinking aloud had a significant impact on HL learners' writing as compared to that of a group that composed silently. Results showed that the writing of learners who thought aloud was significantly more fluent and accurate than that of learners who wrote silently. The authors reasoned that thinking aloud provided HL learners with additional chances to be aware of linguistic forms during production and to "monitor their own writing processes and acquire helpful strategies" (Yanguas and Lado 2012, 393). Indeed, it makes perfect sense that having HL learners tap into one of their strongest skills (speaking) while writing would have a positive effect.

These are the only two studies to date that have used TAs to investigate HLs' processing, and both did so to understand how HLs compose in their heritage language. No study has yet been done to empirically investigate how HLs process aspects of instruction, such as feedback of varying explicitness or rule presentation, and this is the gap that the present study seeks to fill.

## Methodology

### Research Questions

The data for the current chapter are drawn from a larger study that examined how HL learners process linguistic data in Spanish and investigated whether +/− explicit feedback affects performance (Zamora 2017). This study was performed with a pretest / posttest / delayed posttest design, and participants in the larger study also included comparison groups of L2 learners of Spanish at a similar proficiency level. This chapter addresses the research question, "How do Spanish HL learners process instruction containing explicit and implicit feedback in their heritage language?"

## Participants

Participants were ninety-four HL learners enrolled in a Spanish for Heritage Spanish Speakers course at a public university in Miami, Florida. The class met three times a week for fifty-minute-long sessions, and other than self-identifying as a heritage speaker of Spanish, no other placement criteria were required to enroll in the class. These HL participants had not received formal instruction on the target structure, the past subjunctive, before beginning the study. The program was communicative in nature and placed an emphasis on the holistic instruction of listening, speaking, reading, and writing. Of the original ninety-four participants, nine were excluded from the final sample for one of the following reasons: (1) not scoring above 15 (out of 20) on the distractor items of the controlled production pretest to ensure a baseline, (2) not demonstrating a low level of prior knowledge of the target item (fewer than 5 out of 20 on the controlled production pretest), or (3) not following instructions. The HL participants' biographical information, self-rated proficiency, and Diploma de Español como Lengua Extranjera (DELE) scores are summarized in table 4.1.

## Linguistic Target

Similar to Elena Rosa and Ronald Leow (2004), the target structure for the current study was the Spanish contrary-to-fact conditional in the past. Whereas factual conditional sentences express situations that are at least viewed as having the possibility of occurring, contrary-to-fact conditional sentences are viewed as being completely hypothetical or impossible. These sentences may refer to past, present, or future time frames. The 'if' clause is typically found in a past subjunctive tense, and a variation of the conditional tense is used for the main verb. Following Rosa and Leow (2004), the experimental treatment featured two different types of contrary-to-fact conditional sentences in Spanish:

1. Those with results in the present or future, with the imperfect subjunctive in the subordinate clause and the conditional tense in the main clause:
   *Si yo fuera rico, compraría una casa.*
   [If I were rich, I would buy a house.]
2. Those with results in the past, with the pluperfect subjunctive in the subordinate clause and the conditional perfect in the main clause:
   *Si hubiera estudiado más para el examen,*
   *no habría estado tan nerviosa.*
   [If I were to have studied more for the exam,
   I wouldn't have been so nervous.]

These types of conditional sentences are considered to be highly complex and problematic structures for both native speakers and L2 learners of Spanish (e.g.,

**TABLE 4.1.** Participant Characteristics

| Group | Age (SD) | Gender (M, F, other) | Years of formal Spanish study (SD) | Self-rated listening ability (SD) | Self-rated speaking ability (SD) | Self-rated reading ability (SD) | Self-rated writing ability (SD) | DELE score out of 50 (SD) |
|---|---|---|---|---|---|---|---|---|
| + Explicit feedback | 20.65 (2.6) | 16, 21, 1 | 1.06 (1.24) | 2.48 (0.51) | 2.45 (0.51) | 2.23 (0.56) | 1.81 (0.65) | 30.71 (9.64) |
| − Explicit feedback | 20.21 (3.0) | 4, 14, 0 | 0.96 (1.22) | 2.47 (0.51) | 2.42 (0.51) | 2.21 (0.63) | 1.68 (0.67) | 33.32 (9.96) |
| Control group | 20.95 (3.0) | 11, 9, 0 | 1.91 (1.45) | 2.43 (0.51) | 2.35 (0.49) | 2.35 (0.65) | 1.61 (0.66) | 34.04 (8.79) |
| Maturational control group | 20.11 (3.9) | 4, 5, 0 | 1.33 (1.41) | 2.33 (0.50) | 2.25 (0.46) | 2.50 (0.53) | 1.33 (0.50) | 34.78 (10.06) |

*Note*: Means are presented first, with standard deviations in parenthesis. Maturational control group participants completed the pretest and delayed posttest but were absent for the experimental treatment and immediate posttest.

Collentine 2003; López Ornat 1994). They are not very widely used in Spanish and are usually not taught in the first couple of years of language study (Rosa and Leow 2004). Moreover, the subjunctive morphemes are not as salient as other structures, and learners find that native speakers are able to comprehend them despite not producing the subjunctive correctly.

In addition to not being frequent, there is substantial variation in how contrary-to-fact conditional sentences, particularly those in the past, are expressed in Spanish-speaking communities. Estrella Montolío Durán (1999) notes that this structure is most commonly seen in writing (i.e., newspapers and literature) and tends to appear most often in the form presented in the aforementioned examples. Colloquially, however, the structure takes on various manifestations:

1. Si + pluperfect subjunctive form used in Spain + conditional
   *Si hubiese estudiado más para el examen, no estarías tan nerviosa.*
2. Si + pluperfect subjunctive + pluperfect indicative
   *Si hubiera estudiado más para el examen, no había estado tan nerviosa.*
3. Si + pluperfect indicative + pluperfect indicative
   *Si había estudiado para el examen, no había estado tan nerviosa.*

The semispontaneous picture description pretest utilized in this study also provided a glimpse into how this meaning is expressed specifically in the local HL community:

4. Si + pluperfect subjunctive + pluperfect subjunctive
   *Si hubiera estudiado más para el examen, no hubiera estado tan nerviosa.*
5. #Si + present indicative + *ir* + a + infinitive
   *Si estudio más para el examen, no voy a estar tan nerviosa.*
6. #Si + present indicative + future
   *Si estudio más para el examen, no estaré tan nerviosa.*
7. Si + conditional + conditional
   *Si estudiaría más para el examen, no estaría tan nerviosa.*
8. #Si + imperfect subjunctive + conditional
   *Si estudiara más para el examen, no estaría tan nerviosa.*

The sentences indicated with a pound symbol, although grammatically correct, are not semantically equivalent to the proposed structure.

## Procedure

This study followed a pretest (week 1)–immediate posttest (week 2)–delayed posttest (week 4) design. In week 1, during class, participants were presented with an explicit review of contrary-to-fact conditional sentences in the present (e.g., *Si yo fuera rico, compararía una casa*) by the researcher. Then they completed a language background questionnaire and the pretests.

During week 2, participants were randomly assigned to one of three experimental conditions: +Explicit Feedback (+EF), –Explicit Feedback (–EF), or the control group. Participants in the feedback groups were asked to complete a think-aloud warm-up, followed by the treatment. Immediately after completing the instructional treatment, they took the two posttests. Then, in week 4, the learners returned and completed the two delayed posttests.

## Materials

### Explicit Review Session

During the first session, prior to the pretest and before starting the treatment, all participants were presented with a review of contrary-to-fact conditional sentences resulting in the present (the distractor item, e.g., *Si tuviera más dinero, compraría una casa*) in a classroom setting. Participants viewed a PowerPoint presentation providing explicit rules about and input containing this structure, as well as its uses. The tenses reviewed were the imperfect subjunctive in the main clause and the conditional in the subordinate clause. After the review, participants were asked to conjugate the verbs for the contrary-to-fact conditional sentences within the PowerPoint and were provided with the correct answers so that they could check their progress.

### Treatment

Participants were randomly assigned to one of three experimental conditions: +Explicit Feedback, -Explicit Feedback, or Control Group. Participants in the +/– explicit feedback groups were also further divided into a +Think-Aloud group (and asked to think aloud throughout the treatment in the language(s) in which they felt most comfortable), or a –Think-Aloud group, which completed the treatment silently. Silent and TA groups' results could therefore be compared to determine whether there were reactivity (i.e., whether thinking aloud had impacted performance). Results of this aspect are beyond the scope of this chapter but, as reported in Zamora (2017), silent and TA groups had comparable performance on posttests, suggesting that the act of verbalizing did not significantly affect learners' processing or performance.

> Participants in the feedback groups saw the following instructions: This activity consists of 2 short stories that you must help complete. You will

first read a brief paragraph that will introduce you to the scenario. Please keep this scenario in mind as you continue the task. You will then see a screen with a sentence. You will notice that one of the two parts of each sentence is missing. At the bottom of the screen, you have four sentence fragments. ONLY ONE OF THOSE FRAGMENTS IS APPROPRIATE TO COMPLETE THE SENTENCE. Your task is to try to complete each sentence by selecting the sentence fragment that you think best completes it. You will know whether you have completed the sentence correctly based on the feedback you receive.

What you are about to see is a grammatical lesson on how to formulate a specific structure in standard Spanish. There are many varieties of Spanish, and therefore, there are many different ways of saying the same thing (think about English- you could order a soft drink, a soda, or a pop, and they're all correct). If you have a different way of expressing this thought, it doesn't necessarily mean that your way is wrong. This is just an alternative way in which to do so.

Participants in both feedback groups had to complete sentences by selecting from the multiple-choice options provided, as follows:

____________________, se habría recordado que tenía que estudiar en vez de ir a una fiesta.

a) Si Angela hubiera escrito
b) Si Angela escribiera
c) Si Angela escribiría
d) Si Angela habría escrito

If a participant selected an incorrect answer, they received a message saying that the answer was incorrect. In the +Explicit feedback group, this was followed by a prompt to consider whether the sentence was in the present or past tense. In the –Explicit feedback group, no further information was provided (e.g., "Oops, wrong. Try again!"). All participants were then redirected to the previous screen to try again. Participants were provided with an unlimited number of tries until they reached the correct answer, at which point they were presented with a message saying that they had chosen the right answer (e.g., "¡Muy bien!"), and (in the +Explicit Feedback group only) provided with an explicit grammatical rule (e.g., "¡Muy bien! The condition expressed in this sentence refers to the PAST. In sentences like this, you use "SI + HUBIERA + PARTICIPLE"). There were 2 scenarios, each with

20 sentences, which included 10 distractors (a mix of imperfect subjunctive, preterit, and imperfect indicative) and 10 target items (the pluperfect subjunctive).

Participants in the control group were asked to read the same two stories described above, but with all correct verb forms already included (appendix). After reading the stories, they answered comprehension questions. This exposed the learners to the target forms in a natural, meaningful way without any feedback.

## Assessments

In order to ascertain whether the target grammatical structure was learned, participants completed a battery of assessments in a pretest / immediate posttest / delayed posttest design. The pretests also served to determine the participants' eligibility to participate in the experiment. All of the tests were pen-and-paper, and there was no time limit.

Controlled production task (CPT): A fill-in-the-blank test with contrary-to-fact conditional sentences served as the controlled production task. All three versions (pretest, immediate posttest, and delayed posttest) comprised scenarios similar to those used in the treatment. There were six different scenarios in total, and they were randomly assigned to the participants throughout the three sessions to account for any test effects. The CPT consisted of two scenarios, 40 sentences total: 20 distractors, which included the imperfect subjunctive, imperfect indicative, and preterit indicative; and 20 target items, which included the pluperfect subjunctive. Unlike the treatment activity, only the verb in the main clause was left blank. The ordering of the main clause and the subjunctive clause was randomized throughout the scenario (when grammatically allowed).

Semi-spontaneous picture description task (SSPDT): To complement the explicit nature of the CPT, and to descriptively view what HL learners produce when creating contrary-to-fact conditional sentences in the past, a semi-spontaneous picture description task was created. The task was administered to all participants immediately following the CPT in all three sessions. The task consisted of ten pairs of pictures (taken by the researcher), where each pair represented an 'if, then' clause. Below the pictures, blank lines were provided for participants to write a sentence describing what was occurring in the two pictures. In order to facilitate this, participants were also provided a 'si' (if) in either the beginning or middle of the lines to aid them in placing the main clause. In addition, to control as much as possible the answers that could be provided, two verbs in the infinitive were provided in parentheses under the pictures. Similar to the CPT, three different versions of the task were created to control for test effects. Please refer to the larger study (Zamora 2017) for complete materials.

## Results and Discussion

*How do Spanish HL learners process instruction containing explicit and implicit feedback in their heritage language?*

In order to determine how HL learners processed data in their heritage language, a qualitative approach to analyzing the think-alouds was taken, which consisted of utilizing Grounded Theory (see Glaser and Strauss 1967). Think-alouds from the thirty-four participants in the +TA group were transcribed and cleaned to remove false starts and pauses. Transcriptions were analyzed, and, once patterns were found, comments were classified into metalinguistic and nonmetalinguistic categories, as illustrated in table 4.2. The metalinguistic categories included "explicit grammar," "comparison grammar," and "prior knowledge that had been formally learned"; whereas the nonmetalinguistic categories included "intuition" and "prior knowledge that had been informally acquired." One comment could potentially be coded as belonging to more than one category.

The researcher coded the transcriptions and a colleague separately coded 20 percent of the data in order to establish inter-rater reliability. Initial inter-rater agreement was high, at 98 percent, and was calculated by dividing the number of episodes transcribed and coded identically over the total number of items transcribed and coded by both researchers. The two raters met to discuss the cases of disagreement (four instances), which were all resolved by discussing what should be considered as a verbalization of a grammatical rule. In addition, to further ensure the reliability of the transcriptions and the coding, 20 percent of the think-aloud protocols were randomly selected two months after the original transcription. They were retranscribed and recoded by the original researcher. The intra-rater agreement was determined via the same procedure listed for inter-rater agreement above and was found to be 100 percent.

One transcription could include comments belonging to more than one category. For instance, Participant 172 had two episodes that were categorized as "Intuition," one as "Prior Knowledge," and three as "Previous Lessons." In this case, Participant 172's transcription, therefore, would be identified as "Intuition / Prior knowledge / Previous lesson," without specifying which occurred with greater frequency. Table 4.3 shows the total number of HL participants whose transcription was identified as including one of the aforementioned categories. While this chapter focuses on how HL learners process input in Spanish, it is worthwhile to briefly mention how their L2 counterparts processed on the same task, in order to give more weight to the uniqueness of the HL process. Indeed, there is a noticeable difference between the types of

**TABLE 4.2.** Processing Categories Identified in the Think-Aloud Data

| Category | Subcategory | Descriptors | Examples |
|---|---|---|---|
| *Metalinguistic* | Explicit grammar | Makes mention of explicit grammatical structures, grammatical rules | "I think it's C because it would be if he was not . . . well I don't remember. Because uh tuvieron is **preterit third person plural** . . . not sure what tirar is. But habr*í*a is in that tense so the answer should be . . . comiera." (Participant 1) |
| | Prior knowledge (learned) | Alludes to previous grammatical instruction, either from the experimental pretest lesson, or prior formal instruction | "So if Esteban had returned home with the cake. Oh! It's in the past! That's why. It's in the past. Ok ok. So it's preterit, and it's pluperfect now. Ok. . . . so it's double past. Just like when I learned pluperfect. Okay, that makes sense. That makes sense." (Participant 5) |
| | Comparison grammar | Compares current input grammar to grammar of other languages | "Starting to think this is like what I learned in Portuguese with **tivesse** like that super complicated form. Was it in the past? Or the future? Should've taken Spanish instead of Portuguese." (Participant 134) |
| *Nonmetalinguistic* | Intuition | Makes references to participant's "gut instinct" and/or feelings of the validity of the grammatical structure | "Don't remember if patience should go with haber or tener, but my gut is telling me to go with um tener. But potentially, if I look at all of these different verb conjugations, it could guide me to the correct answer, too." (Participant 19) |
| | Prior knowledge (acquired) | Mentions previous instances where participant heard or was exposed to the target structure | "Wait . . . I know this. Isn't this that super fancy word that they use in the bible? 'Si hubiese tenido something something like that' about love and [expletive] in the Corinthians. Oooooh! I think it IS. Dale!" (Participant 149) |

TABLE 4.3. Processing Strategies Used by HL and L2 Learners

| Category | Subcategory | Number of HL (% out of 34) | Number of L2 (% out of 50) |
|---|---|---|---|
| *Metalinguistic* | Explicit grammar | 10 (29%) | 48 (96%) |
| | Previous lesson | 12 (35%) | 24 (48%) |
| | Comparison grammar | 1 (3%) | 5 (10%) |
| *Nonmetalinguistic* | Intuition | 30 (88%) | 6 (12%) |
| | Prior knowledge | 20 (59%) | 0 (0%) |

TAs employed by HL and L2 participants. While the vast majority of HL participants employed nonmetalinguistic strategies (intuition, 88 percent; prior knowledge, 59 percent), the L2 participants employed more metalinguistic strategies (explicit grammar, 96 percent; previous lesson, 48 percent; comparison grammar, 10 percent), particularly their understanding of explicit grammatical rules and how to apply them to the current input. Aside from the prior knowledge category, which no L2 learner utilized as a processing strategy in this experiment, each category occurred at least once in each group (HL or L2).

Tables 4.4 and 4.5 separate the processing categories even further by experimental condition, in order to answer the second part of the research question. As can be seen in table 4.4, HL participants in the +EF condition employed more explicit grammar strategies (59 percent) than the −EF condition (0 percent); however, those in the −EF condition employed more processing using previous lessons (47 percent) than those in the +EF condition (24 percent). The same pattern can be seen within the L2 participants in table 4.5, where those in the +EF condition employed the explicit grammar strategy (100 percent) more than the −EF condition (91 percent), whereas those in the −EF condition employed more processing in the previous lesson category (77 percent) than those in the +EF condition (25 percent). The HL −EF condition saw one participant employ the comparison grammar strategy (3 percent) compared to none in the +EF condition (0 percent), and the opposite is seen within L2, where the −EF condition saw a smaller number of participants employ the comparison grammar strategy (5 percent) compared to the +EF condition (14 percent).

With respect to the nonmetalinguistic categories, both HL (100 percent) and L2 (14 percent) participants in the +EF condition employed more intuition strategies compared to their −EF counterparts (HL: 76 percent, L2: 9 percent). Furthermore, although no L2 participants in either condition employed any prior knowledge strategies, HL learners in the −EF condition (88 percent) employed this strategy more than those in the +EF condition (29

**TABLE 4.4.** Processing Strategies Used by HL Learners (According to Experimental Condition)

| Category | Subcategory | Number of HL in +explicit feedback condition (% out of 17) | Number of HL in −explicit feedback condition (% out of 17) | Total number of HL (% out of 34) |
|---|---|---|---|---|
| *Metalinguistic* | Explicit grammar | 10 (59%) | 0 (0%) | 10 (29%) |
| | Previous lesson | 4 (24%) | 8 (47%) | 12 (35%) |
| | Comparison grammar | 0 (0%) | 1 (3%) | 1 (3%) |
| *Nonmetalinguistic* | Intuition | 17 (100%) | 13 (76%) | 30 (88%) |
| | Prior knowledge | 5 (29%) | 15 (88%) | 20 (59%) |

**TABLE 4.5.** Processing Strategies Used by L2 Learners (According to Experimental Condition)

| Category | Subcategory | Number of L2 in +explicit feedback condition (% out of 28) | Number of L2 in −explicit feedback condition (% out of 22) | Total number (% out of 50) |
|---|---|---|---|---|
| *Metalinguistic* | Explicit grammar | 28 (100%) | 20 (91%) | 48 (96%) |
| | Previous lesson | 7 (25%) | 17 (77%) | 24 (48%) |
| | Comparison grammar | 4 (14%) | 1 (5%) | 5 (10%) |
| *Nonmetalinguistic* | Intuition | 4 (14%) | 2 (9%) | 6 (12%) |
| | Prior knowledge | 0 (0%) | 0 (0%) | 0 (0%) |

percent). Some patterns arose in the data: explicit grammar strategies had a larger presence in the +EF condition in both HL (59 percent) and L2 (100 percent) than the −EF condition (HL: 0 percent, L2: 91 percent). More pertinent to this study were the specific patterns in both experimental conditions in the HL group. For example, more metalinguistic strategies were used by participants in the +EF condition (*N*= 14) than the −EF condition (*N*= 9).

And, although both conditions elicited nonmetalinguistic strategies, the data show that more participants in the –EF condition (88 percent) used the prior knowledge strategy than those in +EF (29 percent). In the +EF condition, 100 percent of learners used the intuition strategy, compared to 76 percent of learners in the –EF condition.

Although some L2 participants used nonmetalinguistic strategies to process the Spanish input (i.e., intuition), none of them produced anything that could be categorized as prior knowledge in this category. Although prior knowledge is defined as "an internal cognitive act in which a linguistic form is related to some bit of existing knowledge (or gap in knowledge)" (Gass 1997, 4), and could therefore include the metalinguistic category of "Previous Lesson" (which 48 percent of the L2 participants produced), it was decided to divide these two into separate categories, to be able to discern a metalinguistic statement of previously *learned* information to a previous *experience* or *acquisition*. The data indicated that although both types of participants can use prior knowledge by making a connection to the target form, one is metalinguistic and learned, whereas the other is nonmetalinguistic and experienced. HL participants employing prior knowledge to facilitate processing made references to various types of cultural components (e.g., music lyrics, parents and/or grandparents using the form, church sermons and/or prayers, famous quotes from *telenovelas* [soap operas]). L2 participants referencing previous lessons, on the other hand, alluded to formal grammatical instruction from current or previous semesters, homework assignments, or books, as shown in the excerpt below from the think-aloud of one L2 participant:

Participant 18: "'Habría comido' seems to be a lot like 'había comido', I think I remember reading that había comido is the past of the past. So maybe this is like the past of the past that is conditional?"

This can be contrasted with an excerpt from an HL participant's think-aloud:

Participant 196: "I'm like pretty sure Yayita used this word every time she talked about how life would be like if Castro hadn't come to Cuba. So maybe it's like . . . what could've been in the past, but that it's too late to change?"

Interestingly, however, whether think-alouds were employed metalinguistically or nonmetalinguistically, the majority of participants whose think-aloud protocol alluded to prior knowledge [L2: $N$ = 22 (of 24); HL: $N$ = 19 (of 20)] obtained high scores on both the immediate and delayed posttests. This is in keeping with previous studies that show the importance of the role of prior knowledge in L2 processing (e.g. Gass 1997; Leow 1998, 2015; Robinson 1995). Control group participants, who were exposed to the same instances of the target structure, but in a reading passage, did not have such gains. In fact, their scores were at floor level on all tests.

Elena Rosa and Michael O'Neill (1999) postulated that different kinds of instruction differing in explicitness may lead to different input processing, such that a more explicit type of instruction could promote data-driven processing, and a less explicit type could facilitate conceptually driven processing. Although the present study deals with +/− explicit feedback rather than instruction, it could be hypothesized that when participants receive just correct/incorrect feedback (as in the −EF condition), they may require more cognitive effort to process the linguistic input deeply and thereby employ processing strategies known to facilitate deeper processing (e.g., intuition, prior knowledge) when compared to participants provided with explicit grammatical information (such as those in the +EF condition), who employed more metalinguistic processing strategies.

Simply being exposed to the target structure in a reading (in the case of the control group) did not lead to learning gains. Although the control group did not perform think-alouds, and therefore it was not possible to observe how they processed the target form, it is likely, based on past research linking low posttest scores to shallow processing, that just reading the forms did not drive learners to process deeply enough to drive learning. This is similar to findings in Fernández Cuenca and Bowles (chapter 5 in this volume), which showed that an input flood technique did not result in lasting learning gains.

An additional finding that emerged from the data had to do with affective concerns. Two of the thirty-four HL participants' think-alouds manifested a feeling of cognitive overload, whereby they complained that the input was too confusing and complex for them to comprehend, or that they lost the motivation to attempt to process at a high level. This was far more prevalent among the L2 group, where the think-alouds of twelve out of fifty learners expressed such feelings, as shown below.

Participant 83 (L2): "Why is this so hard . . . I'm really not getting this. This is tiring me out."

Participant 104 (L2): "Whatever. This is over my head and I can't wrap it around my head at this point . . . ugh."

Both L2 and HL participants' think-alouds also revealed instances in which they would compare the input to their own variety of Spanish:

Participant 152 (HL): "Hm, like, I think I get what this is trying to say. But I wouldn't say it like any of the options here. So, I wonder if I've been saying it wrong this whole time [*laughs*]"

Participant 133 (HL): "This doesn't make sense, because I've never conjugated these verbs in these ways before."

Participant 41 (L2): "I remember we had to talk in this way [past subjunctive] in my high school Spanish class. But I am certain it wasn't with any of these. How the hell did we do it then? I know I haven't used these before. What did I use? How *would* I say this?"

Despite reminding HL participants that the forms to which they would be exposed in this experiment were *one* way of expressing this meaning, think-alouds from twenty HL learners revealed that they nevertheless doubted their own Spanish abilities due to the complexity of the exercise; this was an interesting finding, especially given that this response barely occurred with L2 participants, where there were only three participants who expressed similar doubts in their think-alouds:

Participant 168 (L2): "That just sounds really weird to me. Whatever. I'll go for it. Oh, I got it right! Yes, I actually know some Spanish! I'm not as bad as I thought I was in the beginning."

Participant 190 (HL): "This doesn't make any sense to me. This is some weird past tense shit. Clearly my family was right that I don't know how to speak Spanish."

These think-aloud excerpts stress that great care must be taken when designing a task, particularly when considering how HL learners may interpret and compare new input to their own variety (or knowledge) of Spanish.

Results from the think-alouds produced insights into the processing strategies that HL learners used in the current study. A large proportion of HL participants employed nonmetalinguistic strategies (primarily intuition) to attempt to process the target items, and though at least one participant used each category of processing strategy at least once, it was apparent that many HL participants did not use metalinguistic knowledge nearly as much as the L2 participants, particularly their understanding of explicit grammatical rules and how to apply them to the current input. The qualitative results of how HL learners process incoming data in Spanish are not surprising, given what has been reported in previous research (e.g., Rothman 2009) insofar as HL learners not being exposed to much metalinguistic or explicit information. Although HL participants employed both types of strategies in order to process the input, there was a clear preference for HL learners to use nonmetalinguistic strategies, particularly compared to the strategies that their L2 counterparts employed.

## Implications

This study has implications for research and pedagogy in the field of heritage language learning. First and foremost, this study emphasizes the significance of collecting concurrent data (e.g., verbal reports by participants while performing the task) if researchers are interested in the learning process, rather than just outcomes. Without concurrent data, analyses that explain participants' levels of processing, cognitive overload, intuition, and connecting the language to prior experiences would not have been possible or would have been anecdotal at best. The findings presented here may not come as a surprise to seasoned HL instructors, whose experiences in the classroom working with learners may resonate with some of the comments from the TAs. Nevertheless, this is the first time HL learners' engagement with +/– explicit feedback has been documented empirically, and this is an important step on the path toward understanding how HL learners respond to aspects of instruction and, by extension, how instruction can be designed so it is maximally effective for HLs.

An additional conclusion to contemplate is that of choosing appropriate pedagogical approaches for HL learners. Although intuition was commonly used in both +/– EF groups, TAs revealed that learners did sometimes refer to the explicit information from the lesson to make connections and complete the task. Indeed, 59 percent of HL learners in the +EF group made reference to explicit grammar strategies in their TAs. The fact that learners in both feedback groups made significant (and similar) pre/posttest gains indicates that HL learners in this study were not confused by the explicit feedback they received, in contrast to findings from some past research (Beaudrie 2009). Furthermore, activation of prior knowledge appeared to be advantageous for both groups, as it facilitated deeper processing of the target structure. However, HL and L2 learners tended to activate different sources of prior knowledge, with HL learners relying on knowledge from the same/previous lesson, or on cultural connections and/or associations, and L2 learners tending to refer back to previous explicit grammatical instruction in high school or other college courses. This finding highlights the personal nature of the learning process for all language learners and suggests that rather than simply relying on grammatical explanations from a textbook, teachers should encourage HL learners to draw on their own experiences to make connections with the content. The findings here reinforce the use of top-down (macro) approaches to teaching HLs that "take into account the learners' global knowledge of the language, and grammar and vocabulary instruction is provided within the context of discourse-level activities (Beaudrie, Ducar, and Potowski 2014, 70). Such practices could simultaneously reinforce the value of the HL knowledge learners bring to the classroom and help them to engage in deeper processing and have more durable learning gains. There are many different techniques that teachers could use to accomplish this, including having learners brainstorm in pairs or small groups at the beginning of a new lesson, or even using realia from pop culture references, such as songs or even excerpts from US Spanish corpora (see Vergara Wilson, chapter 6 in this volume). Teachers should remember that given the varied experiences of HL learners, the prior knowledge they bring to class varies, and such techniques could highlight those differences in a positive way and elevate and legitimize their home varieties.

## Conclusion

The present study sought to investigate how HL learners process input in their heritage language. Analyses showed that they employ a variety of approaches to process information in the target language. Whereas few HL learners utilize metalinguistic strategies involving previous lessons and explicit grammatical knowledge, the majority of HL learners in the study employed primarily nonmetalinguistic strategies, including prior knowledge (e.g., cultural connections, prior experience with the language) and intuition. Investigating HL learners' processing may afford instructors and researchers alike the opportunity to determine how different pedagogical interventions (not just feedback, as in this study) affect learners and could be beneficial for instruction, regardless of whether HL learners are placed in mixed or separate classrooms. Future research on processing should address not only how instruction affects learners' linguistic knowledge but also how it impacts their motivation and self-esteem, as these issues clearly emerged for HL learners in the TAs in this study.

## Appendix

### Excerpt of Control Group Treatment

**Scenario 1:** Ángela, a University of Miami student, forgot that she had a major test in her Spanish class last Monday. Now she realizes the consequences of forgetting about her exam, and of not studying for it.

Si Ángela hubiera escrito la fecha del examen en su agenda, se habría recordado que tenía que estudiar en vez de ir a una fiesta. Su compañera de cuarto le habría recordado de su examen si Ángela le hubiera dicho a su compañera de cuarto que iba a salir a una fiesta. Pero, cómo no le comentó nada en esta ocasión, su compañera de cuarto no se lo recordó. De cualquier modo, habría podido estudiar si no hubiera bebido tanto durante las fiestas. La última vez que Ángela tomó mucho, tuvo un gran dolor de cabeza, y durmió mucho. Si Ángela hubiera estudiado para su examen durante el fin de semana, no habría sacado una mala nota. Si hubiera hecho la guía de estudio antes de ir a la fiesta, tal vez habría sacado una mejor nota. Si hubiera puesto la alarma la noche anterior, no se habría despertado tarde el día del examen. Se habría despertado más temprano sin su alarma si no hubiera cubierto la ventana con una sábana. Si hubiera vivido en un dormitorio más cerca a la universidad, habría llegado a tiempo para el examen. Si no se olvidaría de sus responsabilidades escolares, tal vez sería aceptada a un programa de estudiar el extranjero. Si ella quisiera estudiar en Argentina, necesitaría una aplicación con buenas notas y una buena carta de recomendación. Si Ángela produjera una buena nota en la clase, su profesora le escribiría una buena carta de recomendación para su aplicación de estudiar en el extranjero. Pero, cómo no estudió lo suficiente, la profesora no se la escribió. Si hubiera asistido a las sesiones con el tutor de español, la habría ayudado a sacar mejores notas en la clase. El comité la aceptaría al programa si su aplicación para el programa de estudiar en el extranjero fuera mejor. Le iría mejor en la clase si prestara más atención a los anuncios de su profesora de español. Además, si no hubiera sacado una mala nota en su clase, no habría perdido la beca. Si continuara con su beca, Ángela no tendría que trabajar para pagar la matrícula. Este examen le enseñó a Ángela sobre la importancia de no salir a fiestas cuando tienes que estudiar.

Preguntas de comprensión:

1. ¿Por qué es importante que Ángela reciba buenas notas en su clase de español?
2. ¿Qué papel tuvo la compañera de cuarto de Ángela en este cuento?
3. ¿Cuál fue el resultado de Ángela perdiendo su beca?
4. ¿Cuál crees que fue el evento más importante que pasó / no pasó?
5. ¿Cómo cambiaría ese evento (en la pregunta #4) el resultado del cuento?

## References

Beaudrie, Sara. 2009. "Receptive Bilinguals' Language Development in the Classroom: The Differential Effects of Heritage versus Foreign Language Curriculum." In *El español en Estados Unidos y otros contextos de contacto: Sociolingüística, ideología y pedagogía*, edited by Manel Lacorte and Jennifer Leeman, 325–45. Madrid: Iberoamericana / Vervuert Verlag.

Beaudrie, Sara M., Cynthia Ducar, and Kim Potowski. 2014. *Heritage Language Teaching: Research and Practice*. New York: McGraw-Hill Education Create.

Bowles, Melissa A. 2010. "The Think-Aloud Controversy in Second Language Research." New York: Routledge.

Carroll, Susanne. 2001. *Input and Evidence: The Raw Material of Second Language Acquisition*. Amsterdam: John Benjamins.

Carroll, Susanne, and Merrill Swain. 1993. "Explicit and Implicit Negative Feedback." *Studies in Second Language Acquisition* 15(3): 357–86.

Cohen, Andrew D. 2000. "Exploring Strategies in Test Taking: Fine-Tuning Verbal Reports from Respondents." *Learner-Directed Assessment in ESL*, edited by G. Ekbatani and H. Pierson, 127–50. Mahwah, NJ: Lawrence Erlbaum.

Collentine, Joseph. 2003. "The Development of Subjunctive and Complex-Syntactic Abilities Among FL Spanish Learners." In *Studies in Spanish Second Language Acquisition: The State of the Science*, edited by Barbara A. Lafford and Rafael Salaberry, 74–97. Washington, DC: Georgetown University Press.

Ellis, Nick C. 1993. "Rules and Instances in Foreign Language Learning: Interactions of Explicit and Implicit Knowledge." *European Journal of Cognitive Psychology* 5(3): 289–318.

———. 2006. "Selective Attention and Transfer Phenomena in L2 Acquisition: Contingency, Cue Competition, Salience, Interference, Overshadowing, Blocking, and Perceptual Learning." *Applied Linguistics* 27(2): 164–94.

Ericsson, K. Anders, and Herbert A. Simon. 1993. *Protocol Analysis: Verbal Reports as Data*, rev. ed. Cambridge, MA: MIT.

Gass, Susan M. 1997. *Input, Interaction, and the Second Language Learner*. Mahwah, NJ: Lawrence Erlbaum.

Glaser, Barney G., and Anselm L. Strauss. 1967. *The Discovery of Grounded Theory: Strategies for Qualitative Research*. Chicago: Aldine Publishing.

Leow, Ronald P. 1998. "Toward Operationalizing the Process of Attention in SLA: Evidence for Tomlin and Villa's (1994) Fine-Grained Analysis of Attention." *Applied Psycholinguistics* 19(1): 133–59.

———. 2015. *Explicit Learning in the L2 Classroom: A Student-Centered Approach*. New York: Routledge.

Leow, Ronald P., Sarah Grey, Silvia Marijuan, and Colleen Moorman. 2014. "Concurrent Data Elicitation Procedures, Processes, and the Early Stages of L2 Learning: A Critical Overview." *Second Language Research* 30(2): 111–27.

Lightbown, Patsy, and Nina Spada. 1999. *How Languages Are Learned*. Oxford: Oxford University Press.

López Ornat, Susana. 1994. "La adquisición gramatical: Un esquema." In *La adquisición de la lengua española*, edited by Susana López Ornat, Pilar Gallo, Almuneda Fernández, and Sonia Mariscal 101–26. Madrid: Siglo XXI de España Editores.

Montolío Durán, Estrella. 1999. "¡Si nunca he dicho que estuviera enamorada de él! Sobre construcciones independientes introducidas por si con valor replicativo." *Oralia* 2(1): 37–69.

Montrul, Silvina. 2010. "Current Issues in Heritage Language Acquisition." *Annual Review of Applied Linguistics* 30(1): 3–23.

Robinson, Peter. 1995. "Attention, Memory, and the 'Noticing' Hypothesis." *Language Learning* 45(2): 283–331.

Rosa, Elena E., and Ronald P. Leow. 2004. "Computerized Task-Based Exposure, Explicitness and Type of Feedback on Spanish L2 Development." *Modern Language Journal* 88(2): 192–217.

Rosa, Elena E., and Michael D. O'Neill. 1999. "Explicitness, Intake, and the Issue of Awareness." *Studies in Second Language Acquisition* 21(4): 511–56.

Rothman, Jason. 2009. "Understanding the Nature and Outcomes of Early Bilingualism: Romance Languages as Heritage Languages." *International Journal of Bilingualism* 13(2): 155–63.

Sanz, Cristina. 2004. "Computer Delivered Implicit vs. Explicit Feedback in Processing Instruction." In *Processing Instruction: Theory, Research, and Commentary*, edited by Bill VanPatten, 245–60. Mahwah, NJ: Lawrence Erlbaum.

Sanz, Cristina, and Kara Morgan-Short. 2004. "Positive Evidence versus Explicit Rule Presentation and Explicit Negative Feedback: A Computer-Assisted Study." *Language Learning* 54(1): 35–78.

Schwartz, Ana M. 2003. "No me suena! Heritage Spanish Speakers' Writing Strategies." In *Mi Lengua: Spanish as a Heritage Language in the United States*, edited by Ana Roca and M. Cecilia Colombi, 235–56. Washington, DC: Georgetown University Press.

Yanguas, Iñigo, and Beatriz Lado. 2012. "Is Thinking Aloud Reactive When Writing in the Heritage Language? *Foreign Language Annals* 45(3): 380–99.

Yilmaz, Yucel. 2012. "The Relative Effects of Explicit Correction and Recasts on Two Target Structures via Two Communication Modes." *Language Learning* 62(4): 1134–69.

Zamora, Celia Chomón. 2017. "The Secret Is in the Processing: A Study of Levels of Explicit Computerized Feedback in Heritage and L2 Learners of Spanish." Ph.D. diss., Georgetown University, Washington, DC.

FIVE

# What Type of Knowledge Do Implicit and Explicit Heritage Language Instruction Result In?

*Sara Fernández Cuenca*
Wake Forest University

*Melissa A. Bowles*
University of Illinois at Urbana-Champaign

Due to increases in immigration in the last two decades, the US has seen a rise in heritage speaker enrollment in world languages courses built as foreign language courses (Carreira and Kagan 2011, 41). Although the role of language instruction in the language acquisition process has been extensively studied in the field of second language acquisition (Li 2010; Norris and Ortega 2001; Spada and Tomita 2010), there is little research on the effects that language instruction has on adult heritage learners (HLs). Therefore, there is an important need to investigate the effects that language instruction has on HLs to ensure that the learning needs of this student population are met.

## Previous Research on Instructed Heritage Language Acquisition

To date there have been few empirical studies that explored the effects of specific pedagogical interventions on HLs; these are briefly reviewed below. Kim Potowski, Jill Jegerski, and Kara Morgan-Short (2009) compared the effects of traditional output-oriented language instruction (TI) and processing instruction (PI) on second and heritage learners' knowledge of the imperfect subjunctive using a battery of tests that tapped into interpretation, production, and acceptability of this target form. Learners assigned to the PI group received explicit information (explanation of the rule) as well as information describing processing strategies that could interfere with their ability to notice this target form, followed by structured input activities. HLs assigned to the TI group also received an explicit explanation of the target form but did not receive information regarding processing strategies, and instead of receiving structured input practice, they completed output-focused practice, similar to what is found in many Spanish HL textbooks. Results showed that HLs in both experimental groups made significant learning gains from pre- to posttest when compared to a control group that completed the tests but did not receive instruction. No difference was found between experimental groups. In other words, HLs benefited equally from both instructional interventions. However, these learning gains were only found on the interpretation and production tasks. Ratings on the acceptability judgment tasks (AJTs) did not change significantly over time. Overall, these findings suggest that both traditional instruction and processing instruction were beneficial for HLs in the sense that they helped them interpret and produce the target form more accurately over time; however, neither of these instructional approaches affected HLs' acceptability ratings.

Silvina Montrul and Melissa Bowles (2010) tested forty-five HLs on their knowledge of Differential Object Marking (DOM) in Spanish and *gustar*-type verbs. They used explicit instruction, which consisted of an explicit grammar explanation followed by a practice exercise, in which immediate explicit corrective feedback was provided. Language learning was gauged using written production and acceptability judgment pre- and posttests. Results showed that HLs in the experimental group made significantly larger gains than those in the tests-only control group, who received no instruction but completed the tests. Furthermore, gains were larger in the written production task than in the AJT. HLs who received instruction improved at identifying grammatically correct sentences containing DOM but did not consistently do as well rejecting ungrammatical sentences with inanimate objects (containing an *a-personal*). The authors concluded that HLs can benefit from explicit language instruction in adulthood, but instruction did not seem to affect HLs' acceptability ratings as much as it did their written production of the target form.

Another study that examined the impact of instruction on HLs is Torres (2018), who examined the effects of task-based instruction on HLs' knowledge of subjunctive and indicative in Spanish adjectival clauses. A total of thirty-four heritage and forty-nine second language (L2) learners completed oral and written production pretests, immediate posttests, and delayed posttests (1–2 weeks after instruction) and were divided into a control group and two experimental groups that received computerized task-based instruction on the target form with written feedback and that differed based on the task complexity used to assess learning gains (±complex task). Results yielded comparable gains in oral production for instructed heritage and L2 learners that were sustained in the delayed posttest; however, L2 learners showed larger gains from pre to delayed posttest in written production than did HLs. (See also Torres, chapter 1 in this volume.) Data from the debriefing questionnaire suggested that HLs had approached the task differently than L2 learners. Whereas L2 learners were concentrating more on language form and trying to find patterns or rules, HLs focused more on the meaning-making aspect of the task. In addition, HLs did not seem to understand the written recast feedback as corrective, similar to what Susan Gass and Kim Lewis (2007) found with a small-scale task-based interaction study with Italian HLs who received oral corrective feedback.

The findings from these three studies suggest that grammar instruction can be beneficial for adult HLs, but they also reveal that language instruction affects L2s and HLs differently. Furthermore, the lack of systematicity among these studies, as well as the different linguistic nature of the target forms studied, make it difficult to draw any firm conclusions about the effectiveness that different instructional interventions may have on HLs. Finally, only one of the three studies included a delayed posttest, and without this data it is not possible to conclude whether instruction can lead to durable, long-term learning gains.

## Where to Go from Here?

Bowles (2018, 331) calls for a systematic research agenda to empirically establish the best pedagogical practices for this growing student population. The two major questions that she states are fundamental to moving the field forward are: Is classroom instruction beneficial for HL learning? And, if so, what makes this instruction maximally effective? The present study aims to contribute to this line of research by examining not only whether explicit and implicit instruction have differential effects on Spanish HL learners but also what kind of knowledge (explicit or implicit) each type of instruction results in. In order to build incrementally on the existing literature, we chose to focus on the same structure as in Kim Potowski, Jill Jegerski, and Kara Morgan-Short (2009) and to have an explicit instruction group based on PI, as they did.

HLs have a different linguistic profile from L2 learners. Most heritage speakers learn the HL primarily aurally, in their homes and/or communities from an early age, and largely in a naturalistic environment. On the other hand, classroom L2 learners typically begin to learn the language later in life, with their main sources of input being written text and limited teacher input in a formal classroom environment. Thus, these differences in language acquisition context likely influence both the nature of L2's and HL learners' linguistic knowledge and how they approach language learning in a classroom setting. Research has shown that L2 learners tend to rely more on explicit language knowledge, whereas heritage learners tend to rely more on implicit language knowledge (Bowles 2011; Montrul, Bhatt, and Girju 2014; Torres 2018).

Rod Ellis (2005) operationalized the constructs of explicit and implicit knowledge and conducted a psychometric study with English native speakers and L2 learners to determine which tasks target primarily explicit knowledge and which tasks target primarily implicit knowledge. He found that an elicited imitation task, timed AJT, and oral narration task loaded heavily on one factor, which he labeled as being associated with implicit knowledge. On the other hand, an untimed AJT and a metalinguistic knowledge test loaded on another factor, which he labeled as being associated with explicit knowledge. Bowles (2011) adapted the battery of tests from Ellis (2005) to examine how Spanish native, L2, and HL learners would perform. She found that the Spanish HLs in her study, who had learned Spanish at home naturalistically and had received very little formal instruction, scored higher on tests designed to measure implicit knowledge and lower on explicit knowledge tests; whereas, Spanish L2 learners showed the opposite pattern.

Thus, the present study aims to contribute to the subfield of instructed heritage language acquisition proposed by Bowles (2018) by expanding on Bowles (2011) and previous research that assessed the outcomes of heritage language instruction. We examine how Spanish HLs perform when completing two tests that tap into explicit and implicit knowledge, before and after receiving explicit or implicit language instruction on the Spanish past subjunctive in adjectival clauses. Specifically, we posit the following two research questions:

1. Compared to a tests-only control group, do heritage learners benefit from explicit or implicit instruction on the past Spanish subjunctive?
2. If so, are the learning gains in explicit or implicit knowledge?

## Methods

### Target Form

The target form we chose for this study is the Spanish past subjunctive adjectival clauses. This subjunctive form was previously examined in Potowski, Jegerski, and Morgan-Short (2009, 540), and it has been shown to be unstable or sometimes absent in Spanish heritage speakers' grammars (Silva-Corvalán 1994). In the case of (in)existential clauses in the past tense, the subjunctive can be found in the subordinate clause when the entity mentioned in the main clause refers to something that is unknown or nonspecific (example 1a). On the other hand, if the entity in the main clause refers to something specific and known, the use of the indicative mood is required (example 1b).

(1a) Joanne no encontró ningunos pantalones <u>*que*</u> le gusta**ran**
Joanne-subj neg find-PST-3SG any pants that-REL she-DAT like-PST-SBJV
"Joanne didn't find any pants (that) she liked"

(1b) Joanne encontró unos pantalones <u>*que*</u> le gusta**ban**
Joanne-subj find-PST-3SG some pants that-REL she-DAT like-PST-IND
"Joanne found some pants (that) she liked"

(1c) *Joanne no encontró unos pantalones <u>*que*</u> le gusta**ban**
Joanne-subj neg find-PST-3SG some pants that-REL she-DAT like-PST-IND
"Joanne didn't find any pants (that) she liked"

The use of the subjunctive is not always categorical, meaning that very often what seems to be an obligatory linguistic context for the subjunctive to occur for one native speaker might not be for another. The use of subjunctive, as well as its subjectivity, has been found to vary across different Spanish speaking varieties (Gudmestad 2012). In order to ensure that negation would trigger the use of the Spanish past subjunctive in these sentences, we asked a group of thirty monolingually raised Spanish speakers to judge the stimuli for this study using a 5-point Likert scale and to correct any sentences they deemed ungrammatical. These Spanish native speakers (NS) were born and raised in a variety of different Spanish-speaking countries (Spain, Colombia, Ecuador, Venezuela, Puerto Rico, Honduras, and Mexico) and had obtained a bachelor's degree or higher in science or humanities. Their responses showed that negation very often triggered the use of the past subjunctive. When the sentence contained negation in the matrix clause and the verb in the relative clause was in the past subjunctive (example 1a), NS judged these sentences as "acceptable" 96 percent of the time and as "unacceptable" just 4 percent of the time. Participants who marked such sentences as "unacceptable" seemed to be reacting to the use of a relative clause and not to the verb in the relative clause. That is, they tended to reduce the relative clause, especially in sentences containing the verb *ser* (to be), so participants who rejected a sentence like *Ana no encontró una chaqueta que fuera bonita* corrected it by eliminating the relative clause, *Ana no encontró una chaqueta bonita*. When the sentence contained negation in the matrix clause and the verb in the relative clause was in the indicative imperfect form (example 1c), NS judged these sentences as "unacceptable" 74 percent of the time and as "acceptable" 26 percent of the time. We took the NS results as an indication that mood choice is relatively uniform for this structure; also, in a study of spontaneous speech, Kevin Martillo Viner (2018) found that second-generation Caribbean Spanish heritage speakers in New York City used the subjunctive in this context in 64 percent of cases. Nevertheless, we decided to ask our HL participants to correct as well any sentences they judged unacceptable so that we could have some insight into what aspect of the sentence their judgment was based on.

## Participants

The initial pool of participants consisted of sixty-six Spanish HLs enrolled in advanced content-based university-level Spanish courses required to obtain a Spanish minor or major. Although Spanish learners at this level have received some instruction on the past subjunctive (according to the Spanish program curriculum), we predicted that they would not have a good command of the past subjunctive with our target structure. All participants completed a prescreening test, which revealed that six of the learners (about 9 percent of the initial pool) were already using past subjunctive consistently in this context. These participants were removed from the initial participant pool, leaving us with a total of sixty heritage learners (45 females, 15 males) with an average age of nineteen. All of them reported having learned Spanish from birth, and 45 percent were simultaneous bilinguals, who reported also learning English from birth. The remaining 55 percent reported that they began learning English subsequently, between ages three and six. Ninety-three percent of the learners reported being born in the US and having grown up in Illinois; the remaining 7 percent were born in Spanish-speaking countries (two in Mexico, one in Guatemala, and one in Spain) but came to the US before the age of six. Therefore, all of the learners could be considered second-generation HL learners. Information regarding language use showed that the HLs used Spanish less often than English, with fewer speakers, and in a more restricted range of contexts. Not surprisingly, the HLs self-rated their English abilities higher than their Spanish abilities. On a 10-point scale, HLs gave themselves a mean self-rating of 8.9 or higher on all English abilities: understanding ($M = 9.5$), reading ($M = 9.5$), speaking ($M = 9.5$), writing ($M = 9.4$), and pronunciation ($M = 8.9$). In contrast, they gave themselves lower ratings across the board on all Spanish abilities: understanding ($M = 8.4$), reading ($M = 7.7$), speaking ($M = 7.9$), writing ($M = 7.0$), and pronunciation ($M = 7.6$).

## Materials

Each pretest, posttest, and delayed posttest consisted of an elicited imitation task (EIT) meant to tap implicit knowledge, followed by an acceptability judgment task (AJT) meant to tap explicit knowledge. See excerpts in appendix 1 and 2. Each task (either AJT or EIT) contained eight experimental items (half grammatical and half ungrammatical) and eight distractors.

Participants first completed the EIT, which was administered with a PowerPoint that contained audio files and allowed participants to work at their own pace. The sentences used as stimuli were recorded by a monolingually raised Salvadoran male, and the vocabulary was restricted to words that were mutually understood across different Spanish dialects. In the task, participants had to (1) listen to a statement; (2) state whether the statement applied to them or not—when they were a child—by saying out loud "yes," "no," or "does not apply"; and (3) repeat the statement correctly. In keeping with past research using EITs (Ortega 2003; Yan et al. 2016), we incorporated several aspects into the design of the task to help ensure that the EIT was tapping into language knowledge rather than serving as a memory test. First, the sentences were complex, containing relative clauses that likely exceeded working memory span. Second, because participants had to make an intervening judgment (about whether the statement applied to them or not) between the time they heard the sentence and the time they had to repeat it, this pushed participants to both focus on sentence meaning rather than just form and to reconstruct the sentences using their own grammar rather than repeating from memory.

After completing the EIT, participants moved on to the AJT. The AJT was presented in a bimodal design, which allowed participants to both read and hear the sentences, which had been audio-recorded by a monolingually raised speaker of Spanish. This format has been used in previous research (Montrul, Bhatt, and Girju 2015) to accommodate heritage speakers who might prefer aural to written stimuli. This task was administered as an online survey (built in Survey Gizmo) and used a 5-point Likert scale, with 1 being "totally unacceptable" and 5 being "perfectly acceptable." In addition, participants were asked to correct each sentence to which they had assigned a rating of less than 5, by providing the corresponding modification(s) in a text box placed below the Likert scale. This step enabled us to get insight into not only which sentences were considered ungrammatical but also on what basis the judgment was made.

## Pedagogical Intervention

There were twenty participants in each experimental group (explicit or implicit instruction), and twenty participants in the control group, who did not receive instruction but completed all tests. The explicit group completed a lesson designed following PI guidelines, consisting of explicit information about the target form and accurate processing strategies followed by structured input practice (VanPatten 2004). For an excerpt, see appendix 3. In order to ensure that participants understood the explicit information (EI) that was presented, there were a few EI comprehension items embedded in the lesson, and accuracy on these items was used to confirm that participants understood the explicit explanation provided. The structured input portion of this treatment consisted of four practice and sixty-two experimental items. As shown in example 2 below, every item contained the end of a statement, the first word of which was the subjunctive or indicative imperfect form followed by a multiple choice of four possible beginnings for this sentence: (a) an affirmative statement, (b) a negative statement, (c) a statement in the present tense, and (d) an option allowing a, b, and c. The order of these choices was randomized across all sixty-two items. Participants received corrective feedback ("correct" or "incorrect") after every item. All the items in the structured input practice were put together as a story in which a character named Michael and his brother visited Chicago for a weekend. The explicit instruction intervention (explicit information + structured input) was administered using the psychology software Paradigm.

(2) hablara dos lenguas . . .

*[spoke-PST SUBJ two languages]*

| | |
|---|---|
| a) Había gente que | (*There were people that*) |
| b) No había gente que | (*There weren't people that*) |
| c) Hay mucha gente que | (*There are many people that*) |
| d) a, b, y c | (*a, b, and c*) |

Participants in the implicit condition did not receive any explicit information about the target structure. For an excerpt, see appendix 4. They read the same sixty-two items that the participants in the explicit treatment saw, but these were in the form of a written story followed by a series of comprehension questions. All items were grammatical, and no feedback was provided. This pedagogical intervention was meant as an input flood treatment, since it exposed the learners to the same number of instances of the target structure in a meaningful way without explicitly drawing their attention to it. This intervention was administered with paper and pencil.

Participants also completed a language background questionnaire and a debriefing questionnaire. The language background questionnaire was used to collect participants' demographic data as well as self-reported proficiency. We also administered a debriefing questionnaire at the end of session 3 in which we asked participants if they had used their intuition or a rule to complete the posttests. If they used a rule, they were asked to describe it.

## Procedure

In the course of the study, participants came into the laboratory on three occasions. During session 1, participants signed a consent form and completed the pretest and the language background questionnaire. During session 2, participants were exposed to explicit or implicit instruction, followed by an immediate posttest; control group participants took the immediate posttest but did not receive any instruction. Finally, in session 3, held one week later, participants completed a delayed posttest and filled out a debriefing questionnaire. Total testing time was approximately three hours, and participants received their choice of either extra credit or $30 monetary compensation.

## Results

### Data Analysis and Coding

The present study examined accuracy scores in the EIT task and ratings in the AJT task over time. In the EIT task, we coded every target item for each participant, assigning it a 1 or a 0 and fitted a Bayesian mixed-effects logistic regression.[1] In the AJT, we entered ratings assigned for each item and fitted a Bayesian linear regression. For all primary analyses, the fixed effects were instruction (explicit, implicit, control), test (pretest, posttest, delayed posttest), and grammaticality (grammatical, ungrammatical); participant and item were included as random effects (intercepts only). Statistical analysis was carried out using R (R Development Core Team 2019) with the *brms* package (Bürkner 2017, 2018). Pairwise comparisons were obtained using the *tidybayes* package for R (Kay 2020). Finally, data processing and visualization were conducted using the *tidyverse* package (Wickham 2021).

AJT responses were entered based on participants' numeric selection of ratings from the Likert scale provided for this task, which ranged from 1 (totally unacceptable) to 5 (perfectly acceptable). See full Likert scale and sample items in appendix 2. In the EIT, we assigned a 1 to ungrammatical items that participants corrected with past subjunctive, and a 0 to ungrammatical items that were repeated verbatim or with a verb form other than the past subjunctive. If an item was grammatical and participants accurately repeated it, we assigned it a 1. Out of the initial 2,816 responses analyzed in both tasks, a total of 18 responses (0.6 percent) were excluded from analysis for the EIT for one of the following reasons: (a) participants simplified the sentence, eliminating the relative clause; (b) participants made the statement positive, thereby disallowing the past subjunctive; or (c) the verb was not uttered or was inaudible. These exclusions resulted in a total of 2,798 tokens, which were used in the final analysis. Of these 2,798 tokens, 1,700 were coded as inaccurate because participants did not use the past subjunctive. Ninety-two percent of the incorrect responses contained the imperfect indicative. The remaining 8 percent contained other forms such as the preterit, conditional, or present indicative and subjunctive. Descriptive results for each task can be seen in figures 5.1 and 5.2 below.

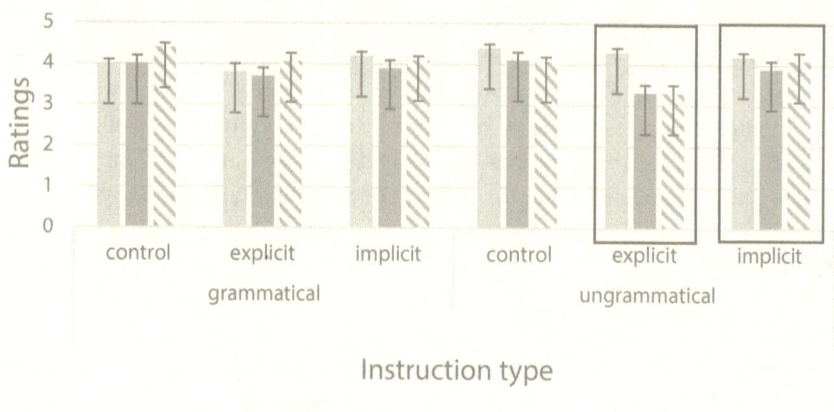


**FIGURE 5.1.** Mean ratings for AJT task over time. Error bars represent standard error. Boxed groups represent true differences.

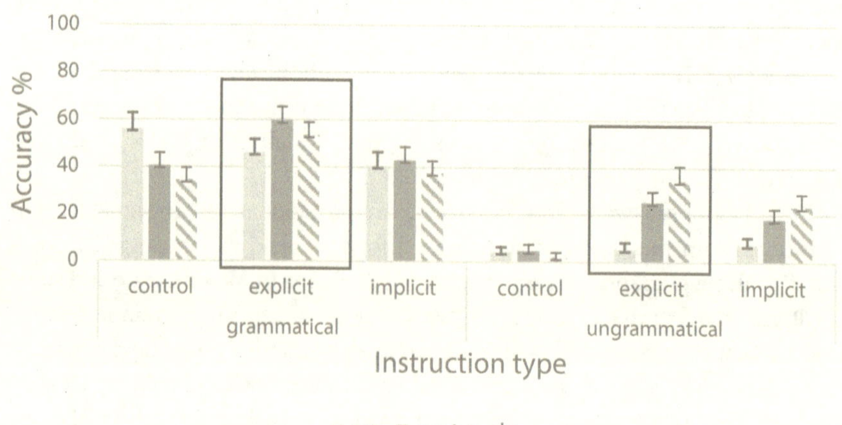


**FIGURE 5.2.** Mean accuracy for EIT task from pre- to posttests. Error bars represent standard error. Boxed groups represent true differences.

## Analyses

Since the main goal of this study was to test potential gains of explicit and or implicit knowledge examined via two different tasks as the result of instruction, we ran separate analyses with the AJT and EIT data. In addition, in order to answer our first research question, which asked if language instruction (explicit or implicit) is beneficial for HLs, we compared the two experimental groups to a tests-only control group, which was therefore set as the reference level for the variable of instruction in the analyses. Self-rated proficiency scores (out of fifty), for both experimental and control groups, were also calculated and proficiency was included as a covariate in the analysis of AJT and EIT responses to determine whether the effects of instruction were mediated by proficiency.[2]

## AJT Results

Explicit knowledge gains were assessed with the AJT data. We ran a Bayesian mixed-effects linear regression with test, instruction, and grammaticality as predictors. The output of this model, which showed that there was a difference in grammaticality, can be seen in table 5.1. Overall, ungrammatical items were rated higher than grammatical items and interacted with time and instruction,

**TABLE 5.1.** Output Bayesian Model: Ratings for AJT Task (Explicit Knowledge)

| | Estimate | EE | Lower-95% CrI | Upper-95% CrI |
|---|---|---|---|---|
| Intercept | 3.83 | 0.22 | 3.37 | 4.24 |
| Instruction (explicit) | −0.20 | 0.27 | −0.70 | 0.32 |
| Instruction (implicit) | 0.22 | 0.26 | −0.30 | 0.72 |
| Test (dp) | 0.45 | 0.24 | −0.03 | 0.93 |
| Test (post) | 0.17 | 0.25 | −0.31 | 0.66 |
| Grammaticality (ungram) | 0.78 | 0.31 | **0.22** | **1.38** |
| Instruction (exp)*Test (dp) | −0.19 | 0.32 | −0.81 | 0.45 |
| Instruction (imp)*Test (dp) | −0.55 | 0.31 | −1.17 | 0.07 |
| Instruction (exp)*Test (post) | −0.14 | 0.33 | −0.79 | 0.50 |
| Instruction (imp)*Test (post) | −0.43 | 0.31 | −1.05 | 0.18 |
| Instruction (exp)* Grammaticality (ungram) | 0.19 | 0.31 | −0.41 | 0.80 |
| Instruction (imp)* Grammaticality (ungram) | −0.34 | 0.31 | −0.94 | 0.27 |
| Test (dp)* Grammaticality (ungram) | −0.66 | 0.35 | −1.33 | 0.03 |
| Test (post)* Grammaticality (ungram) | −0.64 | 0.35 | −1.32 | 0.05 |
| Instruction (exp) *Test (dp)* Grammaticality (ungram) | −0.69 | 0.47 | **−1.61** | **−0.22** |
| Instruction (imp) *Test (dp)* Grammaticality (ungram) | 0.56 | 0.46 | −0.35 | 1.45 |
| Instruction (exp) *Test(post)* Grammaticality (ungram) | −0.53 | 0.45 | **−1.41** | **−0.35** |
| Instruction (imp) *Test (post)* Grammaticality (ungram) | 0.41 | 0.44 | **−0.46** | **−1.28** |

*Note*: Credible intervals not crossing 0 are bolded.

as shown by the credible intervals, which do not cross 0. We ran pairwise comparisons of instruction by time for grammatical items and ungrammatical items. Our results revealed that the general difference in ratings for ungrammatical items by the explicit group between the pre- and posttest was 1.13 rating points, 95% CrI [0.69, 1.58], showing that ungrammatical items were rated lower in the posttest than the pretest. Similarly, the difference in ratings for ungrammatical items for the explicit group between pre- and delayed posttest was 1.0 rating points, 95 percent CrI [0.64, 1.51], showing that ratings in the delayed posttest were also lower than in the pretest. Finally, the difference in ratings for ungrammatical items in the implicit group between pre- and posttest was 0.49 rating points, 95% CrI [0.02, 0.93], showing that the implicit group's ratings for ungrammatical items were also lower in the posttest than the pretest. By the time of the delayed posttest, this difference for the implicit group had disappeared. No other differences were evidenced. To account for proficiency, a second model with proficiency as a covariate was run, and goodness of model fit was assessed using the leave-one-out (LOO) method. This approach involves leaving one data point out and running the model, which is then used to predict that data point, and calculating the difference between the predicted and actual value. The model with the lowest LOO value (also known as LOOIC; leave-one-out cross-validation criterion) is considered to have the best performance. Our first model (not containing proficiency) yielded a lower LOOIC value, $LOOIC = 5010.3$, than the second model, which contained proficiency as a covariate, $LOOIC = 5012.6$ , suggesting that participants' proficiency did not modulate their AJT responses. The output of the second model, containing proficiency as a covariate, can be seen in appendix 5.

## EIT Results

Implicit knowledge gains were assessed with the EIT data. We ran a Bayesian mixed-effects logistic regression with test, instruction, and grammaticality as predictors. The output of this model, which can be seen in table 5.2, shows that there was a difference in grammaticality, with ungrammatical items being less accurate than grammatical items, as well as a Test and Instruction interaction, with HLs who received explicit instruction being more accurate in tboth posttests. Pair-wise comparisons of instruction by time with grammatical and ungrammatical items revealed that the general difference in ratings for grammatical items by the explicit group between pre- and posttest was 0.20%, 95% CrI [−0.40, −0.01], showing that accuracy was higher in the posttest than the pretest. Similarly, the difference in accuracy for grammatical items for the explicit group from pre- to delayed posttest was 0.14%, 95% CI [−0.33, −0.00], showing that accuracy in the delayed posttest was higher than in the pretest for this group.

**TABLE 5.2.** Output Bayesian Model: Accuracy for EIT Task (Implicit Knowledge)

| | Estimate | EE | Lower-95% CrI | Upper-95% CrI |
|---|---|---|---|---|
| Intercept | −1.18 | 0.65 | −2.52 | 0.04 |
| Instruction (explicit) | −0.23 | 0.70 | −1.64 | 1.15 |
| Instruction (implicit) | −0.46 | 0.69 | −1.81 | 0.91 |
| Test (dp) | −0.71 | 0.54 | −1.74 | 0.35 |
| Test (post) | −0.19 | 0.53 | −1.21 | 0.85 |
| Grammaticality (ungram) | −1.95 | 0.89 | **−3.69** | **−0.21** |
| Instruction (exp)*Test (dp) | 1.51 | 0.68 | **0.13** | **2.84** |
| Instruction (imp)*Test (dp) | 0.88 | 0.65 | −0.40 | 2.14 |
| Instruction (exp)*Test (post) | 1.22 | 0.70 | **0.15** | **2.60** |
| Instruction (imp)*Test (post) | 0.40 | 0.65 | −0.86 | 1.66 |
| Instruction (exp)* Grammaticality (ungram) | 0.18 | 1.03 | −1.89 | 2.23 |
| Instruction (imp)* Grammaticality (ungram) | 1.13 | 0.96 | −0.75 | 3.05 |
| Test (dp)* Grammaticality (ungram) | −1.14 | 1.65 | −4.87 | 1.69 |
| Test (post)* Grammaticality (ungram) | −0.17 | 1.16 | −2.57 | 2.03 |
| Instruction (exp) *Test (dp)* Grammaticality (ungram) | 2.93 | 1.83 | −0.39 | 6.89 |
| Instruction (imp) *Test (dp)* Grammaticality (ungram) | 2.12 | 1.76 | −0.98 | 6.03 |
| Instruction (exp) *Test(post)* Grammaticality (ungram) | 1.49 | 1.43 | −1.23 | 4.51 |
| Instruction (imp) *Test (post)* Grammaticality (ungram) | 0.90 | 1.35 | −1.71 | 3.59 |

*Note*: Credible intervals not crossing 0 are bolded.

Regarding ungrammatical items, we found that the general difference in accuracy by the explicit group from pre- to posttest was −0.26%, 95% CI [−0.52, −0.09], showing that accuracy was higher in the posttest than the pretest. Similarly, we found a difference in accuracy from post to delayed posttest for the explicit group of 0.32%, 95% CI [−0.58, −0.12], showing that accuracy was higher at the delayed posttest than at the posttest. No other differences were evidenced. In addition to this model, a second model with proficiency as a covariate was run to account for proficiency differences within and among groups. The output of this second model can be seen in appendix 6. The LOOIC value for the initial model (without proficiency) yielded a lower LOOIC value, *LOOIC* = 1112.0, than the second model, *LOOIC* = 1114.0, suggesting that proficiency did not affect EIT responses.

## Discussion

Our first research question asked if HLs benefit from explicit and implicit instruction. Overall, descriptive and inferential statistical analyses showed that explicit instruction led to more consistent learning gains over time. HLs in the explicit group improved significantly from pre- to posttests on both tasks. Specifically, after instruction they rated ungrammatical sentences lower in the AJT and showed an increase in accuracy in the EIT with grammatical and ungrammatical items. These findings supporting the benefits of explicit grammar instruction are consistent with previous research (Montrul and Bowles 2010; Potowski, Jegerski, and Morgan-Short 2009). Notably, Potowski and colleagues' PI group was most similar to our explicit instruction group, yet in their study there were no significant pre-posttest gains on the AJT, whereas in our study there were. We believe that a likely explanation is that Potowski et al.'s AJT was written, whereas ours was bimodal. Similar to findings by Julio Torres (2018), the present study also included a delayed posttest that took place one week after instruction. The results from our analyses, which showed that HLs' learning gains were maintained a week after the instruction, are consistent with Torres (2018), suggesting that some explicit instructional interventions can lead to learning gains that last beyond the immediate posttest stage.

Results from the AJT also revealed learning gains for HLs in the implicit group; namely, that they gave ungrammatical items lower ratings on the posttest than on the pretest. To the best of our knowledge, this is the first study to examine the effects of an input flood on HLs. Our findings suggest that although the gains were not as substantial or as long lasting as those resulting from the explicit instruction, since they had disappeared a week after instruction, input flood did have some benefit for HL learners.

In order to answer our second research question, which asked what knowledge results from implicit and explicit instruction, we examined ratings for the AJT and accuracy scores for the EIT separately. The present study found that HLs in the explicit group showed learning gains in both tasks. HLs in the explicit group showed learning gains with only ungrammatical items in the AJT, which according to previous research are more likely to tap into explicit knowledge than grammatical items (Gutiérrez 2013). This finding suggests that explicit language instruction led to explicit knowledge.

This is the first study to employ an elicited imitation task to examine the effects of language instruction on HLs. If we assume AJTs tap into explicit knowledge, and EITs tap into implicit knowledge, our findings suggest that explicit language instruction led to both explicit and implicit knowledge, and implicit instruction led only to explicit knowledge, which was not maintained at the time of the delayed posttest one week after instruction.

As this is the first study to examine the relationship between the explicitness of HL instruction and the type of knowledge that results (explicit or implicit) from it, caution must be taken in interpreting the findings. Future research should be conducted to determine whether similar results are obtained with other HL learners, on other grammatical structures, and with a wider range of assessments. We chose to use untimed AJTs in this study both because they have been shown to measure explicit knowledge in L2 and HL populations (Bowles 2011; Ellis 2005) and because they have been widely used in previous instructional and experimental HL studies. Similarly, we decided to use EITs as a measure of implicit knowledge, but other instruments, such as serial reaction time tests (e.g., Suzuki and DeKeyser 2015), could also be used.

John Norris and Lourdes Ortega (2001) argued that the types of measures use to assess learning gains in L2 language instruction research are often biased toward explicit knowledge; instructed HL research appears to suffer from the same problem and this poses a problem for HL learners who, based on our results and on previous research (Bowles 2011), are more likely to draw on implicit knowledge. Future research should employ a wide variety of tasks designed to tap into explicit and implicit knowledge, in both written and oral modalities, in order to capture the full range of potential learning experienced by HLs (Keating, Jegerski, and VanPatten 2011, 2016; Montrul et al. 2014).

Explicit or implicit knowledge aside, the issue of task modality is one that needs to be explored further. (See also Torres, chapter 1 in this volume.) Although previous studies show advantages for L2 learners on written tasks and HLs learners on oral tasks, we believe the distinctions might need to be more nuanced. In our study, the EIT involved auditory stimuli that learners responded to orally, and the AJT was bimodal, involving written and auditory stimuli that learners responded to in writing. Perhaps it is not just the modality of the stimuli themselves but also response modality that is important.

Along these lines, researchers who work in incidental and implicit learning often use subjective measures to assess which cognitive mechanisms learners were drawing from when completing different tasks (Rebuschat 2013). In our study, we asked HLs to complete a debriefing questionnaire after session 3 that asked them to describe (subjectively) whether they used their intuition or rules to complete the EIT and AJT. Interestingly, one of the participants in the explicit group responded, "I used the rule for the written part, and more intuition for speaking" (participant 1603); this response suggests that different knowledge sources may be used depending on the task at play, providing further support for the AJT and EIT tapping into different knowledge sources. Hence, the role of response modality is a variable that merits further investigation.

## Pedagogical Implications

This study was conducted not in a classroom setting but rather in a laboratory where we controlled the nature of the explicit information students received, the stimuli, and the type of feedback provided. It involved a lesson that lasted 40 minutes or less and was focused on one grammatical feature. In that sense, like those of Potowski, Jegerski, and Kara Morgan-Short (2009), Montrul and Bowles (2010), and Torres (2018), this study was isolated and not part of a broader curriculum, but this separation allowed us to make fine-grained comparisons. In conjunction with past findings, our study's results suggest that HL learners benefit from explicit instruction, which serves to orient them toward form; exposure alone, even when the input is seeded with many exemplars of the target structure, as it was in this case, may be insufficient to promote the development of explicit or implicit knowledge that lasts beyond the immediate term.

Because of the focused nature of our study, we feel the need to limit our claims to grammar, since the same results might not apply to other subdomains of language, such as vocabulary or pragmatics. In supporting the use of explicit instructional methods to teach grammar, including Processing Instruction, we are not advocating that grammar be a primary focus in Spanish as a heritage language (SHL) classes. Rather, it should be included in small doses, where needed. We concur with Sara Beaudrie, Cynthia Ducar, and Kim Potowski (2014, 172), who state, "Focus on form and explicit instruction in grammar can be useful for heritage learners in restructuring parts of their internal grammatical systems." Our findings show that explicit methods appear to have a greater and longer-lasting impact than implicit ones in those cases. For instance, in academic writing, HL learners of Spanish often use the passive voice in situations that would be more naturally expressed by *se-impersonal.* Our results imply that having students simply read texts containing examples of *se-impersonal* would not be as effective as a focus on form approach that explicitly drew learners' attention to the structure and contrasted its use to the English passive voice. We remind the reader that focus on form approaches such as the ones in this study draw attention to form *in the context of meaningful language use*; language form is never isolated and decontextualized, nor should it be, in the HL classroom.

Indeed, our findings are in line with suggestions in Beaudrie, Ducar, and Potowski (2014) that highlight a role for a variety of focus on form techniques on targeted structures in the HL classroom. The targets of instruction may include those that are most commonly found in Spanish textbooks for HL learners (Carreira and Potowski 2011), but instructors must be sensitive to the differing needs of the learners they teach and determine appropriate targets of instruction based on their learners' proficiency level, needs, and goals. For instance, the preterit and imperfect forms in Beaudrie and Holmes's study in chapter 2 of this volume were appropriate targets for their receptive HL learners but would have been too simple for the learners in our study.

It is also important to stress that any focus on form should be part of a sociolinguistically informed pedagogical approach that is aware of and responsive to norms in local Spanish language communities. Our goal should always be to empower learners to make informed choices about which language forms they choose to use in which contexts (see Holguín Mendoza, chapter 7 in this volume).

Certainly, lab-based studies such as this one should be conducted alongside research conducted in intact HL classrooms, which are necessarily not as controlled environments but provide ecological validity and can speak to broader questions about the efficacy of a particular curriculum or SHL program (e.g., Bowles and Bello-Uriarte 2019 and Bello-Uriarte, chapter 3 in this volume, for a semester-long study on how genre-based instruction impacts HL learners' writing). The two kinds of research complement each other to inform pedagogy.

## Limitations and Future Research

Finally, we would also like to acknowledge a few limitations to our study and some implications these could have on our findings. First, we did not use a standardized proficiency test to examine HLs' linguistic knowledge prior to assigning them to an experimental or control group. We did not do this due to time constraints and to avoid participant fatigue, given that total testing time was three hours, and participants had to come to the lab on three different occasions within a short time frame. Second, there is sociolinguistic variability in the target form; although Spanish NS accepted the past subjunctive form 96 percent of the time, they also accepted the indicative imperfect form as grammatical 26 percent of the time. Third, implicit knowledge has proven to be a difficult construct to measure, and even though several studies have found that the performance on EITs loads onto a factor that is often associated with implicit knowledge (Bowles 2011; Ellis 2005), there is some debate about whether the EIT truly measures implicit knowledge or merely automatized explicit knowledge (e.g., Suzuki and DeKeyser 2015). Finally, both of our treatments (explicit and implicit) had the same number of items so that we could compare them on equal footing; however, it is possible that with a larger number of instances of the target structure, implicit instruction might be more effective, since implicit learning studies (albeit with L2 learners) have shown that compared to explicit conditions, many more exemplars are often required for learning to take place (Doughty 2003).

Future research should continue to undertake focused investigations to understand what aspects of instruction are most effective for HL learners, and these should include a wider range of assessments, including not only AJTs but other oral and written measures of explicit and implicit knowledge. We also advocate that online and offline methods be used to investigate not only how instruction affects HL learners' outcomes (in terms of posttest scores) but also how it impacts their processing. This investigation can be done with a variety of psycholinguistic and behavioral measures—including eye-tracking, think-alouds, and reaction times—which have been found to be instrumental in explaining variability in learning outcomes for L2 learners (Leow et al. 2014; Leow 2019).

## Appendix 1

Excerpt from elicited imitation task

> Listen to the following sentences carefully and indicate whether these sentences are consistent with your personal experience by saying "Sí" "No" or "No se aplica" then repeat them out loud in correct Spanish. (Sometimes this will mean repeating the sentence exactly as you heard it, and sometimes this will mean changing some part of the sentence).
>
> Cuando era más joven . . . (context)
> Practice item: – No me gustaba pasar tiempo con mis padres.
>
> 1. No tenía amigos que hablaran chino mandarín.
> 2. Tenía muchas fiestas de cumpleaños.
> 3. No tenía hermanos que escuchaban mis problemas.
> 4. Mis hermanos jugaba con juguetes peligrosos.

## Appendix 2

Excerpt from acceptability judgement task

> Read the following sentences and using the scale below indicate what you think their acceptability is. If you think that a sentence is not totally acceptable, please make the necessary corrections to make it sound better.

1. En mi escuela, no había profesores que hablaran bien español.

1–totally unacceptable 2–unacceptable 3–neutral 4–acceptable 5–perfectly acceptable

| |
|---|
| |

2. Susana no compró un televisor que costaba $2.000 dólares en Amazon.

1–totally unacceptable 2–unacceptable 3–neutral 4–acceptable 5–perfectly acceptable

| |
|---|
| |

## Appendix 3

Excerpt from explicit instructional treatment

What does the past subjunctive look like?
To form the past subjunctive, begin with the form (ellos/ellas) in the past tense (preterit). Example: *ellos hablaron*. The **-ron** ending is eliminated and the past subjunctive endings **-ra, -ras, -ra, -ramos, -ran** are added. All spelling changes in the *ellos* form that occur in the past (such as vowel changes in the verb root) will also stay in the corresponding past subjunctive forms; check out the verb *saber* and *venir* below.

| Example: | (cantar) | cantaron | canta**ra**, canta**ran** |
|---|---|---|---|
| | (saber) | supieran | supie**ra**, supie**ran** |
| | (venir) | vinieron | vinie**ra**, vinie**ran** |

Location of the subjunctive
The past subjunctive is generally located in subordinate clauses (clauses that depend on the main clause for existence) and these subordinate clauses are generally introduced by "que"

Example: Joanne no encontró unos pantalones <u>*que*</u> le gusta**ran**

Sample of structured input item
[They read:] ". . . tuviera acento de Chicago"
[They see:]
a. Había mucha gente que . . .
b. No había mucha gente que . . .
c. Hay mucha gente que . . .
d. ninguna

## Appendix 4

Excerpt from implicit instruction

> En esta actividad vas a leer una entrada en el diario de Michael en la que habla de su viaje a Chicago. Lee atentamente y responde a las preguntas que aparecen después del texto.
>
> Un verano en Chicago:
> La semana pasada fui a visitar Chicago con mi hermano. Nunca había estado en Chicago y mi impresión de la ciudad fue impresionante. Mi hermano y yo probamos la pizza estilo deep dish y fuimos al loop. Los ciudadanos de Chicago fueron muy amables todo el tiempo. En mi viaje conocí a mucha gente que había nacido y crecido en Chicago. Charlé con gente que viajaba en autobús al trabajo todos los días. Por lo general, no había mucha gente que tuviera un acento fuerte de Chicago. Como era de esperar, conocí a mucha gente que seguía el equipo de los Cubs. Mi hermano y yo hablamos con muchas chicas que eran muy simpáticas y habladoras.
> Preguntas de comprensión:
> 1. El autor del diario no viajó solo a Chicago ¿Con quién viajó?
> 2. ¿Qué tipos de comida probó? Lista por lo menos 3 tipos de comida diferentes.
> 3. ¿Visitó el autor del diario algún edificio alto en el loop?

## Appendix 5

**TABLE 5.3.** Output Bayesian Model: Rating for AJT Task with Proficiency as a Covariate

| | Estimate | EE | Lower-95% CrI | Upper-95% CrI |
|---|---|---|---|---|
| Intercept | 4.05 | 0.44 | 3.16 | 4.89 |
| Instruction (explicit) | −0.18 | 0.26 | −0.69 | 0.33 |
| Instruction (implicit) | 0.21 | 0.26 | −0.28 | 0.72 |
| Test (dp) | 0.44 | 0.24 | −0.03 | 0.92 |
| Test (post) | 0.17 | 0.24 | −0.29 | 0.65 |
| Grammaticality (ungram) | 0.78 | 0.31 | **0.21** | **1.42** |
| Proficiency | −0.01 | 0.01 | −0.02 | 0.01 |
| Instruction (exp)*Test (dp) | −0.18 | 0.32 | −0.80 | 0.43 |
| Instruction (imp)*Test (dp) | −0.55 | 0.31 | −1.16 | 0.05 |
| Instruction (exp)*Test (post) | −0.13 | 0.31 | −0.75 | 0.49 |
| Instruction (imp)*Test (post) | −0.44 | 0.30 | −1.02 | 0.16 |
| Instruction (exp)* Grammaticality (ungram) | 0.20 | 0.31 | −0.41 | 0.82 |
| Instruction (imp)* Grammaticality (ungram) | −0.34 | 0.31 | −0.97 | 0.26 |
| Test (dp)* Grammaticality (ungram) | −0.64 | 0.34 | −1.32 | 0.02 |
| Test (post)* Grammaticality (ungram) | −0.64 | 0.36 | −1.35 | 0.05 |
| Instruction (exp) *Test (dp)* Grammaticality (ungram) | −0.71 | 0.45 | −1.61 | 0.16 |
| Instruction (imp) *Test (dp)* Grammaticality (ungram) | 0.55 | 0.45 | −0.31 | 1.45 |
| Instruction (exp) *Test(post)* Grammaticality (ungram) | −0.54 | 0.45 | −1.44 | 0.34 |
| Instruction (imp) *Test (post)* Grammaticality (ungram) | 0.42 | 0.43 | −0.43 | 1.27 |

*Note*: Credible intervals not crossing 0 are bolded.

## Appendix 6

**TABLE 5.4.** Output Bayesian Model: Accuracy for EIT Task with Proficiency as a Covariate

| | Estimate | EE | Lower-95% CrI | Upper-95% CrI |
|---|---|---|---|---|
| Intercept | −2.73 | 1.40 | −5.42 | −0.04 |
| Instruction (explicit) | −0.27 | 0.69 | −1.59 | 1.10 |
| Instruction (implicit) | −0.31 | 0.69 | −1.66 | 1.11 |
| Test (dp) | −0.66 | 0.55 | −1.74 | 0.39 |
| Test (post) | −0.15 | 0.53 | −1.16 | 0.91 |
| Grammaticality (ungram) | −1.91 | 0.87 | **−3.62** | **−0.23** |
| Proficiency | 0.04 | 0.03 | −0.02 | 0.10 |
| Instruction (exp)*Test (dp) | 1.46 | 0.69 | **0.16** | **2.81** |
| Instruction (imp)*Test (dp) | 0.83 | 0.66 | −0.46 | 2.14 |
| Instruction (exp)*Test (post) | 1.18 | 0.70 | −0.22 | 2.57 |
| Instruction (imp)*Test (post) | 0.37 | 0.66 | −0.92 | 1.67 |
| Instruction (exp)* Grammaticality (ungram) | 0.11 | 1.01 | −1.89 | 2.06 |
| Instruction (imp)* Grammaticality (ungram) | 1.07 | 0.95 | −0.70 | 2.99 |
| Test (dp)* Grammaticality (ungram) | −1.15 | 1.58 | −4.88 | 1.52 |
| Test (post)* Grammaticality (ungram) | −0.22 | 1.11 | −2.41 | 1.89 |
| Instruction (exp) *Test (dp)* Grammaticality (ungram) | 2.95 | 1.77 | −0.18 | 6.80 |
| Instruction (imp) *Test (dp)* Grammaticality (ungram) | 2.11 | 1.69 | −0.91 | 5.97 |
| Instruction (exp) *Test(post)* Grammaticality (ungram) | 1.55 | 1.40 | −1.13 | 4.33 |
| Instruction (imp) *Test (post)* Grammaticality (ungram) | 0.94 | 1.30 | −1.60 | 3.53 |

*Note*: Credible intervals not crossing 0 are bolded.

This study would have not been possible without the help of a very talented group of undergraduate research assistants: Ashley Carreon, Austin Billimack, Clarissa Roa, Etta Alblinger, Ivan Carrasco, Jacqueline San Diego, Jazmine Velazquez, José Amador, Kate Parks, Katelyn Wonderlin, Kaylee Tucker, Lauren Michelle Allesee, Lizette Mojica, and Nicole Pudlo. They played an important role in participant recruitment and data collection.

## Notes

1. We initially planned to run linear mixed effects models, which are becoming a standard in linguistics. However, our model for the EIT data did not converge, due to the large number of 0 scores in the dataset. Following Eager and Roy (2017), we opted for a Bayesian analysis and rather than present linear mixed effects for the AJT and a Bayesian analysis for the EIT, we decided to present Bayesian statistics for both tasks.
2. We would like to thank an anonymous reviewer for suggesting that we include proficiency as a covariate in our analyses.

## References

Beaudrie, Sara M., Cynthia Ducar, and Kim Potowski. 2014. *Heritage Language Teaching: Research and Practice*. New York: McGraw-Hill Education Create.

Bowles, Melissa A. 2011. "Measuring Implicit and Explicit Linguistic Knowledge: What Can Heritage Language Learners Contribute?" *Studies in Second Language Acquisition* 33, no. 3 (September): 247–71.

———. 2018. "Outcomes of Classroom Heritage Language Instruction: State of the Field and an Agenda for the Future." In *The Routledge Handbook of Spanish as a Heritage/Minority Language*, edited by Kim Potowski, 331–44. New York: Routledge.

Bowles, Melissa A., and Adrián Bello-Uriarte. 2019. "What Impact Does Heritage Language Instruction Have on Spanish Heritage Learners' Writing?" In *Evidence-Based Second Language Pedagogy: A Collection of Instructed Second Language Acquisition Studies*, edited by Masatoshi Sato and Shawn Loewen, 219–39. New York: Routledge.

Bürkner, Paul-Christian. 2017. "Brms: An R Package for Bayesian Multilevel Models Using Stan." *Journal of Statistical Software* 80(1): 1–28.

———. 2018. "Advanced Bayesian Multilevel Modeling with the R Package brms." *R Journal* 10, no. 1 (July): 395–411.

Carreira, Maria, and Olga Kagan. 2011. "The Results of the National Heritage Language Survey: Implications for Teaching, Curriculum Design, and Professional Development." *Foreign Language Annals* 44, no. 1 (February): 40–64.

Carreira, Maria, and Kim Potowski. 2011. "Commentary: Pedagogical Implications of Experimental SNS Research." *Heritage Language Journal* 8(1): 134–51.

Doughty, Catherine. 2003. "Instructed SLA: Constraints, Compensation, and Enhancement." In *The Handbook of Second Language Acquisition*, edited by Catherine Doughty and Michael Long, 206–57. New York, NJ: Blackwell.

Eager, Christopher, and Joe Roy. 2017. "Mixed Effects Models Are Sometimes Terrible." Poster presented at the 2017 Linguistics Society of America.

Ellis, Rod. 2005. "Measuring Implicit and Explicit Knowledge of a Second Language: A Psychometric Study." *Studies in Second Language Acquisition* 27, no. 2 (June): 141–72.

Gass, Susan, and Lewis, Kim. 2007. "Perceptions about Interactional Feedback: Differences between Heritage Language Learners and Non-Heritage Language Learners." In *Conversational Interaction in Second Language Acquisition*, edited by Alison Mackey, 173–93. Oxford: Oxford University Press.

Gudmestad, Aarnes. 2012. "Toward an Understanding of the Relationship between Mood Use and Form Regularity: Evidence of Variation across Tasks, Lexical Items, and Participant Groups." In *Selected proceedings of the 14th Hispanic Linguistics Symposium*, edited by Kimberly Geeslin and Manuel Díaz-Campos, 214–27. Somerville, MA: Cascadilla Proceedings Project.

Gutiérrez, Xavier. 2013. "The Construct Validity of Grammaticality Judgement Tests as Measures of Implicit and Explicit Knowledge." *Studies in Second Language Acquisition* 35, no. 3 (September): 423–49.

Kay, Matthew. 2020. "tidybayes: Tidy Data and Geoms for Bayesian Models." Accessed March 15. https://cran.r-project.org/web/packages/tidybayes/index.html.

Keating, Gregory D., Jill Jegerski, and Bill VanPatten. 2011. "Who Was Walking on the Beach? Anaphora Resolution in Spanish Heritage Speakers and Adult Second Language Learners." *Studies in Second Language Acquisition* 33, no. 2 (June): 193–221.

———. 2016. "Online Processing of Subject Pronouns in Monolingual and Heritage Bilingual Speakers of Mexican Spanish." *Bilingualism: Language and Cognition* 19, no. 1 (January): 36–49.

Leow, Ronald P., ed. 2019. *The Routledge Handbook of Second Language Research in Classroom Learning.* New York: Routledge.

Leow, Ronald P., Sarah Grey, Silvia Marijuan, and Colleen Moorman. 2014. "Concurrent Data Elicitation Procedures, Processes, and the Early Stages of L2 Learning: A Critical Overview." *Second Language Research* 30, no. 2 (April): 111–27.

Li, Shaofeng. 2010. "The Effectiveness of Corrective Feedback in SLA: A Meta-analysis." *Language Learning* 60, no. 2 (May): 309–65.

Montrul, Silvina, Rakesh Bhatt, and Roxana Girju. 2015. "Differential Object Marking in Spanish, Hindi and Romanian as Heritage Languages." *Language* 91, no. 3 (September): 1–47.

Montrul, Silvina, and Melissa Bowles. 2010. "Is Grammar Instruction Beneficial for Heritage Language Learners: Dative Case Marking in Spanish." *Heritage Language Journal* 7, no. 1 (Winter): 47–73.

Montrul, Silvina, Justin Davidson, Israel de la Fuente, and Rebecca Foote. 2014. "Early Language Experience Facilitates Gender Agreement Processing in Spanish Heritage Speakers." *Bilingualism: Language and Cognition* 17, no. 1 (January): 118–38.

Norris, John, and Lourdes Ortega. 2001. "Does Type of Instruction Make a Difference? Substantive Findings from a Meta-analytic Review." *Language Learning* 51, no. 5 (July): 157–213.

Potowski, Kim, Jill Jegerski, and Kara Morgan-Short. 2009. "The Effects of Instruction on Linguistic Development in Spanish Heritage Language Speakers." *Language Learning* 59, no. 3 (August): 537–79.

R Development Core Team. 2019. "R: A Language and Environment for Statistical Computing." R Foundation for Statistical Computing. Vienna, Austria. https://www.r-project.org/.

Rebuschat, Patrick. 2013. "Measuring Implicit and Explicit Knowledge in Second Language Research." *Language Learning* 63, no. 3 (September): 595–626.

Silva-Corvalán, Carmen. 1994. *Language Contact and Change: Spanish in Los Angeles.* Oxford Studies in Language Contact. Oxford: Clarendon Press.

Spada, Nina, and Yasuyo Tomita. 2010. "Interactions between Types of Instruction and Type of Language Feature: A Meta-analysis." *Language Learning* 60, no. 2 (June): 263–308.

Suzuki, Yuichi, and Robert DeKeyser. 2015. "Comparing Elicited Imitation and Word Monitoring as Measures of Implicit Knowledge." *Language Learning* 65, no. 4 (December): 860–95.

Torres, Julio. 2018. "The Effects of Task Complexity on Heritage and L2 Spanish Development." *Canadian Modern Language Review* 74, no. 1 (February): 128–52.

VanPatten, Bill. 2004. "Input Processing in Second Language Acquisition." In *Processing Instruction: Theory, Research, and Commentary*, edited by Bill VanPatten, 5–31. Mahwah, NJ: Erlbaum.

Viner, Kevin Martillo. 2018. "The Optional Spanish Subjunctive Mood Grammar of New York City Heritage Bilinguals." *Lingua* 210–211 (July–August): 79–94.

Wickham, Hadley. 2021. "Tidyverse: Easily Install and Load the 'Tidyverse.'" Accessed March 20. https://cran.r-project.org/web/packages/tidyverse/index.html.

# PART II

## Social and Educational Outcomes

SIX

# "Incorporating Our Own Traditions and Our Own Ways of Trying to Learn the Language": Beginning-Level Spanish as a Heritage Language Students' Perception of Their SHL Learning Experience

*Damián Vergara Wilson*
University of New Mexico

Heritage language students who have been exposed to foreign language learning environments engage in the Spanish as a Heritage Language (SHL) experience with perceptions and attitudes that are shaped by that previous experience. Outdated methodologies relying on decontextualized, rote activities and drills that students encounter in some Spanish as a foreign language classes shape perceptions toward the heritage language but fail to validate them. (These correspond to focus on forms approaches described in Bowles's introduction to the volume and are not well suited for either L2 or heritage learners.) The opportunity to study in a heritage language context provides an opportunity to facilitate a shift in the way these students perceive and interact with the language. Often for the first time in their educational career, students experience an orientation toward Spanish in which the heritage variety is recognized as valid and students are seen as resources.

The current study presents a qualitative analysis of thirty-five semiguided interviews with beginning-level Spanish as a Heritage Language Learners (SHLLs) in which students describe their learning experience and perceptions of an SHL program at a large southwestern university. Although these interviews provide a rich panorama of information, the focus here is on the contrast between a beginning-level SHL class and courses taken previously by the participants. The main goal of this chapter is to contribute to the understanding of beginning-level SHLLs, who possess receptive skills in the HL and are therefore not true beginners. To better understand this group, we examine how students construct perceptions of their own language experiences and bilingualism. Instead of exclusively focusing on the community experience, as is done in other studies on receptive bilinguals (e.g., Beaudrie 2009), we analyze depictions of previously taken courses. By examining how participants construct these prior experiences, we gain insight into the following conundrum from the student perspective: Why did previously taken courses not prepare students for higher levels of Spanish?

## Context of Investigation: The Spanish as a Heritage Language Program

The study takes place in the context of the Sabine Ulibarrí Spanish as a Heritage Language (SUSHL) program at the University of New Mexico, a large university in a border state of the American Southwest. This program has been in continuous existence since the 1960s. Currently the program offers four levels of lower division instruction (SHL I, II, III, and IV) and fluctuates between eight and twelve sections across levels. For purposes of recruitment that is inclusive of receptive bilinguals, this program uses a wide definition to identify SHLLs: "SHL learners seek to explore and develop their connection to the Spanish language. Such a connection to the language may come through community, family, or cultural heritage" (Wilson and Martínez 2011, 128). Despite a focus on a specific context, the findings of this study apply to a wide range of educational circumstances regarding US Spanish-speaking communities (see DeFeo 2015) and to the understanding of educational experiences faced by receptive bilinguals.

The SUSHL program attempts to combine notions of critical pedagogy and sociolinguistically oriented teaching with communicative learning outcomes. Task-based speaking and writing activities are part of almost every class period. In SHL I, the beginning-level course in question, the communicative goals revolve around improving the students' abilities to describe their daily lives, where they are from, what they study, how they identify, and frequent activities. Students are positioned as bringing important *funds of knowledge* (Moll et al. 1992; Gonzalez, Moll, and Amanti 2006) to the course, especially regarding the target language and culture.

This course syllabus, and all others in the SUSHL sequence, includes a student learning outcome aimed at raising critical language awareness. Recent research has pointed out that building critical language awareness helps to combat alienation felt by SHLLs in the face of traditional Spanish language educational experiences and that it contributes to fostering agency and understanding of power dynamics and promotes activism (see Beaudrie, Amezcua, and Loza 2019; Holguín Mendoza 2018; this volume). This critical awareness goal is approached through a variety of in-class activities and is characterized by the final project for each level, which involves community engagement. For the group of students interviewed, the final project was an examination of translingual practices in their communities through observation and interviews.

The placement exam that all students are required to take at the beginning of the semester is an important factor. Described in Damián Wilson (2012), this online multiple-choice placement exam was created "in-house" and included a rigorous item analysis process that maximized test reliability and validity. Students are placed in the corresponding level SHL course based on their test score, and instructors informally verify that the placement is appropriate at the beginning of each term.

## Literature Review

This study connects to others that examine receptive bilinguals who are able to understand significant amounts of the heritage language due to exposure to it but who produce very little of the language. Sara Beaudrie (2009) and Beaudrie and Cynthia Ducar (2005) represent two efforts that specifically examined receptive bilinguals in the SHL context. (See also Beaudrie and Holmes, chapter 2 in this volume.) Beaudrie and Ducar (2005) examined attitudes held by receptive bilinguals and found that participants' lack of confidence in the language contrasted with a strong motivation to raise fluency. Beaudrie (2009) examined the linguistic profiles of receptive SHLLs according to immigrant generation. While Beaudrie did not find great differences in self-reported language skills between generational groups, she did find strong links between identity and the HL that was countered by participants' low regard for home varieties of Spanish. Notably, Beaudrie (2009) points out that there is a paucity of research on receptive bilinguals. Both of these studies relied chiefly on survey data, but Beaudrie and Ducar (2005) included interviews in order to qualitatively bolster their pedagogical suggestions.

The present endeavor is connected to previous research on students in the same program. Wilson (2013) administered Likert surveys to beginning-level SHLLs and found that identity labels were a significant explanatory variable in rating four attitudinal dimensions of heritage language maintenance. For example, participants who used the label *mexicano/a* rated the sentimental and language loyalty dimensions of the language as more important to them than their peers who did not use that label. This result led Wilson (2013, 194) to conclude that the social context influencing an individual to use a certain label may also engender certain attitudes.

However, the surveys used to study attitudes and identity labels (Wilson 2013; Wilson and Martínez 2011; Hudgens-Henderson, Wilson, and Woods 2020) occasionally provided conflicting points of information. The surveys provided participants with a space to write comments, and many students wrote remarks that contradicted their other survey responses. For example, many students who highlighted the instrumental dimension of language maintenance on the survey wrote comments such as, "I just want to speak with my grandmother." Such mismatches highlighted the necessity to compliment quantitative survey work with a qualitative dimension in order to give voice to the participants.

In order to highlight the student voice, Wilson and Carlos Ibarra (2015) analyzed student perceptions of the SUSHL program through interview data. Specifically, the researchers hypothesized that students might not be cognizant of the goals and orientations of the SUSHL program. This study concluded that the students were both aware of and responded positively to these goals (also see Beaudrie and Ducar 2005, 14–16).

Research on the student perspective is scarce but important. Beaudrie (2012, 214) proposes that in order to reconcile a mismatch between student and educator positions, "student voices must be incorporated into the design of SHL programs." We emphasize that efforts to include the student voice will counterbalance and enhance findings from studies that rely on tasks that do not elicit free expression. Research on student perspectives provides valuable information to practitioners of SHL as we consider program design and orientations toward the students. In fact, we consider the elevation of the student voice in research to be an important element in recognizing students' funds of knowledge. See Wilson and Ibarra (2015) for a more complete review of studies that highlight the SHLL student perspective (e.g., Beaudrie 2009; Beaudrie, Ducar, and Relaño-Pastor 2009; Ducar 2008; Potowski 2002; Schwarzer and Petrón 2005).

## Methods

The data come from semiguided interviews conducted with thirty-five students enrolled in a beginning-level SHL course, SHL I, and were part of a project, La perspectiva estudiantil, that collected panoramic qualitative data on SHLL learner experiences (e.g., Perara-Lunde and Melero-García 2015; Wilson and Ibarra 2015). All interviewers, regardless of the level of their participants or research goals, presented a fixed set of Protocol Questions that elicited biographical and educational background information in addition to asking about identity labels. After the Protocol Questions, each set of researchers asked Investigator Questions particular to their own project and were designed to elicit data for qualitative analysis of emergent themes yet to be identified by the researchers and are not research questions, per se.

The Investigator Questions for the present study are

- IQ1: If you were going to describe the SHL program to someone outside of UNM, how would you describe it?
- IQ2: In your experience, what do you see as the goals of the program?
- IQ3: How would you describe the student body? OR, what do you think makes someone a candidate for the SHL program?
- IQ4: Have you taken Spanish in the past? How does this compare?
- IQ5: Spanish in the classroom. Does it match what you hear in the community? How do you describe Spanish in the community?

The transcribed data were analyzed through iterative and recursive qualitative data analysis. Beginning with a global thematic analysis in order to develop a sense of the overall set and identify themes, the author returned to the individual transcriptions. Doing so allowed for determination of whether the potential themes identified could be sustained upon closer analysis (e.g., Hatch 2002, 179–91). After refining the themes in this recursive step, the data were coded by assigning segments to a pertinent theme. As stated by Lioness Ayres (2008, 867), "Thematic analysis is primarily a descriptive strategy that facilitates the search for patterns of experience within a qualitative data set; the product of a thematic analysis is a description of those patterns and the overarching design that unites them." The coding aims to segment and categorize the data in order to apply plausible themes to the data. Typically, as is the case here, the researcher approaches the data with a priori themes that they believe will be supported by the data. However, the researcher engages in an inductive examination of the coding within and across data segments with the goal of revising a priori themes and identifying emergent ones. This recursive process involves applying themes to the data as a whole as well as to individual cases.

The thirty-five participants were students enrolled in a beginning-level SHL course (SHL I) during the fall semester of 2014 with 21 (60 percent) females and 14 (40 percent) males spanning an age range of 18 to 33. Notably, 32 of the participants had previously taken at least one year of Spanish with an average of 2.27 years of previous instruction across these participants; one outlier had taken seven years of Spanish prior to enrolling in SHL I. Two had taken courses in other postsecondary institutions. None of the participants had taken SHL courses previously.

All but two participants had lived in New Mexico for at least eight years prior to the interview. While many participants claimed Albuquerque, the home city of the university located near the center of the state, as their place of origin ($N = 14$, 40 percent), there were a substantial number of participants from northern New Mexico ($N = 12$, 34 percent) and a smaller number from the southern part of the state ($N = 7$, 20 percent). Only two participants hailed from out of state: one from Colorado and another from Arizona (see Wilson and Ibarra 2015 for more detail, especially regarding identity labels provided).

## Results

### Receptive Learners in a Bilingual Community

The elicited perceptions provide evidence that our participants have receptive skills in the heritage language that are greater than their productive skills. Despite stronger receptive skills, receptive bilinguals may be able to participate in basic conversations on familiar topics (Beaudrie 2009, 86). The participants provided descriptions of their receptive skills at various points in the interview data.

First, in the Protocol Questions we asked participants whom they speak the most Spanish with and whom they overhear the most. According to the responses, the participants have widespread access to Spanish speakers and overhear a great deal. All but 4 students cite their immediate family as sources of overhearing the language, with 22 saying they overhear grandparents and 16 listing parents or other relatives, such as aunts or uncles. In terms of speaking, we see a similar trend for grandparents as the main sources of language usage, with 19 participants reporting that they speak with grandparents and 16 reporting that they speak with parents. At the same time, 8 participants do not claim to speak Spanish with filial relatives. However, of these 8, only 2 describe a background in which there were limited opportunities to speak (or overhear) Spanish: one receives input only from school and work (Mandy), and another did not begin learning Spanish until she married a Spanish-speaking man (Alexis). The other 6 who do not report speaking to family list friends or go on to state that regardless of not speaking, they overhear a great deal from family. For example, James, an eighteen-year-old freshman from rural New Mexico, emphatically claims that he speaks Spanish with nobody. However, he contrasts this claim by stating that "everyone at home" speaks Spanish and that he can understand it. He then describes a common dynamic in New Mexico in which elders use Spanish as a secret language to talk about things they do not want the children to understand.

In a different line of questioning, when asked to describe their strengths in Spanish, twelve participants elucidated that understanding oral language was a strength. Christine describes her receptive abilities in the following manner:

1) But like reading the sentence I can mostly understand it or if I'm driving somewhere and I see like a Spanish billboard I can understand it,

or like if someone is saying something to me I can for the most part understand.

Despite the fact that only twelve interviewees indicated comprehension of oral language as a strength, there are many other indicators of receptive capabilities. James, our SHLL who speaks to nobody but overhears everybody, acknowledges his receptive capabilities but does not list them as a strength; he describes his strength as being vocabulary. In fact, given the variety of strengths listed, the fact that twelve listed oral comprehension as a strength shows that some students are aware of, and value, their receptive skills.

Translanguaging practices may provide another source for experiencing the heritage language, and there is ample evidence that participants engage in translanguaging outside the classroom. For this discussion we follow Ricardo Otheguy, Ofelia García, and Wallis Reid's (2015, 281) definition of translanguaging linguistic behavior as "the deployment of a speaker's full linguistic repertoire without regard to watchful adherence to the socially and politically defined boundaries of named languages." In responding about whom the participants speak with, thirteen included elements of translingual behavior in these descriptions. Many described mixing at a more conversational level, such as answering a grandparent in Spanish and then deploying English out of necessity. Others stated that they incorporated Spanish words into what we infer is mainly English discourse, as described by Ethan:

2) Probably just with my friends, messing around, mmm like throw in a word once in a while to [provide] a little emphasis or something like *corazón* or *rápido* or something.

Others described using words or chunks of the heritage language for pragmatic purposes, especially with elders, mainly in the form of requests, greetings, or leave taking. At least three others mention participating in some sort of translingual behavior elsewhere, and the overall data give a clear impression that these participants have come to value translanguaging practices. Out of all participants, only two openly expressed negative views toward translingual practices, which participants tend to call "Spanglish" in both positive and negative depictions (Wilson and Ibarra 2015). Given that the overall group is very New Mexican, and given that translingual behavior is widespread in New Mexico to the point of being a community norm in some situations (see Gonzales 1999; Torres Cacoullos and Travis 2018), it is probable that much of the heritage language that the students are exposed to, and in which they participate, will display translanguaging of some form or other. Cassandra describes a situation in which translanguaging in the workplace serves as comprehensible input:

3) I find Spanglish to be a lot easier to follow. At my old job everybody there spoke primarily Spanish but knew English, you know, and they would just speak Spanglish to each other. I'd be standing there, they'd be having a conversation in English, they'd go to Spanish, and then back to English. And I thought that was really cool and could kind of follow the conversations especially now with this . . . uuu . . . with my Spanish class.

Overall, these students overhear the HL and participate in conversations. While the data show that participants perceive their speaking to be limited, it at least demonstrates that most have chances to experience the heritage language outside the classroom and that some of this experience will involve translanguaging. Yet, most descriptions of receptive bilinguals focus on community experience and do not recognize that another avenue of exposure may come from educational contexts.

## Description of Previously Taken Courses

In this section we analyze the depictions of previous courses as they compare to SHL I. The data for this segment come chiefly from IQ4: "Have you taken Spanish in the past? How does this compare?" However, we also gain important data from other portions of the interviews.

A thematic depiction of rote learning in previously taken courses emerges in the data that contrast with communicative learning in the SHL program. One of the key indicators of rote learning comes from the mention of mechanical work that students produced in class, which is most typified by a focus on worksheets in the high school context. The emergent theme of *mechanical work* includes all depictions of class activities in which the student participates in a cloze writing activity that does not require interaction. Depictions of mechanical work refer to discrete work that requires the student to "fill in the blanks." Although the category of mechanical work is most typified by the term *worksheets*, we also included the mention of activities such as filling out conjugation tables and working out of the textbook during class. A total of thirteen participants overtly mentioned production of mechanical work in their characterizations of previously taken courses, as exemplified by Erica, Ethan, and Ana:

4) In high school it was mostly just videos and worksheets. So, of course, you know I never really did anything. (Erica)
5) Mmmm yeah. Or they'd just talk and give us a worksheet. And then once in a while we'd give like a speech in Spanish. But it was just like four sentences. . . . We never talked to each other. (Ethan)
6) He had like PowerPoint slides and he would like choose everyone in class like okay now fill in this blank, or like what do you use in this instance

and stuff. But I think that's mostly fill in the blank. So sometimes people would just see the word like, "okay since its plural you have to conjugate it like this, or if its past you conjugate like this." So, people would go through the worksheets fast without like thinking. (Ana)

A secondary theme tied to the portrayal of rote learning in previously taken courses has to do with memorization, mentioned by seven participants. In this category of *memorization* we included this nominalized form as well as the verbal form, 'memorize', which is frequently tied to the activity of filling out worksheets. On the one hand, we separate the two here because memorization is an internal process, whereas completing worksheets involves external production. On the other hand, these two pedagogical tasks are frequently mentioned together in their depictions of previous educational experiences. For example, Marcus begins by comparing his previously taken courses to beginning chemistry and biology, describing them as facilitating rote learning, and then goes on to state:

7) Like here's a list of words, memorize this list of words, when you see this you do that, when you do this you do that. When it's future you do this. When it's present you do this. When it's you, you do this. When it's somebody else . . . and just strict memorization. How do you conjugate. Memorize some words. I don't remember ever in class having to speak more than a sentence. (Marcus)

According to our participants, therefore, this SHLL population has been exposed to considerable instruction in Spanish, but those classes tended to foster rote learning and failed to draw from the funds of knowledge possessed by the students. These findings reflect those of Lucy Tse (2000), who examined autobiographical essays from students in college-level foreign language classes. Students described previous courses as implementing extensive rote memorization and cloze answer worksheets, which led Tse to propose that communicative language teaching is not as widespread in practice as educators might believe.

Despite prevalent reports of rote learning, there is evidence that students had mixed experiences with previous courses, with some valuing it and others not. Most discourse surrounding descriptions of rote learning tends to cast it as lacking in a perceived benefit for the learner. In one characteristic example, Elena describes how she learned vocabulary and some structure but that "it was kind of like do the work, memorize and then kind of forget it." On the other hand, there is evidence that some students believed that previous courses served as a base upon which they could expand. A total of four students mentioned that previous coursework had prepared them for SHL I. Of interest, when asked where they had learned the most Spanish, a total of thirteen participants responded that they had learned the most in previously taken classes.

The finding that thirteen students mentioned that they had learned the most in previous courses, and that four claimed that previous courses prepared them for SHL I, raises some important questions. We repeat that SHL I is a beginning-level class and that, ideally, effective instruction should have enabled students to place into a higher level. Yet, we also see that some students valued these previous courses. Is it possible that the students draw some sort of comfort from noncommunicative activities, which do not bring up the anxiety they have when speaking? A total of twenty-one students mentioned some aspect of speaking when asked to explain their weaknesses in the heritage language. Some students overtly mentioned some type of anxiety related to speaking: as Erica puts it, "It's frickin scary." In a more detailed example Ethan says:

8) Interviewer: Do you like the approach we use where we push people to talk?
Ethan: Yeah. It makes me uncomfortable a little bit. But I think it really helps me to learn.
Interviewer: So . . . Do you feel like you're put on the spot? Or . . . ?
Ethan: No . . . it's just kind of weird speaking Spanish it's just. I can't do it as good so . . .

This perceived weakness in speaking is contrasted with a perception that elements of rote learning are described as a strength. We are left with the question as to whether students may cling to noncommunicative learning as a compensation for low oral skills. As stated by Christine in Example 1, when someone is speaking, she "can for the most part understand." Logically, a receptive bilingual may not understand everything that they hear, and the anxiety triggered by both a lack of comprehension and speaking apprehension may cause them to view language experiences, such as rote learning, as less intimidating.

One element did not surface in the data to the level at which we had hypothesized: depictions of deliberate attempts to eradicate southwestern dialectal features. The teaching of SHL initially emerged as an effort to maintain the heritage language in hostile sociolinguistic circumstances, including efforts by many educators to eliminate features of US Spanish varieties (e.g., Sánchez 1976; Valdés-Fallis 1976). Often cloaked by concern for the well-being and success of the students, an eradicationalist uses prescriptive teaching in order to cleanse students of their dialectal features and replace those with prestige norms (Valdés-Fallis 1976, 20). Because eradicationalism documented in early SHL research bears strong parallels to standard language ideologies that surface in modern pedagogical materials (e.g., Leeman and Martínez 2007; Ducar 2009), we hypothesized that these approaches would remain active in New Mexico and that students would be aware of them. However, there were no reports of educators overtly diminishing the value of New Mexican Spanishes. There were, however, two instances where students described a discrepancy between the Spanish taught by their previous instructors and the Spanish of their communities. In both of these cases, participants reported that instructors who spoke Spanish from Spain attempted to teach peninsular norms that conspicuously diverged from the Spanish of SHLL communities. In Example 9, Cassandra describes a course she took at a nearby community college:

9) You know, she lectured. She gave us lists of words and . . . you know, stem vowel changes of course and everything, you know. She kind of just taught us. Whereas this one [SHL I] we are kind of participating in. . . . We kind of helped each other out instead of just having the teacher tell us how it is. She was very specific, she had a specific Spanish she was trying to teach us, you know. She lived in, I think she said she lived in Spain so that's what she was trying to teach us was the Spanish in Spain.

Here Cassandra raises the issue that the Spanish taught by her teacher was perceptively different from that of the learning community. She then elucidates a contrast to SHL I in which the students participated and "helped each other out" instead of being positioned as being told "how it is." In Cassandra's previous class, students were positioned as passive learners who have no agency in what variety of Spanish they were learning. Cassandra goes on to say:

10) I think it confused us because this is New Mexico and we speak a, I think we speak a very different form of Spanish, you know. Ours isn't so formal. We're very informal I think, you know. I mean we've got formality but . . . um . . . She was teaching us very formal things and the right way.

In this excerpt we see that Cassandra goes on to ideologize that New Mexican Spanish is somehow less formal than Peninsular Spanish. By casting Peninsular Spanish as formal and "the right way," she positions the Spanish of New Mexico as less correct and less formal. The finding that only one participant overtly described a dynamic that involved a prestige language ideology was surprising but may point to another issue. Hierarchical ideologies may be so prevalent in our society, in language classrooms and other "mainstream avenues" (Beaudrie, Amezcua, and Loza 2019, 2) that they do not rise to the level of salience for our participants.

## Descriptions of the SHL Experience: SHL I

One tangible contrast was in casting previous learning as noncommunicative and SHL learning as communicative. The two main themes in the category of active learning are an engagement in *speaking activities* and inclusion of the *culture of local speech communities*, which fosters active learning through engagement. In building up the category of speaking activities, we included descriptors such as interaction, using the language, practicing, or any other description that clearly implied speaking, as in the following example:

> 11) The most . . . the most speaking we did in [a noncommunicative] class was the teacher would walk in, "hola como estás." And that's pretty much the whole speaking from what I remember of it. So that contrasted to this where I feel like there is more of an emphasis on speaking . . . even to the point where I wish there was more speaking in the class. To be honest with you. (Marcus)

The category of speaking activities was one of the most salient and most frequently mentioned elements in their perception of SHL I. When asked to compare previous versus current educational experiences (IQ4), twenty-three students mentioned speaking the heritage language in class as a differentiating characteristic of SHL I. In addition, thirteen students mentioned speaking when asked to describe the program (IQ1), and another thirteen did so when asked to describe the objectives of the program (IQ2). Only seven students did not volunteer descriptions of speaking as a characteristic of SHL I. What is more, opportunities to speak the heritage language in the classroom encourage more usage in the community. A total of eleven students stated that their learning experience in SHL I had contributed to their capability and motivation to communicate with family and community members.

## Discussion

This study confirms findings of others (e.g., Beaudrie 2009; Beaudrie and Ducar 2005) that many beginning-level students experience the heritage language in the community. Beyond those findings, this study delves into their perceptions of previously experienced courses, which pertain to the teaching of Spanish as a foreign language. Two salient differences between the two educational contexts are the speaking opportunities and cultural validation present in SHL I. The overarching tendency for SHL students to describe SHL I as having an emphasis on the heritage culture (see also Wilson and Ibarra 2015) implies that this was absent in previous classes and returns us to the theme of valorization. In SHL I, the inclusion of culture comes from the students themselves, whom we position as possessing funds of knowledge, and also from selected curricular materials instead of exclusively from teacher-fronted instruction or mass-produced textbooks.

In responses about previous courses, there were no descriptions of blatant attempts to uplift or downgrade local bilingual communities just as there were no descriptions of previous courses containing context-based instruction. Even though educators may not overtly disparage New Mexican Spanish, the depictions of previous Spanish classes reveal contexts that potentially fostered sociolinguistic erasure: "the process in which ideology, in simplifying the sociolinguistic field, renders some persons or activities (or sociolinguistic phenomena) invisible" (Irvine and Gal 2009, 404). Although it is indirect evidence, the usage of cultural validation as a prominent difference between the two educational experiences points to a situation in which local cultures were simply absent from previous curricula. Erasure is not necessarily a deliberate strategy and may occur when an element is unobserved or ignored; action is taken to openly downgrade an incongruent element only when that element is presented as a threat to a given ideological context (Irvine and Gal 2009).

On a larger scale, the teaching of Spanish as a foreign language in the US facilitates erasure for SHL communities because of the way it neglects the varieties of Spanish that surround learners (see DeFeo 2015). However, instead of blaming teachers, we must consider the context in which they teach and the factors leading up to classroom instruction. Ideally, researchers in SHL will nudge the field of teacher training to foster more engaging teaching methods that recognize learners as bringing funds of knowledge to the classroom. Alan Brown and Gregory Thompson (2018) and Maria Carreira and Olga Kagan (2018) argue that the field of teacher training should evolve to focus more on heritage speakers and their communities' circumstances in the US, even in the context of curricula aimed at traditional foreign language teaching (DeFeo 2015). The traditional teaching methods the students described in their past Spanish courses should not be the norm in second language, heritage language, or mixed classrooms, and teacher training and professional development are key to changing that.

In contrast to numerous participant depictions of traditional teaching methods, participants held unanimously positive views toward their SHL course, and several expressed the belief that they had learned more in the SHL program than in all their previous classes combined. The data reveal a perception by the students that the SHL environment was comfortable at an affective level and that their heritage language speech communities were validated. Many participants reported that they were inspired to seek new contexts for using Spanish, such as conversing in Spanish with elders or texting in Spanish. All but two of the participants reported that their view of translingual norms of bilingual speech communities became more positive, often viewing it as a practice in which they could now engage.

## Pedagogical Implications

Aside from pointing out the inadequacy of rote teaching methodologies in developing receptive SHLLs' language skills, we must also examine the ways in which receptive bilinguals are best served. Clearly, we have evidence here that years of memorizing lists of grammatical elements for later production on cloze item activities has not capitalized on the vast knowledge of the heritage language that these students hold as a group. At the same time, thirteen of the thirty-five students interviewed told us that they had learned the most Spanish in those prior courses (as opposed to any other setting, like in their homes). It is difficult to reconcile these findings, but since students' attitudes and beliefs are shaped by past experiences, we think it is possible that the explanation lies in their understanding of what "learning" consists of. If they see learning as something that happens primarily in a formal classroom setting, they may not think of all of the exposure at home that led them to be able to understand Spanish as "learning." Then, when the students were exposed to Spanish in the classroom settings described before they enrolled in SHL I, the traditional approach came to be what they conceived of as "learning a language" de facto because it was their only experience in such a setting. The way that many participants juxtaposed their experiences in prior courses with those in SHL I supports this idea and suggests that being exposed to a new approach and actually using Spanish to communicate meaning, rather than to fill in blanks, opened their eyes to other ways of "learning a language." In this regard, it may be helpful for instructors to explicitly discuss why they use the methods they use with students at the beginning of the term.

By the same token, students' comments indicate that they embrace speaking activities while simultaneously feeling anxieties toward speech, which raises issues related to effective linguistic input and innovative methodologies for these students. The most obvious pedagogical suggestion is to provide task-based communicative instructional opportunities for SHLLs in a way that recognizes the variation present in their speech communities (see Wilson and Ibarra 2015 and Leeman and Serafini 2016). Local community use was conspicuously absent from their descriptions of past courses and helped lead students to hypothesize that their home varieties must not have been formal. In addition to providing students with critical language awareness instruction that addresses concepts such as formality and prestige varieties (see Holguín Mendoza, chapter 7 in this volume), SHL instructors may also wish to explore the use of corpora as a way to bring local varieties into the classroom and to do so in a meaning-based, contextualized way that encourages the use of macro-teaching principles.

Wilson (2018), in a task that compared elicited production of SHLLs to frequently produced constructions from a concordance of the *New Mexico / Colorado Spanish Survey* (Bills and Vigil 2008), found that SHL I students have a great deal of knowledge of frequently occurring forms and a less rich knowledge of infrequent ones. He argues that language corpora represent great potential for receptive bilinguals to be able to make connections between their present knowledge and production of the HL by more fluent members of the speech community. Tim Johns (1994) and Paul Nation (2001) propose that corpora provide rich, authentic input for L2 learners, which we contend is particularly applicable to SHLLs, who may otherwise receive input in the HL from a restricted number of speakers.

There are many publicly available corpora representing regional Spanish varieties, such as the *New Mexico / Colorado Spanish Survey* (NMCOSS) (Bills and Vigil 2008). The *Spanish in Texas Corpus* (Bullock and Toribio 2013) is designed for learners and consists of video interviews with transcriptions that are tagged for parts of speech and topics. By using these corpora, the language of US Spanish speakers is elevated as being worthy of instructional focus. Also, we hypothesize that the language experience of the students will be reflected in these corpora, which will enhance the potential for cognitive benefit and sociolinguistic awareness. For example, many students are confronted with a rejection of the subjunctive verb *haiga* 'may there be' (from existential *haber* 'there is'). But if students perform a query using the *Corpus del español* (Davies 2002) they see that *haiga* is not restricted to the American Southwest and northern Mexico, but is seen across time and attested in diverse regions, including Spain and South America. The *Spanish in Texas* corpus allows the user to modify transcripts to exclude certain elements for listening comprehension activities. In an anecdote, an instructor in SHL I reported that students reacted enthusiastically to a comprehension activity using the *Spanish in Texas* corpus, with one student saying, "This is exactly what my brain needs." Johns (1994) and Nation (2001) promote using queries for words and phrases in corpora as a way to capture variable and polysemous instances of items that the students may analyze in an inductive process. We go so far as to propose that if we teach our students to use corpora, they may use them in independent language queries beyond the classroom, which positions them as agents guiding their own learning.

## Future Research

The discussion on eradication raises questions related to the receptive bilingualism documented here. Perhaps participants did not produce enough of their home varieties in the classroom to provoke evaluations of their home variety, positive or negative, from the instructor. Do more proficient students gain more reproach from educators based on their production of community forms? The overwhelming depictions of unengaging rote learning prior to entering SHL I also raise another question: Is there a group of K–12 educators who are providing engaging and effective education in the heritage language that propels their students into higher levels when testing in to the SHL program? We believe that it would be fruitful for future explorations to examine students who come into our program and place into higher levels as freshmen in order to further explore these questions.

This research also highlights the need to better document the nature of receptive bilinguals' knowledge of the heritage language and language experience. While sociolinguistic interviews and corpora give great insight as to what the community norms are, we also recognize that they do not always reflect daily language usage. For example, command forms and vulgarisms are very rare in corpora such as the NMCOSS (Bills and Vigil 2008) but surface frequently in preliminary documentation of receptive bilingualism (Wilson 2018). Additionally, we need to better understand the exposure and language expectation experienced by receptive bilinguals in the US: Do community members use certain strategies to elicit the HL from receptives? How and why do receptive bilingual SHLLs use the HL in the community?

Finally, we hope to have conveyed the utility of qualitative research, especially in regards to SHLLs, as an avenue for complementing quantitative research and explaining what would otherwise be inexplicably contradictory student response behaviors.

## Note

I would like to acknowledge the excellent reviews of this work that greatly enhanced its quality. I am indebted to Carlos Enrique Ibarra, who helped collect and transcribe the data for this research under the Perspectiva estudiantil project. Melissa A. Bowles, the editor of this volume, has provided a level of attention, encouragement, and insight that is rare among editors. I am most grateful to the participants, members of our Spanish as a Heritage Language learning community, who shared their perspectives and insights into the learning process: ¡Muchísimas gracias a ellos!

## References

Ayres, Lioness. 2008. "Thematic Coding and Analysis." In *The SAGE Encyclopedia of Qualitative Research Methods*, edited by Lisa M. Given, 868–69. Thousand Oaks, CA: SAGE Publications.

Beaudrie, Sara. 2009. "Spanish Receptive Bilinguals: Understanding the Cultural and Linguistic Profile of Learners from Three Different Generations." *Spanish in Context* 6(1): 85–104.

———. 2012. "Research on University-Based Spanish Heritage Language Programs in the United States: The Current State of Affairs." In *Spanish as a Heritage Language in the US: State of the Field*, edited by Sara Beaudrie and Marta Fairclough, 203–21. Washington, DC: Georgetown University Press.

Beaudrie, Sara, Angelica Amezcua, and Sergio Loza. 2019. "Critical Language Awareness for the Heritage Context: Development and Validation of a Measurement Questionnaire." *Language Testing* Online 36(4): 573–94.

Beaudrie, Sara, and Cynthia M. Ducar. 2005. "Beginning Level University Heritage Programs: Creating a Space for All Heritage Language Learners." *Heritage Language Journal* 3(1): 1–26.

Beaudrie, Sara, Cynthia Ducar, and Ana María Relaño-Pastor. 2009. "Curricular Perspectives in the Heritage Language Context: Assessing Culture and Identity." *Language, Culture and Curriculum* 22(2): 157–74.

Bills, Garland, and Neddy Vigil. 2008. *The Spanish Language of New Mexico and Southern Colorado: A Linguistic Atlas*. Albuquerque: University of New Mexico Press.

Brown, Alan V., and Gregory L. Thompson. 2018. *The Changing Landscape of Spanish Language Curricula: Designing Higher Education Programs for Diverse Students*. Washington, DC: Georgetown University Press.

Bullock, Barbara E., and Almeida Jacqueline Toribio. 2013. *The Spanish in Texas Corpus Project*. University of Texas at Austin: COERLL. www.spanishintexas.org.

Carreira, Maria, and Olga Kagan. 2018. "Heritage Language Education: A Proposal for the Next 50 Years." *Foreign Language Annals* 51(1): 152–68.

Davies, Mark. 2002. "Corpus Del Español: 100 Million Words, 1200s–1900s." www.corpusdelespanol.org.

DeFeo, Dayna J. 2015. "Spanish Is Foreign: Heritage Speakers' Interpretations of the Introductory Spanish Language Curriculum." *International Multilingual Research Journal* 9(2): 108–24.

Ducar, Cynthia M. 2008. "Student Voices: The Missing Link in the Spanish Heritage Language Debate." *Foreign Language Annals* 41(3): 415–33.

———. 2009. "The Sound of Silence: Spanish Heritage Textbooks' Treatment of Language Variation." In *Español en Estados Unidos y otros contextos de contacto: Sociolingüística, ideología y pedagogía*, edited by Manel Lacorte and Jennifer Leeman, 347–68. Madrid: Iberoamericana Editorial.

Gonzales, María D. 1999. "Crossing Social and Cultural Borders: The Road to Language Hybridity." In *Speaking Chicana: Voice, Power, and Identity*, edited by D. Galindo and M. D. Gonzales, 13–38. Tucson: University of Arizona Press.

Gonzalez, Norma, Luis C. Moll, and Cathy Amanti, eds. 2006. *Funds of Knowledge: Theorizing Practices in Households, Communities, and Classrooms*. Mahwah, NJ: Routledge.

Hatch, J. Amos. 2002. *Doing Qualitative Research in Education Settings*. New York: State University of New York Press.

Holguín Mendoza, Claudia. 2018. "Critical Language Awareness (CLA) for Spanish Heritage Language Programs: Implementing a Complete Curriculum." *International Multilingual Research Journal* 12(2): 65–79.

Hudgens-Henderson, Mary, Damián Vergara Wilson, and Michael R. Woods. 2020. "How Course Level, Gender, and Ethnic Identity Labels Interact with Language Attitudes towards Spanish as a Heritage Language." *Hispania* 103(1): 27–42.

Irvine, Judith T., and Susan Gal. 2009. "Language Ideology and Linguistic Differentiation." In *Linguistic Anthropology: A Reader.* 2nd ed., edited by Alessandro Duranti, 402–34. Malden, MA: Wiley-Blackwell.

Johns, Tim. 1994. "From Printout to Handout: Grammar and Vocabulary Teaching in the Context of Data-Driven Learning." In *Perspectives on Pedagogical Grammar,* edited by Terence Odlin, 293–313. Cambridge: Cambridge University Press.

Leeman, Jennifer, and Glenn Martínez. 2007. "From Identity to Commodity: Ideologies of Spanish in Heritage Languages Textbooks." *Critical Inquiry in Language Studies* 4(1): 35–65.

Leeman, Jennifer, and Ellen J. Serafini. 2016. "Sociolinguistics for Heritage Language Educators and Students: A Model for Critical Translingual Competence." In *Innovative Strategies for Heritage Language Teaching: A Practical Guide for the Classroom,* edited by Marta Fairclough and Sara M. Beaudrie, 56–79. Washington, DC: Georgetown University Press.

Moll, Luis C., Cathy Amanti, Deborah Neff, and Norma Gonzalez. 1992. "Funds of Knowledge for Teaching: Using a Qualitative Approach to Connect Homes and Classrooms." *Theory into Practice* 31(2): 132–41.

Nation, Paul. 2001. *Learning Vocabulary in Another Language.* Rowley, MA: Newbury House Publishers.

Otheguy, Ricardo, Ofelia García, and Wallis Reid. 2015. "Clarifying Translanguaging and Deconstructing Named Languages: A Perspective from Linguistics." *Applied Linguistics Review* 6(3): 281–307.

Perara-Lunde, Molly, and Fernando Melero-García. 2015. "Identidades gramaticales: Perspectivas estudiantiles hacia el aprendizaje y uso de la gramática en una clase de SHL." *EuroAmerican Journal of Applied Linguistics and Languages* 2(2): 67–84.

Potowski, Kim. 2002. "Experiences of Spanish Heritage Speakers in University Foreign Language Courses and Implications for Teacher Training." *ADFL Bulletin* 33(3): 35–42.

Prada, Josh, and Blake Turnbull. 2018. "The Role of Translanguaging in the Multilingual Turn: Driving Philosophical and Conceptual Renewal in Language Education." *ELUA. Estudios de Lingüística Universidad de Alicante* 5(2): 8–23.

Sánchez, Rosaura. 1976. "Spanish for Native-Speakers at the University: Sugerencias." In *Teaching Spanish to the Spanish Speaking: Theory and Practice,* edited by Guadalupe Valdés-Fallis and Rodolfo García-Moya, 95–107. San Antonio, TX: Trinity University Press.

Schwarzer, David, and Maria Petrón. 2005. "Heritage Language Instruction at the College Level: Reality and Possibilities." *Foreign Language Annals* 38(4): 568–78.

Torres Cacoullos, Rena, and Catherine E. Travis. 2018. *Bilingualism in the Community: Code-Switching and Grammars in Contact.* Cambridge: Cambridge University Press.

Tse, Lucy. 2000. "Student Perceptions of Foreign Language Study: A Qualitative Analysis of Foreign Language Autobiographies." *Modern Language Journal* 84(1): 69.

Valdés-Fallis, Guadalupe. 1976. "Pedagogical Implications of Teaching Spanish to the Spanish-Speaking in the United States." In *Teaching Spanish to the Spanish Speaking:*

*Theory and Practice*, edited by Guadalupe Valdés-Fallis and Rodolfo García-Moya, 3–27. San Antonio, TX: Trinity University Press.

Wilson, Damián V. 2012. "Developing a Placement Exam for Spanish Heritage Language Learners: Item Analysis and Learner Characteristics." *Heritage Language Journal* 9(1): 27–50.

———. 2013. "The Intersection of Identity, Gender, and Attitudes toward Maintenance among Beginning Spanish as a Heritage Language Students." *International Journal of the Linguistic Association of the Southwest* 31(1): 177–97.

———. 2018. "Formulaic Language and Receptive Bilinguals: What Constructions Do Beginning Spanish as a Heritage Language Learners Know?" Paper presented at the 3rd International Conference on Heritage/Community Languages. UCLA, Los Angeles, February 16–17.

Wilson, Damián V., and Carlos E. Ibarra. 2015. "Understanding the Inheritors: The Perception of Beginning-Level Students toward Their Spanish as a Heritage Language Program." *EuroAmerican Journal of Applied Linguistics and Languages* 2(2): 85–101.

Wilson, Damián V., and Ricardo Martínez. 2011. "Diversity in Definition: Integrating History and Student Attitudes in Understanding Heritage Learners of Spanish in New Mexico." *Heritage Language Journal* 8(2): 115–32.

SEVEN

# Beyond Registers of Formality and Other Categories of Stigmatization: Style, Awareness, and Agency in SHL Education

*Claudia Holguín Mendoza*
University of California, Riverside

Numerous experts in the field have advocated for the incorporation of sociolinguistics in Spanish as a Heritage Language (SHL) curricula as a way to validate students' home and community varieties while also helping them become proficient in standard varieties and formal registers in order to achieve social, academic, and professional success (Valdés 1981; Potowski 2005; Beaudrie, Ducar, and Potowski 2014). However, not only does this tension between validating students' linguistic varieties and imparting an understanding of real-world language expectations perpetuate dominant sociolinguistic and cultural hierarchies—by relegating students' own varieties of Spanish, and hence a good deal of their authentic selves, to informal contexts (Villa 2003; Leeman 2005)—it also conflates notions of register and notions of style and mischaracterizes these simply as questions of formality and informality (Leeman 2005, 2018; Leeman and Serafini 2016). Thus, pedagogical resources among SHL language educators that use the notion of appropriateness in order to explain sociolinguistic variation to students differ from critical language and literacy approaches in the sense that the former do not question our linguistic choices, nor our cultural assumptions immersed in structures of power and difference in relation to class or ethnoracial categories, among others (see Freire 1973; Fairclough 1995; Lippi-Green 1997; Martínez 2003; Leeman 2005; Cho 2018). In addition, this SHL pedagogical discourse often omits questions of prestige and stigma and fails to consider style as a "dynamic resource for identity performance" (Mortensen, Coupland, and Thøgersen 2017, 2).

In this chapter, I first discuss current understanding of style and register, as well as prestige and stigma, and the way that these are related to, but distinct from, questions of formality. Next, I describe a critical pedagogical SHL curriculum that incorporates Critical Language Awareness (CLA) of these sociolinguistic constructs (Holguín Mendoza 2018; see also Leeman and Serafini 2016). Critical pedagogies including CLA, are becoming increasingly widespread in SHL education in the US (see Martínez 2003; Leeman, Rabin, and Román-Mendoza 2011; Parra 2016, Velázquez 2013; Del Valle 2014; Leeman and Serafini 2016; Loza 2017). Sara Beaudrie, Angélica Amezcua, and Sergio Loza (2019), in a study measuring outcomes of CLA in an SHL classroom, found positive effects of instruction on a sample of nineteen students. The authors state that "several recent studies have contributed to defining the construct of CLA by describing instructional programs to teach CLA in various contexts, but few studies have sought to study empirically the results of teaching CLA in either the English or the HL context" (5). Thus, I present the results from a qualitative study utilizing an attitudinal survey to investigate students' sociolinguistic attitudes during and after completing the two-course SHL sequence in a CLA-based SHL program (2018). The interrelated goals of the study were (1) to explore students' awareness of these sociolinguistic constructs prior to instruction, and (2) to investigate the impact of SHL instruction on students' sociolinguistic awareness.

The qualitative results from the attitudinal survey reveal that since the beginning stages of the program, students ($n$ = 33) were able to differentiate categories of social stigmatization among particular linguistic forms. In addition, the data indicate that after students ($n$ = 31) took more than one SHL course,[1] there was an attitudinal shift from dominant sociolinguistic and culture ideologies to a deeper understanding of social meanings and behaviors informing language use and social perceptions. These results have profound implications for SHL education; they underscore the benefits of critical pedagogies that incorporate CLA combined with careful attention to students' linguistic confidence and self-esteem.

## Style and Stance

The notion of style became associated with concepts of register and formality since the very early Labovian studies. The construct of stylistic variation came into the field from William Labov's (1966) groundbreaking research study in New York City. In this and in subsequent studies, Labov gave great importance to the study of each speaker's stylistic variation across the socioeconomic hierarchy. He conceptualized the prestigious end of the speaker's range as the result of more formal, careful speech and the stigmatized end as the result of more casual, vernacular, unmonitored speech; "speakers' stylistic activity, therefore, was directly connected to the speaker's place in, and strategies with respect to, the socioeconomic hierarchy" (Eckert and Rickford 2001, 2). Understood as more natural and unmonitored, the vernacular is central to Labovian studies, and the participant's elicitation of a wide range of styles through controlling the topic in sociolinguistic interviews is crucial. As a consequence, other early studies in style, such as Bell's "audience design" framework, centered on audience and how the topic in interactions shifts according to not only the addressee and other overhearers, but other interlocutors present in the speakers' mind (Bell 1977).

Later studies observed how this attention to audience and the social context overlooks speakers' agency and their many strategies in making social meaning. In this way, the focus in many studies has been mostly "on the relation between variation and the speaker's place in the world, at the expense of the speaker's strategies with respect to this place" (Eckert and Rickford 2001, 1). As a result, even though style goes beyond notions of formality by being part of speakers' strategies in interactions, style became associated with notions of speakers' degrees of formality within certain, rather fixed, social contexts (2001). Thus, Nikolas Coupland (1980) later decided to focus on the "identity dimensions" of style and proposes a view of stylistic variation as a "dynamic presentation of the self" (Eckert and Rickford 2001, 4). This focus on identity stresses the important aspect of taking into consideration what the speakers perceive as style; what is more, instead of focusing on the aggregate use of variables, Coupland focuses on the strategies speakers employ in using variables in discourse. This focus created a major change in studies on stylistic variation. Accordingly, many studies centered on performativity and the construction of style through the use of single variables that can be employed at certain moments to construct a speaker's persona (2001). These subsequent studies are part of a movement that views variation as a social practice with a focus on agency and the construction of identities and social meaning; language not only reflects the social but also creates the social (2001). Natalie Schilling-Estes (1998) argues that the study of performance speech may illuminate our understanding of speech styles. She observes how performance speech may display regular patterns in contrast to other studies that have previously understood the vernacular versions of dialects as irregular and exaggerated. Schilling-Estes also demonstrates that style-shifting may be "proactive" rather than "reactive" in the sense that not only does the speakers' style shift in reaction to the formality of the social context and the audience, but also that speakers "highlight features of which they are most aware (whether at the conscious or unconscious level) when they give a speech performance" (1998, 77).

Other more current research in the field has exposed how the notion of stance "becomes a critical mediating concept between linguistic forms and larger social structures" (Bucholtz 2009, 165).[2] Stance has a central role in a speaker's main way of organizing social interactions, including the language speakers use in them (Kiesling 2009). An indexical theory of style underscores how the relationship between stance, style, and identity is conformed to a bidirectional process where local interaction and larger cultural ideologies participate in its creation (Bucholtz 2009). Another relevant theoretical advancement in the field has focused on speakers' awareness and control in language production, including style-shifting, as central aspects in better understanding variation (Babel 2016). By observing and analyzing speakers' metalinguistic commentaries of their own language use as well as that of their interlocutors, it is possible to better understand the connections between the multiple levels of social meaning in the language patterns of different communities, including the ideologies of what is considered appropriate depending on social discourses and contexts (see Álvarez 1991).[3]

## Academic Language and Notions of Formality and Informality

The complexity in acquiring academic language is clearly exposed in the context of Spanish and English bilingual students with different opportunities of access to both languages, many of whom are in Spanish courses for heritage speakers. Daniel Villa (2003) observes that Spanish heritage speakers regularly employ "rural, working class or 'campesino' Spanish, often with a number of recent borrowings from English thrown in. Some scholars consider this 'low' Spanish, unsuited for academic purposes" (90). There is a class-based language difference in the linguistic repertoires of Mexican immigrants who speak stigmatized varieties of Spanish and that serve as models for bilingual students in our classrooms (2003). Hence, even though scholars in the field have already made substantial progress in proposing critical and inclusive approaches in SHL curricula, there are still several problematic issues at stake. One main predicament resides in the fact that as educators we are invested in SHL students' attainment of an ideal proficiency in standard varieties in order to achieve social, academic, and professional success. This goal includes the use of a discourse of appropriateness centered in the acquisition of formal registers and academic language. That strategy may overlook the fact that our students already possess extensive sociopragmatic knowledge and, in addition, that we often may not share with them the same cultural and community-based consensus of what is appropriate and formal for academic and other settings. Furthermore, "discussions of appropriateness typically fail to address the question of who determines what is appropriate, or to mention that appropriateness norms are not universally shared, thus eliding issues of power" (Leeman 2018, 351).

Judith Irvine (1979) has observed how there is not a universal notion of formality and how any preferred definition should be reexamined before its use since its meaning may be vague, variable, and culturally influenced. The author recognizes four aspects of formality that apply to most communities. These are increased code structuring, code consistency, invoking positional identities, and the emergence of a central situational focus. Increased code structuring refers to the extra rules and conventions organizing behavior in a specific social context that possess many and different degrees of displayed structures, such as intonation and lexical items, among others; as a result, since speech events differ in how and when they formalize different linguistic elements, Irvine observes, they cannot just be placed on a continuum from informality to formality. In relation to code consistency, speakers possess a wide array of alternatives to contrast social meaning. In order to delimit meanings in constrained social contexts, certain rules must apply to discourse organization and need to co-occur (using a uniform code) in order to offer consistency to particular contexts. Positional identities have to do with the ability of speakers to invoke a particular identity appropriately within a given situation. Last, the emergence of a central situational focus concerns the participation in the focal activity of a social occasion that possesses its own structure and rules in which main activities and actors are not to be confused with the rest of the event's participants and activities. Thus, notions of formality in different communities may diverge because these various aspects of formality are not exploited and extended in the same manner and on the same occasions. Formality and informality are not a single continuum; "if one type of meeting somehow restricts the political freedom of its participants more than the other, it is not formality in general that brings restrictions, but only one aspect of formality (either centralization of attention or increased structuring of code)" (1979, 784). In this way, given that formality is mostly socioculturally and discursively constructed, as well as context dependent, some of the questions that may arise in the context of the SHL classroom would surely include, How do we define formality in our language courses? Would that definition not be quite variable? More precisely, how many elements, as defined by Irvine, would have to be taken into consideration in order to signal formality to students in a given task?

## Stigma and Prestige

It is crucial to note that notions of formality differ not only from the sociolinguistic notion of style but also from stigmatized and taboo language. Otto Santa Ana and Claudia Parodi's (1998) model of *nested speech-community configurations of language awareness* exposes Mexican Spanish speakers' recognition of the social evaluations of linguistic variables. The authors find that speakers possess different levels of access to variables of a dialect along the socioeconomic value continuum. In the first level of awareness, speakers distinguish between stigmatized and taboo words that possess socially sanctioned semantic content and that tend to be avoided in most contexts, such as 'puta' (whore) (1998, 27). However, speakers in field one do not recognize stigmatized words with no taboo content, including words such as 'mesmo' versus the standard 'mismo' (same) (1998, 27). In field two, speakers are aware of more elements of the linguistic hierarchy than are field one speakers; thus, they are able to identify the items that constitute stigmatized variables of Mexican Spanish. In field three, speakers not only recognize nonstandard stigmatized variables, but also regional variables. In the fourth field, by contrast, speakers favor normative variants over regional ones.

Speakers of Spanish varieties from Latin America who immigrate to the US may lack the language awareness commonly found in field four of Santa Ana and Parodi's formulation, where national standard variants are more favored. Parodi (2011) observes the use of forms prominent in rural and urban popular regions in Mexico and El Salvador and a strong English influence in the Los Angeles metropolitan area. Most of these stigmatized variants are positively evaluated by SHL speakers, in a process of koineization signaling the local prestige that this variety possesses in this speech community (2011). In his study of SHL learners' evaluations of nonstandard forms and following Santa Ana and Parodi's (1998) model, Armando Guerrero Jr. (2018) finds that by using their own linguistic resources and strategies, SHL students index their Mexicanness through different sociolinguistic styles. Second-generation SHL students traveling to Mexico as part of a study abroad program of a university in California, and with different levels of awareness before and after their trip, include in their stylistic performances their own variety's nonstandard variables with the purpose of reaffirming their *mexicanidad* (Guerrero 2018). After continuous social and institutional challenge, students acquire higher metalinguistic awareness of the "rural" and "popular" features, which allows them to assertively engage the pertinent variants and use them in the construction of their identities as stylistic practices (Guerrero 2018).

These central studies for the critical understanding of Spanish in the US show that despite speakers' relatively low awareness of stigmatized forms in field four for Mexico and other regions, these speakers in the US already possess their own nested field of language awareness with their own particular categorization of variants.

## Stylistic Practices and Agency among Bilingual SHL Learners

Moreover, speakers' degrees of language awareness incorporate multiple levels, since linguistic forms are semantically and pragmatically multidimensional by featuring attitudinal stances as well as other sociopragmatic meanings (see

Terkourafi 2011). These meanings are signaled by speakers' stances at the level of the linguistic variables and at the level of the different language styles used, which may involve more than one language (Holguín Mendoza 2011); this is precisely the case of bilingual speakers who codeswitch from Spanish to English and vice versa within a single conversation, simultaneously expressing personal stances and indexing their US Latinx identities. Central to SHL education is the learners' ability and agency to choose different alternatives within their own linguistic repertoires to communicate specific interactional stances, as well as to use language to index hybrid cultural identities (Leeman and Serafini 2016). These bilingual stylistic practices—including instances of language contact features as well as features otherwise categorized as "rural" or "popular" linguistic forms—conform, in themselves, a code (see Álvarez 1991). In Irvine's (1979) terms, in many communities around the world, a consistent code seems to be perceived to have a greater social significance and seriousness as opposed to other conversations where speakers could rearrange variants to achieve certain effects. This may be why codeswitching, instead of code consistency, is often used as a parenthetic device, and therefore a detachment from the social persona implied by a single code. The persistence of conceiving bilingual practices, including codeswitching, as informal no longer applies if these practices are not perceived and understood by educators as separate codes but, instead, in terms of natural stylistic communicative practices in all their vast complexity.

As formality is culturally and contextually determined, educators conscious of the linguistic practices of their students may aim to prioritize in their curriculum opportunities for their students to understand their own sociolinguistic experiences, which are affected by social structures of difference and power. After critical pedagogic language instruction, students are free to decide which variety to use according to their own critical assessment of a particular sociolinguistic, political, and ideological context.[4] Critical-pedagogy-based education must not continue to be understood as "anything goes" linguistic practices. This is an epistemological fallacy in the field, since allowing for teacher and student agency does not equal social anarchy. This type of agency is based on continuous self-reflection (see Velázquez 2013). As Hyesun Cho (2018) observes, "reflexivity in meaning possibilities and the multiplicity of interpretations should be allowed to make critical pedagogy productive and transformative for students and teachers alike" (228). Answering some of the critics of critical literacy and pedagogy, Cho adds that critical literacy

> acknowledges multiple axes of knowledge and difference production.... Teachers are not just ideologically informed agents who have the requisite knowledge to guide students to empowerment; rather, they must become border crossers, along with their students, who consistently reflect on and

> negotiate competing discourses in academia. Teachers cannot engage in students' transformation without first moving beyond the teacher's self, allowing disagreement, disharmony, and dissonances within the self and with students. (228)

Moreover, this type of interdisciplinary work committed to human emancipation has already been well established across disciplines (Leeman 2016), including in critical theory, feminism, postcolonial criticism, and queer theory, as well as critical literacy and CLA-based pedagogies (e.g., Horkheimer 1993; Fairclough 1995; Osei-Kofi, Shahjahan, and Patton 2010; Giroux 2011; Darder, Mayo, and Paraskeva 2016). However, this vast body of critical scholarship continues to be understudied by scholars and practitioners in Spanish and SHL education.

## An SHL Curriculum Based on Critical Pedagogies

Working on the creation of a complete curriculum for an SHL program at the University of Oregon, a solid team of instructors and I as the leader extensively trained ourselves in critical pedagogies (cf. Freire 1973), including CLA, Classroom Based Dialect Awareness (CBDA, Martínez 2003), and critical stylistic and sociopragmatic awareness and practice (Holguín Mendoza 2018). Over five years we developed a complete six-course curriculum for SHL learners that takes into account the complexity of stylistic language variation and a deep understanding of social power relations.[5] As an additional outcome, the program also seeks to change the discourse that discourages the use of stigmatized linguistic forms in Spanish such as those considered "rural" and "popular"; thus, educators in this program intend to counteract the harmful effects of such stigmatization on students' confidence in their intellectual abilities and their academic progress as a whole (2018). In order to evaluate the effects of these program pedagogies, a preliminary assessment was conducted through a linguistic attitudinal survey for SHL students in the program (2018). This mixed-methods study was based on the evaluation of sentences carrying stigmatized Mexican Spanish words that are used in varieties of Spanish spoken in the US. This first study exposes how SHL students in this program significantly develop more CLA and positive linguistic attitudes toward stylistic language variation (2018).

## Research Methodology

As a follow-up to the study mentioned above, a qualitative study based on different stigmatized forms was conducted among SHL students in this same program. Students enrolled in two SHL language courses (SPAN 218: Herencia

Latina I, and SPAN 228: Herencia Latina II) in a single term completed a survey assessing their language ideologies and awareness both early in the term ($n = 33$) and again at the end of the term ($n = 31$). Reflecting the broader demographics of the students in the program, participants in this study were mostly of Mexican descent, with a few of Central American descent. They were mostly second generation, with very few reporting to be third generation (91 percent and 9 percent respectively). Most participants have spent almost all their lives in the state of Oregon (79 percent), with a few coming from the state of California (9 percent), and the rest (12 percent) coming from a variety of states, including Illinois, Texas, and New York.

In the survey, after a brief demographic questionnaire, SHL learners were asked to write their opinions about a set of evaluative statements in regard to how people pronounce marginalized variants of adapted English loanwords, as well as other variants from stigmatized varieties. The statements consist of variations of the phrase "Se escucha mal/feo cuando alguien dice . . . " (It sounds ugly/uneducated when someone says . . . ). This wording was chosen because it is indicative of the dominant, standard language ideologies many SHL students come to class having experienced. In consultation with members of the SHL team at this institution, I decided to present students with these types of statements to use as a diagnostic tool. The primary objective was to discover evidence of the presence or absence of the development of critical knowledge and CLA among students in these courses. The questionnaire's purpose was not to "bait" with the sorts of negative attitudes that HL courses seek to eradicate or to perpetuate ideologies, but to provide an exercise in which the student could choose to refute biased statements or affirm them. The dominant paradigm is not new for the vast majority of SHL students (see Rosa 2016); therefore, this survey simply measures the extent of the awareness that students have of the reigning linguistic values and ideologies. Moreover, as can be observed in the Can-Do Statements for Critical Sociocultural Linguistic Literacy, some of the program's main learning objectives are based on students using their critical capacities and developing their abilities to identify sociolinguistic attitudes and ideologies and to dispute them using the material discussed in class (see also Martínez 2003, 2016).[6]

These marginalized linguistic forms fall into particular categories that have already been documented to inhabit different fields of awareness among Mexican and Central American Spanish speakers in a speech community in the US and in other regions (Parodi 2011; Holguín Mendoza 2011). The stigmatized loanwords were taken from various Internet sites featuring the Latinx community in the US (these websites include Mitú, https://wearemitu.com/; Flama, https://www.youtube.com/c/theflama/videos; and Pocho, https://www.pocho.com.), and they have also been observed to be stigmatized in Mexico in field four of awareness

(2011). These websites are primarily created by second-generation Latinxs who produce satirical comic relief based on their frequently difficult experiences as working-class minorities in the US. These sites often mock the way in which Latinx first-generation individuals, usually the parents and older family members of these sites' creators, adapt to US culture, including the way they speak English. This mocking of first-generation Spanish speakers provides us with a more accurate sense of US second- and later generation SHL speakers' bilingual fields of awareness. Some of the salient mock Spanish elements observed in these websites include the velarization and elision of stops /p t k/, frequent in many varieties, and that often occur in coda position in English borrowings such as 'coca lai' (Coca Light), and 'pecsi' (Pepsi) (see Bongiovanni 2014).

The survey statements also included salient stigmatized Spanish words from perceived "rural" varieties such as 'mesmamente' versus 'mismamente' (likely), and another kind of velarization in onset position such as the word 'juiste' for 'fuiste' (you went). Other statements included extended Latin American "popular" forms chosen because speakers are usually less aware of the stigmatization attached to them. These included semantic redundancies such as 'métete para adentro' (get in inside) (see Hidalgo 1987) and the regularization of the paradigm in second person singular such as in 'comistes' vs. 'comiste' (you ate) (see 1987). In order to provide participants a recognizable contrast in formality with these previous forms, the survey statements also included some instances of extended colloquial forms from Mexican Spanish such as the word 'ándale' (hurry up), and the expressions 'echarle ganas' (give it your best shot) and 'tener cruda' (have a hangover). Finally, learners were also asked to comment on a series of straightforward negative statements about bilingual speakers' mixing languages and their identity formations in order to elicit students' more candid assertions regarding their own language ideologies and linguistic confidence. The list of statements can be found in the appendix.

After the term was over, the data were analyzed using thematic analysis (Braun and Clarke 2006). A set of themes was identified across the data, and the themes were then coded and categorized by the author and a research assistant based on an original rubric for critical metalinguistic awareness created for the assessment of the topics covered in our own SHL curriculum. The categories included language ideologies; articulation of historical contexts that contribute to linguistic variation; power structures contributing to linguistic hierarchies; and awareness of stylistic variation, social meaning, and identity formation. The final step in the analysis consisted of selecting representative quotations of each theme in the rubric and in relation to the variants from the different categories of stigmatization included in the survey statements; these quotations are presented in the section below, written as the students wrote them without any modification.

## Results and Discussion

The qualitative results from the attitudinal questionnaire reveal that since the beginning stages of the program, students ($n$ = 33) were able to differentiate categories of social stigmatization among some linguistic forms. The majority of students in the first course in the sequence ($n$ = 18), provided short responses regarding the use of the variants in the survey statements. For the "rural" and "popular" variants, most of the students' comments reflected a lack of awareness of their stigmatization. These included "yo a escuchado todos de estos ejemplos y no suena mal" (I have heard all of these examples and they don't sound bad), "I speak this way, I didn't know it sounded bad," and "no tengo opinion" (I don't have an opinion). Thus, these students seemed unaware of the stigmatization of most such forms. However, their responses differed when they commented on the loanwords, which reflected their language ideologies. These comments include "esta bien que no se oyen bien porque es una lengua diferente" (it is ok that it doesn't sound correct because it is a different language), and "depende, porque no es correcto de grammatica" (it depends, because it is not grammatically correct). Two different students also included significant metalinguistic observations about their community, such as "my mom says that," and "mi mama dice hocdots pero yo no" (my mom says 'hocdots' but I don't). These statements expose how students already come to our classrooms with particular configurations of Spanish and English levels of awareness combined with ideologies and knowledge in regards to these languages' uses among different generations in their speech communities. Some students in this first group also included statements about their own Spanish proficiency that reflected their lack of linguistic confidence, such as "my Spanish can be bad but I want to improve."

At the end of the term, students from this same course ($n$ = 15) showed similar levels of awareness as at the beginning of the term. In other words, there is not a salient or marked difference in their comments. However, they were able to articulate deeper metalinguistic evaluations reflecting their pragmatic abilities in the ways they interpret discourse. This is exemplified in the following comment: "hay veces que digo 'juiste' porque lo escucho, lo digo sin pensar" (there are times when I say 'juiste' because I hear it, I say it without thinking). Other comments reflected articulated sociopragmatic awareness of their bilingual settings, implicating that they do not sanction the use of the stigmatized loanword variants in all social contexts, as in the observation "depiende del 'environment'" ([It sounds ugly/uneducated] depending on the environment) for the form 'pecsi.' This reflects the speakers' awareness of their own US Latino speech community's language uses (see Parodi 2011). One way in which their comments more clearly differ from the beginning of the term was in regards to the participants' positive affective stances as bilinguals. For instance, in "yo hablo completamente en inglés/español y también uso Spanglish" (I completely speak in English/Spanish and I also use Spanglish), or "[e]stamos pidiendo que el uso de spanglish debe de ser aceptado" (we are asking for the use of Spanglish to be accepted). These comments could possibly imply a first step in the students' process of becoming more critically aware of their community's language use, the historical context of language variation, and language hierarchies through direct instruction in CLA.

Students from the second course in the sequence ($n$ = 14), who answered the survey the first time (at the beginning of the semester), showed similar abilities in articulating their awareness of language uses. This perspective is reflected in a commentary on the forms "juiste" and "Jelipe" that states, "[i]t sounds almost the same, I would hardly tell the difference in spanish." This type of response reveals some of the struggles that students may experience while trying to learn to avoid using the marginalized variants. As per the purpose of this qualitative analysis, it is possible to observe a gradual change in students' discourse; as time passed, they showed more critical awareness of language ideologies, as well as expressing their sociopolitical stances. Examples of these comments include "some people have accents, and I catch what they're trying to say. It's an accent, not bad education," "no puedes discredit gente just because of how they speak," and "ay muchas formas de español que no puede ser mal o incorrecto" (there are many forms of Spanish that can't be bad or incorrect). Interestingly, some students also elaborated on their community members' velarization of coda /p t k/. This is exemplified in the comments, "mi papa habla así" (my dad speaks like this) and "[a]lgunas personas que en todas sus vidas han hablando español es dificil saber como se pronuncian palabras pero yo que si se lo digo en ingles" (For some people who have spoken Spanish their whole lives it is difficult to know how to pronounce some words, but I do know since I speak English). This group also showed greater frequency of minimal metalinguistic comments regarding the use of colloquial forms such as in "I grew up with this language" or "it's commonly used." They also wrote clear statements on identity and language use, as in "mezclando español e inglés es la identidad de uno" (mixing Spanish and English is one's identity). It is important to note that these statements do not mean that students have already changed their own language ideologies reflecting social hierarchies, which can be observed in the comment given for the survey statement talking about other students in their classes speaking "better" Spanish, "todos aprendimos español en diferente maneras y como en todo algunos hablan mejor que otros" (we all learned Spanish differently, and, as in everything, some speak better than others) and "I know my spanish is not excellent, but that is why I am taking spanish, in order to improve." This suggests that the ability of a speaker to become more aware of their own language ideologies is a long process, and deciding to change them or their language use may take time or potentially may not ever happen.

It is important to always keep in mind and constantly remind ourselves as critical educators that literacy "can only be known to us in forms which already have political and ideological significance and it cannot, therefore, be helpfully separated from that significance and treated as though it were an 'autonomous' thing" (Cho 2018, 25). As part of the main objectives of the courses in this program, the educators trained in critical pedagogies recognize the nature of literacy practices as sociopolitical in every lesson plan and, thus, constantly problematize this notion (of literacy as isolated from politics and ideologies) during classroom lectures and activities. The importance of finding in this assessment that students themselves are stressing contradictions and are problematizing sociolinguistic practices through their metalinguistic comments becomes crucial, and it is considered a positive outcome. In this way, when the students from the second course in the sequence (*n* = 16), answered the survey the second time (at the end of the term), some of their answers were a little more explicit; in some of their comments, students reflected greater awareness in a critical manner and provided salient sociopolitical stances. In regards to the velarization of the loanwords, for instance, a student commented, "yo no lo diría así (I wouldn't say it like that) but it's hard to pronounce words properly if it's not a language you grew up learning." In some of their comments, students reflected greater CLA and provided salient sociopolitical stances. A student wrote, "[m]i padre dice palabras como picza y pecsi y el sabe todo de inglés y español. Si alguien es bilingue, nadien puede decir que no son inteligentes con los linguajes" (my father says words like picza and pecsi and he knows everything in English and Spanish. If someone is bilingual, no one can say that they are not intelligent with languages), and "[c]reció con mi padre siempre gritando 'echale ganas' cuando yo estaba jugando futbol, por es me encanta la frase" (I grew up with my father always shouting 'échale ganas' when I was playing football; that's why I love this phrase).

In addition, students in this group included more uses of the vocabulary learned in class to convey metalinguistic content and were able to better articulate historical contexts and hierarchies contributing to variation. This evolution is evident in comments such as "[a]prendí español en casa, y en mis clases por eso tengo una combinación de un español mexicano y un español academico con el variación linguistica de España los dos son correctos" (I learned Spanish at home, and in my classes, that's why I have a combination of Mexican and academic Spanish as well as linguistic variation from Spain, both are correct). There were also many more comments in the last items regarding identity formation. In the survey item stating that a person who mixes English and Spanish speaks poorly, several students included affective stances reflecting their process of explaining their linguistic insecurity as part of their own lack of language access. This is exemplified in the comment "[a] veces siento mal porque pienso que mi español no es bueno, pero no es puro por las reglas, es tambien porque mis primos que tienen dos hispanohablantes para padres saben más que yo" (sometimes I feel bad because I think that my Spanish isn't good, but it's not only for the rules, it's also because my cousins, who have two Spanish speakers as parents who know more than me). Another student explained where they had learned these ideologies and indicated that the instructional content in the program had changed them, stating, "[t]hats what some people have told me (in high school) (I have learned from SHL [program] that it is okay)" and "I agree & disagree because I believe all spanish is correct but it is still taught & ingrained in us that one spanish is better than another." Other comments included deeper reflections on power structures such as in "[w]hat is 'correct' Spanish & who gets to decide?" Some comments reflected more on the respondent's critical awareness of stylistic variation and agency, for instance in "[l]a persona que mezcla inglés con español es muy inteligente y todos tienen una identidad nomás porque mezclas los dos idiomas no dice que no tienes una identidad" (a person who mixes English and Spanish is very intelligent and everybody has an identity because if you mix both languages that does not mean that you don't have an identity). An additional comment reflected an understanding of the choices speakers have to index social meanings in relation to what they consider valuable and pleasant from their cultural practices and language uses, "[l]a identidad es de los lenguajes. La cultura latin@ en los Estados Unidos es bonito si usa los dos lenguajes" (identity comes from languages. In the Latin@ culture in the US it is beautiful if you use both languages).

These results indicate that SHL learners are able to develop their analytical abilities in discourse and become more critically aware of their own sociolinguistic resources as well as their choices to index their identities and attitudinal stances. Nevertheless, as mentioned before, it is important to remind ourselves that the ability of individuals to become more aware of society's as well as their own language ideologies is a long process, and deciding to change their beliefs or their language practices may take more than one 10-week course, as demonstrated in this study.

## Pedagogical Implications

This study suggests that after explicit instruction oriented to develop CLA and CBDA, as well as stylistic and sociopragmatic awareness and practice, students can develop a broader, more transcultural communicative competence if and when they are encouraged to discern the social meanings of linguistic styles and to articulate how their own linguistic decisions shape and are shaped by social values that either perpetuate or resist oppressive structures. A speaker's use of a specific style is not only a matter of following social norms. Instead, bilingual speakers may choose a proactive speech performance for political reasons, for instance.

Thus, in the SHL context, "presenting appropriateness as part of a fixed sociolinguistic order with which speakers must comply, without any acknowledgment that it is historically contingent and subject to change, downplays speaker agency in making linguistic choices and denies the possibility of resistance" (Leeman 2018, 351). The complex stylistic practices of SHL learners in language classrooms must no longer be described, assessed, misjudged, or marginalized via vague, or mischaracterized, terminology. Responses such as those also result in the perpetuation of pedagogical approaches that enable, consciously or unconsciously, the endless judgement of student abilities to access the many facets of sociolinguistic capital within the social hierarchy (Bourdieu 1984) that has been and continues to be denied to them (García 1993). Prestigious language—in contrast to marginalized regional and bilingual nonstandard varieties—acquired in conjunction with many other elements of social capital and other class markers should not be the sole and ultimate goal of language education. Instead, we should continue looking at their abilities to perform in certain preinvestigated contexts after they have been offered access to the necessary tools to succeed in such tasks. We must also carefully offer students access to every possible strategy that better equips them to make their own, well-informed decisions in their professional and personal lives. The first steps in order to achieve such goals as educators are to discern and explore any misjudgment we may possess in relation to the real sociolinguistic and cultural knowledge that our students bring to class, to reevaluate our placement and assessment measures, and to truly investigate our own adherences to paradigms of social hierarchies including not only those of a socioeconomic nature, but also nationalistic ideologies and our commitment to linguistic purity and correctness, as well as our ideas about the perceived superior competence of monolingually raised native speakers.

## Appendix

Por favor comente las siguientes frases [please comment on the following phrases].

1. Algunas personas se escuchan mal cuando pronuncian algunas palabras como "Pecsi" en lugar de "Pepsi" (marca de soda) [some people

sound badly/uneducated when they pronounce some words as "Pecsi" instead of "Pepsi"].

2. Se escucha mal cuando algunas personas dicen "súbete para arriba" o "métete para adentro" [it sounds uneducated when some people say "go up above" or "get in inside"].

3. Algunas personas suenan mal cuando dicen "mesmamente" en lugar de "mismo" [some people sound uneducated when they say "similarly" instead of "similar"].

4. Se escucha mal cuando una persona dice "comistes" en vez de "comiste" o "tomastes" en lugar de "tomaste" [one sounds uneducated when using "comistes" instead of "comiste," etc.].

5. Algunas personas se escuchan mal cuando pronuncian algunas palabras como "lactoc" en vez de "laptop" [some people sound uneducated when they pronounce some words like "lactoc" instead of "laptop"].

6. Uno se escucha mal cuando dice "hoc docs" a los "hot dogs" [one sounds uneducated when saying "hoc docs" instead of "hot dogs"].

7. Se escucha feo cuando una persona dice "coca lai" en vez de "coca light" [it sounds ugly when one person says "coca lai" instead of "coca light"].

8. Se oye mal cuando alguien pronuncia "juiste" en lugar de "fuiste" o "Jelipe" en lugar de decir "Felipe" [it sounds ugly when someone says "juiste" instead of "fuiste" or "Jelipe" instead of saying "Felipe].

9. Uno se escucha mal cuando dice "ándale" [one sounds ugly when one says "andale" / hurry up].

10. Se escucha mal cuando alguna persona dice "echarle ganas" [it sounds ugly when a person says "echarle ganas" / give it your best shot].

11. Se escucha mal cuando alguna persona dice "tener cruda" [it sounds ugly when a person says "tener cruda" / be hung over].

12. La persona que mezcla inglés con español es una persona sin identidad [a person who mixes English and Spanish doesn't have an identity].

13. La persona que mezcla español con inglés habla mal [a person who mixes English and Spanish speaks poorly].

14. En las clases de español en las que participo, mis otros compañeros aunque hablan menos, cuando hablan, hablan mejor que yo porque han aprendido un español correcto [in my Spanish classes, my other classmates, even when they speak less, they speak better than me because they have learned the correct Spanish language].

15. El hecho de que yo no sé las reglas gramaticales me hace pensar o me ha hecho pensar en el pasado que mi español no es bueno [the fact that I do not know all the rules has made me think that my Spanish is not good].

## Notes

I would like to acknowledge the members of the SHL program at the University of Oregon for all their work in their training and implementation of our own critical pedagogical approach. I would like to thank Melissa A. Bowles and the anonymous reviewers for their insightful comments on this paper. Special thanks to Jennifer Leeman, Analisa Taylor, Munia Cabal Jiménez, Luz María Ede Hernández, and Craig Ede for all their feedback in the development of this manuscript. All errors remain my own.

1. This refers to ten-week courses within a quarter system at the University of Oregon.
2. Stance has been defined as "a person's expression of their relationship to their talk (their epistemic stance—e.g., how certain they are about their assertions), and a person's expression of their relationships to their interlocutors (their interpersonal stance—e.g., friendly or dominating)" (Kiesling 2009, 3).
3. An anonymous reviewer noted that the field of interactional sociolinguistics developed in anthropology and conversation analysis goes unmentioned in this literature review (e.g., Gumperz 1983; Goffman 1959; or Hymes 1980). The objective of this study is to address the theoretical misinterpretation that seems to exist surrounding constructs such as style and register (in terms of formality and informality) in relation to the notions of academic language and the standard. This misinterpretation resides in the lack of a clearer distinction between the Labovian framework and advances in an indexical theory of style offering a much richer view of style as a multidimensional cluster of sociolinguistic practices (e.g., Eckert 2008; Bucholtz 2009). All these constructs are ideologically mediated and are related to the several categories of stigmatization of variants that many SHL students use. Thus, I decided to center the literature review on this aspect.
4. In relation to the concept of formality, this is the critical approach followed at the SHL program at the University of Oregon described here.
5. These courses are described in Holguín Mendoza (2018) and Holguín Mendoza (in press).
6. Our original Can-Do Statements for Critical Sociocultural Linguistic Literacy rubric has been published as part of an online educational material project by

the Center for Open Education and Resources for Language Learning (COERLL) from the University of Texas at Austin (Holguín Mendoza and Davis 2018). The complete educational material designed to implement critical pedagogies in SHL courses at the University of Oregon as well as other collaborating institutions can be found at "Pedagogías críticas para la enseñanza de lenguas" (n.d.).

## References

Álvarez, Celso. 1991. "The Institutionalization of Galician: Linguistics Practices, Power, and Ideology in Public Discourse." PhD diss., University of California at Berkeley.

Babel, Anna. 2016. *Awareness and Control in Sociolinguistic Research*. Cambridge: Cambridge University Press.

Beaudrie, Sara, Angélica Amezcua, and Sergio Loza. 2019. "Critical Language Awareness for the Heritage Context: Development and Validation of a Measurement Questionnaire." *Language Testing*. https://doi.org/10.1177/0265532219844293.

Beaudrie, Sara, Cynthia Ducar, and Kim Potowski. 2014. *Heritage Language Teaching: Research and Practice*. New York: McGraw-Hill Education Create.

Bell, Allan. 1977. "The Language of Radio News in Auckland: A Sociolinguistic Study of Style, Audience, and Subediting Variation." PhD diss., University of Auckland, New Zealand.

Bongiovanni, Silvina. 2014. "Tomas [pepsi], [peksi] or [pepsi]?": A Variationist Sociolinguistic Analysis of Spanish Syllable Coda Stops." *IULC Working Papers* 14(2): 43–61.

Bourdieu, Pierre. 1984. *Distinction: A Social Critique of the Judgement of Taste*. Translated by Richard Nice. Cambridge, MA: Harvard University Press.

Braun, Virginia, and Victoria Clarke. 2006. "Using Thematic Analysis in Psychology." *Qualitative Research Psychology* 3(2): 77–101.

Bucholtz, Mary. 2009. "From Stance to Style: Gender, Interaction, and Indexicality in Mexican Immigrant Youth Slang." In *Stance: Sociolinguistic Perspectives*, edited by Alexandra Jaffe, 215–59. Oxford: Oxford University Press.

Cho, Hyesun. 2018. *Critical Literacy Pedagogy for Bilingual Preservice Teachers: Exploring Social Identity and Academic Literacies*. Singapore: Springer.

Coupland, Nikolas. 1980. "Style-Shifting in a Cardiff Work-Setting." *Language in Society* 9(1): 1–12.

Darder, Antonia, Peter Mayo, and João Paraskeva. 2016. *International Critical Pedagogy Reader*. New York: Routledge.

Del Valle, José. 2014. "The Politics of Normativity and Globalization: Which Spanish in the Classroom?" *Modern Language Journal* 98(1): 358–72.

Eckert, Penelope. 2008. "Variation and the Indexical Field." *Journal of Sociolinguistics* 12:453–76.

Eckert, Penelope, and John Rickford. 2001. *Style and Sociolinguistic Variation*. Cambridge: Cambridge University Press.

"Pedagogías críticas para la enseñanza de lengua." n.d. Accessed June 18, 2021. https://pedagogiascriticas.ucr.edu/materiales-lessons-plan/.

Freire, Paulo. 1973. *Education for Critical Consciousness*. New York: Seabury Press.

Fairclough, Norman. 1995. *Critical Discourse Analysis: The Critical Study of Language*. London: Longman.

García, Ofelia. 1993. "From Goya Portraits to Goya Beans: Elite Traditions and Popular Streams in U.S. Spanish Language Policy." *Southwest Journal of Linguistics* 12(1–2): 69–86.

Giroux, Henry. 2011. *On Critical Pedagogy.* New York: Continuum International Publishing Group.
Goffman, Erving. 1959. *The Presentation of Self in Everyday Life.* Edinburgh: University of Edinburgh Social Sciences Research Centre.
Guerrero, Armando, Jr. 2018. "The Mexican Diaspora: On Constructing and Negotiating *mexicanidad* in Mexico City." PhD diss., University of California Los Angeles.
Gumperz, John. 1983. *Language and Social Identity* (Studies in Interactional Sociolinguistics). Cambridge: Cambridge University Press. doi:10.1017/CBO9780511620836.
Hidalgo, Margarita. 1987. "Español mexicano y español chicano: Problemas y propuestas fundamentales." *Language Problems and Language Planning* 11(2): 166–93.
Holguín Mendoza, Claudia. 2011. "Language, Gender, and Identity Construction: Sociolinguistic Dynamics in the Borderlands." PhD diss., University of Illinois at Urbana Champaign.
———. 2018. "Critical Language Awareness (CLA) for Spanish Heritage Language Programs: Implementing a Complete Curriculum." *International Multilingual Research Journal* 12(2): 65–79.
———. In press. "Sociolinguistic Justice and Student Agency in Language Education: Towards a Model for Critical Sociocultural Linguistics Literacy." In *Teaching Languages Critically,* edited by Sara Beaudrie and Sergio Loza. Routledge.
Holguín Mendoza, Claudia, and Robert L. Davis. 2018. "Can-Do Statements for Critical Sociocultural Linguistic Literacy." ESL: CSLL Can-Dos. https://docs.google.com/document/d/1o_kJu7-Fmq7BbXVO6ldN7gwgwEtnp5DghPcmX_Qa94k/edit.
Horkheimer, Max. 1993. *Between Philosophy and Social Science: Selected Early Writings.* Cambridge, MA: MIT Press.
Hymes, Dell. 1980. *Language in Education: Ethnolinguistic Essays.* Washington, DC: Center for Applied Linguistics.
Irvine, Judith T. 1979. "Formality and Informality in Communicative Events." *American Anthropologist* 81(4): 773–90. https://doi.org/10.1525/aa.1979.81.4.02a00020.
Kiesling, Scott F. 2009. "Style as Stance: Stance as the Explanation for Patterns of Sociolinguistic Variation." In *Stance: Sociolinguistic Perspectives,* edited by Alexandra Jaffe, 171–95. Oxford: Oxford University Press.
Labov, William. 1966. *The Social Stratification of English in New York City.* Washington, DC: Center for Applied Linguistics.
Leeman, Jennifer. 2005. "Engaging Critical Pedagogy." *Foreign Language Annals* 38(1): 35–45.
———. 2016. "A Critical View of SHL Education: Speaking Back to the Neoliberal University." Lecture, 3rd Symposium on Spanish as a Heritage Language, University of Oregon, Eugene, February 18.
———. 2018. "Critical Language Awareness and Spanish as a Heritage Language: Challenging the Linguistic Subordination of US Latinxs." In *Handbook of Spanish as a Minority/Heritage Language,* edited by Kim Potowski, 345–58. New York: Routledge.
Leeman, Jennifer, Lisa Rabin, and Esperanza Román-Mendoza. 2011. "Identity and Activism in Heritage Language Education." *Modern Language Journal* 4(95): 481–95.
Leeman, J., and E. Serafini. 2016. "Sociolinguistics and Heritage Language Education: A Model for Promoting Critical Translingual Competence." In Innovative Strategies for Heritage Language Teaching, edited by Marta Fairclough and Sara Beaudrie, 56–79. Washington, DC: Georgetown University Press.
Lippi-Green, Rosina. 1997. *English with an Accent: Language, Ideology, and Discrimination in the United States.* London: Routledge.

Loza, Sergio. 2017. "Transgressing Standard Language Ideologies in the Spanish Heritage Language (SHL) Classroom." *Chiricú Journal: Latina/o Literatures, Arts, and Cultures* 1(2): 56–77.

Martínez, Glenn. 2003. "Classroom Based Dialect Awareness in Heritage Language Instruction: A Critical Applied Linguistic Approach." *Heritage Language Journal* 1(1): 1–14.

———. 2016. "Goals and Beyond in Heritage Language Education: From Competencies to Capabilities." In *Innovative Strategies for Heritage Language Teaching: A Practical Guide for the Classroom*, edited by Marta Fairclough and Sara Beaudrie, 39–56. Washington, DC: Georgetown University Press.

Mortensen, Janus, Nikolas Coupland, and Jacob Thøgersen. 2017. *Style, Mediation, and Change: Sociolinguistic Perspectives on Talking Media*. New York: Oxford University Press.

Osei-Kofi, Nana, Riyad A. Shahjahan, and Lori D. Patton. 2010. "Centering Social Justice in the Study of Higher Education: The Challenges and Possibilities for Institutional Change." *Equity and Excellence in Education* 43(3): 326–40.

Parodi, Claudia. 2011. "El otro México: Español chicano, koineización y diglosia en Los Ángeles, California." In *Realismo en el análisis de corpus orales: Primer coloquio de cambio y variación lingüística*, edited by P. Martín Butragueño, 217–43. Mexico City: El Colegio de México.

Parra, María Luisa. 2016. "Critical Approaches to Heritage Language Instruction: How to Foster Students' Critical Consciousness." In *Innovative Approaches in Heritage Language Teaching: From Research to Practice*, edited by Marta Fairclough and Sara Beaudrie. Washington, DC: Georgetown University Press.

Potowski, Kim. 2005. *Fundamentos de la enseñanza del español a hispanohablantes en los EE.UU.* Madrid: Arco Libros.

Rosa, Jonathan Daniel. 2016. "Standardization, Racialization, Languagelessness: Raciolinguistic Ideologies across Communicative Contexts." *Journal of Linguistic Anthropology* 26(2): 162–83.

Santa Ana, Otto, and Claudia Parodi. 1998. "Modeling the Speech Community: Configurations and Variable Types in the Mexican Spanish Setting." *Language in Society* 27(1): 23–51.

Schilling-Estes, Natalie. 1998. "Investigating "Self-Conscious" Speech: The Performance Register in Ocracoke." *Language in Society* 27(1): 53–83.

Terkourafi, Marina. 2011. "The Pragmatic Variable: Toward a Procedural Interpretation." *Language and Society* 40(3): 343–72.

Valdés, Guadalupe. 1981. "Pedagogical Implications of Teaching Spanish to the Spanish-Speaking in the United States." In *Teaching Spanish to the Hispanic Bilingual*, edited by Guadalupe Valdes, Anthony G. Lozano, and Rodolfo García-Moya, 3–20. New York: Teacher's College.

Velázquez, Isabel. 2013. "Getting It: Sociolinguistic Research and the Teaching of U.S. Spanish." *Critical Inquiry in Language Studies* 10(3): 191–214.

Villa, Daniel. 2003. "Heritage Language Speakers and Upper-Division Language Instruction: Findings from a Spanish Linguistics Program." In *AAUSC Issues in Language Program Direction*, edited by Heidi Byrnes and Hiram Maxim, 88–98. Boston: Heinle and Heinle.

# EIGHT

# Toward an Understanding of the Relationship between Heritage Language Programs and Latinx Student Retention: An Exploratory Case Study

*Josh Prada*
Indiana University-Purdue University Indianapolis

*Diego Pascual y Cabo*
University of Florida

While it is common to define US Latinx as a *minority*, this term is progressively becoming a misnomer, particularly in some areas. As of 2018, the United States' Latinx population totaled 58.9 million (the nation's largest "minority" group), up by 2.3 million since 2015, according to the most recent census report (US Census 2018).[1] Given such demographic shifts, it is not surprising that institutions of higher education across the country are developing strategies to connect with the increasing numbers of Latinx high school graduates seeking to further their education at the community college and university level (e.g., Flink 2018; Medina and Posadas 2012; Samuel and Scott 2014). Despite the growth in participation in higher education, the Latinx student body struggles when attempting to navigate these unfamiliar educational environments, which have traditionally disfavored minority groups. As a result, graduation rates are not in keeping with the increase in enrollment (e.g., Flink 2018; Medina and Posadas 2012; Samuel and Scott 2014; Tovar 2015).

College and university enrollment rates among US Latinxs are at an all-time high, but many drop out before graduating (Gramlich 2017). The high dropout rate is, however, not new. Latinx students continue to be among the least likely ethnic and racial groups to graduate from high school, two-year, and four-year colleges (Astin and Oseguera 2005; Fry 2002; Samuel and Scott 2014). In addition to the typical challenges that most adult college students experience, many Latinxs are faced with additional stressors, including, but not limited to, discrimination, stereotyping, or the feeling that they do not belong on campus (e.g., Flink 2018). Other factors contributing to low graduation rates are lack of funding opportunities (Olivas 1997), language barriers (Soto, Smrekar, and Nekcovei 1999), and a frequent need to contribute to the household economy (Sy and Romero 2008). These (and other) challenges have significant negative effects on the students' psychological well-being and, subsequently, on their ability to succeed academically (e.g., Arbona and Jimenez 2014; Cronin et al. 2012; Flink 2018).

This circumstance calls for the identification of institutional structures, educational approaches, and departmental/programmatic configurations that serve students from different backgrounds to successfully move from enrollment to degree completion (and beyond). Recognizing this, it is imperative for higher education institutions across the country to identify ways to provide students with the necessary conditions to facilitate and support their academic integration and development. In this regard, initiatives such as the hiring of more diverse faculty and the creation of Latinx student readiness and mentorship programs are contributors to higher student retention and graduation rates. Connectedly, the support and promotion of Hispanic Serving Institutions (colleges and universities whose enrolled student body is at least 25 percent Latinx) is fundamental, since they are known to contribute to a more welcoming academic environment for Latinx students (e.g., Nichols 2017; Rivera et al. 2017). Similarly, for first-generation Latinx students, taking Chicano studies during the first two years of their college careers may contribute to a supportive academic and social environment during a time when they are most likely to drop out of college (Berkner et al. 2007).

Considering the above, we contribute to the broad question of what we (as faculty in Spanish programs/departments) can do to encourage/facilitate Latinx students' move from enrollment to degree completion. More specifically, this chapter joins the literature on Latinx college *retention* and graduation from the perspective of Spanish/World-Global-Modern-Foreign Languages programs and departments. Along the lines of what Maria Carreira (2007) proposed at the K–12 level, in this report we investigate whether enrolling in Spanish as a Heritage Language (SHL) programs/courses aids Latinx students in completing their undergraduate degrees. Given the scope of this question, herein we discuss some positive parallels obtained by means of a mixed-methods case study conducted at Texas Tech University, a large Research 1 university (R1), Hispanic Serving Institution. These parallels reflect a general positive trend that connects Latinx students who take SHL courses with higher retention and completion rates. In approaching this issue, we contribute to examinations of the extent to which the nature and scope of SHL programs may play a role in Latinx students' successful college experiences. Following Carreira (2007), our argument rests on the premise that embracing and adopting a model for SHL teaching that adheres to best practices in the field (Parra 2017) will lead to an increased sense of belonging and fulfillment, ultimately translating into higher rates of academic success.

We begin by providing an overview of theoretical aspects defining the link between US Latinx students and retention in higher education, followed by a snapshot of what constitutes the Spanish program for heritage speakers at the institution where the case study took place. We continue by reporting on trends connecting Latinx enrollment in an SHL program and retention rates, and compare these to trends concerning Latinx students from the same college, the College of Arts and Sciences, who did not take any courses from the SHL program. We finish by offering some concluding remarks and by outlining future directions for research and administrative activity concerning student retention among heritage speakers.

## Latinx Students and Retention in Higher Education

While early conceptualizations of retention emphasized student agency in navigating the college experience (e.g., Spady 1970, 1971; Tinto 1975, 1982), perspectives soon shifted to include the notion that institutions also hold a degree of responsibility in aiding students to remain in college (e.g., Bean 1983), implying that retention does not "rest with the individual students" alone (e.g., Braxton, Hirschy, and McClendon 2004). Over the 1990s, the period known as "Broadening Horizons" (Oseguera, Locks, and Vega 2009, 27) saw an increase in scholarly activity testing existing theoretical propositions linked to retention among ethnically diverse students, a body of work that has influenced American college campuses by guiding their approaches to keeping students onboard (Berger and Lyon 2005).

John Braxton, Amy Hirschy, and Shederick McClendon (2004) proposed that factors across four categories (i.e., economic, organizational, psychosocial, and sociological) come into play when students decide to leave or to remain in college. These factors include (1) the institution's commitment to students' welfare, (2) institutional integrity, (3) proactivity in social adjustment, (4) psychosocial engagement, and (5) financial ability to cover costs. As a whole, the researchers' argument underscores the positive role of establishing personal connections with faculty and peers, the development of a sense of community, and powerful transitional programs. They continued by proposing retention practices at the programmatic level by recommending three steps with a sharp focus on minority students: (1) to achieve and maintain a sizable mass of enrolled students, (2) to create spaces for diverse students (such as specific programs and events), and (3) to underscore interventions that affirm students' identities through a sense of incorporation, rather than of assimilation, into the college environments.

Similarly, Watson Swail, Kenneth Redd, and Laura Perna (2003) offered a framework for retention that emphasizes persistence and academic achievement to account for academic success among minority students. This model focuses on how institutional services and practices (instead of individual behaviors) affect academic achievement and persistence. Swail and colleagues (2003) connected five elements, namely, (1) financial aid, (2) recruitment and admissions, (3) academic services, (4) curriculum and instruction, and (5) student services. According to this model, institutional strategies should include quality orientations, both precollege and during the college years, admissions that assess the student-environment fit (as opposed to traditional measures of merit), and an ongoing assessment of resources provided for faculty to create and implement pedagogical strategies that develop positive relationships among curricula, instructional strategies, and retention (Swail, Redd, and Perna 2003). A comparison between these two models brings forth three main (if broad) overlapping areas, which might not be surprising to practitioners and administrators who are cognizant of the situation of US Latinxs in higher education. First is the role of economic support and financing. Second are issues related to facilitating the transition into college and navigating college structures. Third is the area of community building, within and beyond the classroom.

Combined, we find the above frameworks to provide a nuanced general perspective on institutional behaviors at multiple levels that may positively impact the well-being of our students in US universities. However, a fundamental characteristic dictates our possibilities as SHL instructors, coordinators, or program directors: the scope of action of SHL programs typically extends over the course of a few semesters at best, with less favorable cases where a single stand-alone course rotates in every second or third semester. Even more difficult is the common situation in which mixed courses are the only option. To that, multiple factors at work at the individual level can be added: whether or not students' majors include language requirements and how that may play into their choosing to take Spanish; and at what juncture students enroll in courses and whether or not they do so in consecutive semesters if the courses are offered regularly. These are overwhelming institutionally defined factors that could contribute but that are beyond the control of instructors and therefore fall outside of the scope of this report.

Barring such individual limitations, the possibilities afforded to a solidly designed SHL program (and even stand-alone SHL courses) when it comes to improving students' educational experience are many (e.g., Carreira 2007). For example, two of the five key elements proposed by Swail, Redd, and Perna (2003), recruitment and admission and curriculum and instruction, can fall (partly or completely) within the scope of action of SHL programs (or Spanish programs in general). Similarly, SHL programs often emphasize and promote mentorship (Zalaquett and Lopez 2006) and close relationships with faculty members and advisors (Tovar 2015), both of which are solidly connected with retention and completion rates.

While a thorough theoretical perspective on how retention among college Latinx students in the US may connect with common practices and configurations of SHL programs falls outside of the scope of the present chapter, a description of the workings of the particular SHL program under study in this report is necessary.[2] We now turn to providing a brief snapshot of the program, its rationale, and the main strategies characterizing it. We then turn to the report describing retention differences among students who enrolled in the SHL program and those who did not.

## Spanish as a Heritage Language Programs

Within the context of the US, educational efforts in Spanish language teaching have been traditionally geared toward the promotion and development of Spanish as a second/foreign language programs, resulting in the long-standing neglect of Spanish students of Latinx origin (e.g., Alvarez 2013; Villa 2002; Carreira and Beeman 2014). This situation has brought about a number of negative by-products beyond the strictly educational ones. For example, in neglecting heritage speakers, the educational system has bolstered the stigmatization of local varieties of Spanish spoken in the US, accentuated old ethnolinguistic tensions, and perpetuated the misconception of US-born Latinx bilinguals as linguistically lacking and problematic in the Spanish language classroom. A compound of these and other reasons—which include but are not limited to negative judgments at home and in the community, poor representations of US Latinxs in popular culture, media, and political discourse—continues to situate the needs of heritage speakers in the periphery of the Spanish language teaching agenda.

Fortunately, an important action toward remedying this situation in language departments across the country has been the creation of courses and programs specifically designed for heritage language learners, students with linguistic and/or familial connections to the Spanish language and the Latinx culture. Taking the early claims by Guadalupe Valdés in the 1970s as a point of departure, most SHL courses and programs are articulated through resources and strategies that traditionally, have not been present in the second / foreign language classroom. For example, and here we are simplifying for the sake of exposition, these programs usually share the following three broad guiding principles: (1) to strengthen the students' linguistic abilities and literacy skills in the HL, (2) to raise critical social and linguistic awareness, and (3) to nurture and support a positive self-image of learners as valid members of their communities (e.g., Beaudrie and Fairclough 2012; Beaudrie, Ducar, and Potowski 2014; Leeman 2015; Leeman and Serafini 2016). Within these broad principles, it is important to note that SHL best pedagogical practices not only emphasize the understanding of why certain linguistic behaviors emerge, teasing out sociolinguistic factors that evolve around linguistic variation, but also and perhaps most important, the celebration of students themselves and their own local varieties. Simply put, while linguistic development is undoubtedly an objective in the Spanish as a heritage language curriculum, elements such as linguistic and cultural self-esteem, sociolinguistic awareness, and the development of a critical view on the sociopolitical factors at play in determining the Latinx community's day-to-day realities are purposely reflected in the SHL classroom. In this manner, the SHL classroom becomes a safe space with foci on socioaffective factors as much (if perhaps not more sometimes) as on linguistic/literacy skills (e.g., Sánchez-Muñoz 2016; Parra 2017). Considering these objectives, we believe that SHL programs fulfill the crucial goal of fostering conditions that support Latinx students' academic success, at whose center is permanence in college and program completion. To explore the retention effects of a specific SHL program, we must first understand the features of the program in question, its context, and its resources. As we see it, an SHL program must reflect its immediate reality: it must emerge from its context and grow organically in dialogue with it. Because of this symbiosis between an SHL course or program and its social, political, economic, and linguistic surroundings, a necessary first step is to describe the structural aspects, resources, and contextual factors integrating/framing the program in question. We now turn to providing such a picture.

The SHL program we report on in this chapter is a midsize program housed within the Department of Classical and Modern Languages and Literatures at Texas Tech University, a public research institution located in Lubbock. The university, established in 1923, has grown substantially from its humble origins as a regional technological college. As of fall 2018, it enrolled over 38,000 students, of whom, according to the university Fact Book, 31,957 were undergraduate, 5,835 graduate, and 417 law students, most enrolled full time and considered traditional students. Additionally, in 2017, Texas Tech met enrollment criteria to qualify as a Hispanic Serving Institution (Texas Tech University Institutional Service 2017).

The Latinx student population at Texas Tech University is representative of the local community, given that 94.8 percent of the student body come from the state of Texas. Therefore, most Latinx students who study Spanish there come from Texas, including Lubbock and the west Texas region, El Paso, Dallas / Fort Worth, Austin, and Houston. In addition, it is common to have students from New Mexico in these classes. Besides US-born and -raised students, the SHL program enrolled between three and seven foreign-born students every semester. These students, while foreign born (often in Mexico), had in most cases been raised in the US. All students enrolled in the SHL program reported having grown up exposed to Spanish at home, with a vast majority of them being functional bilinguals in English and Spanish yet reporting dominance in English, particularly when describing their academic skills. Most students had taken Spanish courses prior to joining Texas Tech University; however, it was common for them to describe their prior learning experiences as "mostly useless" or "too basic to learn anything".

The SHL program began in fall 2014 as a stand-alone course with twenty students at the upper-intermediate level. This course was developed to better address the differing linguistic and socioaffective needs of Spanish heritage speakers. Following best practices in the field, its syllabus was designed to include discussions about Latinx presence in the US, reflections about the political climate, linguistic features, and central questions in bilingualism and language contact, particularly within the US context. Written assignments included creative writing pieces, biographical pieces, and descriptions of Spanish-speaking countries and US regions that reflected the students' backgrounds. The program evolved over the subsequent six semesters into a three-level program with two sections per level, enrolling up to eighty students per semester.

Although after the first semester (fall 2014), the number of students enrolled in SHL courses remained consistent, recruiting students to register for these classes was not always easy. Anecdotally, we can say that students were affected by two issues that will not be foreign to the seasoned practitioners in the field: students either were afraid that their Spanish was not good enough or that SHL classes would be harder/more demanding than Spanish classes for the traditional second language (L2) learner. Methods for student recruitment were fine-tuned over the years. Early efforts consisted of visiting lower-level Spanish classrooms (after receiving approval from each instructor via email) and asking the group if any of the students had grown up speaking and/or hearing Spanish at home, even if they were English dominant. This was done during the first days of the semester. Then, we would ask the student(s) to step outside with us to talk about new learning opportunities. Once we were outside of the classroom, we offered students a quick overview of the available class(es) and left them with an informational flier listing the course number(s) and the people to talk to in the event they wanted to change sections and transfer to the SHL program. This process was streamlined over the semesters as the department administrators and advisors learned about the SHL program, the types of students the program was designed for, and the credits granted by each course.

By the academic year 2017–18, a placement exam adapted from previous related work by Marta Fairclough (2012) and Kim Potowski, Maryann Parada, and Kara Morgan-Short (2012) had been implemented. This exam was not credit bearing; it simply directed students who qualified for the SHL program to enroll in the appropriate level SHL course. Moreover, students who were identified as heritage speakers by their instructors, and those who were found early in the semester by visiting Spanish as a second language classes, had to interview with the program director. The interview consisted of a short informal conversation in which the student provided some background information about themselves. From time to time, and always on an individual basis, some students who were not heritage speakers but had a linguistic profile that could benefit from this type of learning environment were also admitted to the program (e.g., Spanish L2 learners who had enjoyed close interactions with Spanish speakers for a long period of time and showed a strong connection to the language and the culture). We found that these students added much human value to the already diverse nature of each group.

Particular importance was placed on SHL-specific professional development. Instructors in the SHL program were mostly graduate students in Spanish linguistics or literature. Every spring semester, all graduate students were encouraged to apply to become part of the SHL program. The application consisted of writing a formal letter expressing their interest and their qualifications. Before leading their own SHL class, instructors-to-be spent one semester shadowing current SHL instructors and attending the weekly meetings led by the program director. These meetings were used, among other things, to work on materials, brainstorm about solutions to particular problems, share experiences and questions, and provide ongoing training via small group workshops. Additionally, instructors-in-training were asked to support the service-learning program by attending some sessions. Moreover, a graduate seminar entitled "Understanding the Heritage Speaker" was offered to all graduate students on a regular basis. All students and instructors also had access to one-on-one consultations with the program director and the program coordinator.

In the first two sections of this chapter we discussed the difficulties that Latinx students in general face with regards to academic success at the college level beginning with an overview and then shifting the focus to the low retention rates characterizing this student group. In section 3, after presenting best practices of SHL teaching in general, we provided specific details about the SHL program being reported herein. Against this background, questions related to how these SHL courses may connect with and respond to larger social, cultural, and political concerns remain unanswered, leaving the interplay between SHL courses, programs, and institutions largely underexplored. At this juncture, and formulated as a set of broad questions, some of our initial considerations include the following: Do SHL programs contribute to improving SHL students' academic experiences beyond the SHL class? Do SHL programs contribute to shaping SHL students' academic success and persistence at the college level? And last, beyond purely linguistic gains, what are other positive outcomes brought forth by implementing a powerful/successful SHL program? In what follows, we attempt to provide preliminary answers to some of these questions through the analysis of publicly available data from the university, as well as a set of interviews with eight key informants, all of whom had completed at least one semester in the SHL program. Before turning our attention to the report, we would like to acknowledge the limitations of the data to be presented.

On the one hand, our quantitative data, while valuable, only comprise a small number of students followed for four semesters. To be sure, a significantly larger pool of students followed over a longer period of time would be needed to make definite claims regarding any correlation between SHL enrollment and overall student academic success. With that said, we believe the trends we observe may be an indication of how fruitful our efforts prove to be. Also relevant, the interviews conducted with our key informants covered a number of topics besides the effects of attending an SHL program on their overall academic success, which might be useful for other purposes, but the qualitative portion of this report is limited to just the relevant portions of our interview data. Regardless, we understand that, despite its limitations, with this chapter we initiate what we consider a necessary conversation in the area of SHL program administration: an area within our field that remains severely underexplored. More specifically, in what follows, we aim to ascertain the abovementioned positive impact of enrolling in an SHL program on academic success at the college level among Latinx students in terms of retention/persistence.

## Our Report

We start this section by asking ourselves the following question: Can enrolling in an SHL program contribute to increased academic success among Spanish heritage speakers? Our prediction is that given the strong focus on community building, on the development of positive perspectives, and on cross-cultural sensitivity (among other key elements as outlined earlier in the frameworks proposed by Carreira 2007; Braxton, Hirschy, and McClendon 2004; and Swail, Redd, and Perna 2003), SHL students will reap important personal benefits, resulting in more academic success. To be clear, herein we broadly understand *success* as higher student retention rates.

To explore this possibility, we draw on publicly available institutional information obtained from the university website and from the Office of the Registrar. Simply put, we turn to the data (1) to report on retention and drop-out rates of Latinx bilinguals enrolled in the SHL program, and (2) to compare said rates with those of Latinx students that are also completing a degree in the College of Liberal Arts and Sciences but who at the time of our report had not enrolled in the SHL program. Before continuing, a few important points about the scope and limitations of our report require attention. As ours is an exploratory study, we are interested in describing general trends following a methodology that can be easily replicated by colleagues in the field. At this stage, where the *unforeseen/unanticipated benefits of SHL programs* have received little to no attention, our interest is to illuminate possible pathways for research into this topic. We, therefore, acknowledge the limitations of our methodology, which reflects both the scope of our question and the available data.

Notably, in this report we are comparing retention rates among Latinx students who were enrolled in at least one course from the SHL program, and those Latinx students in the College of Arts and Sciences who did not enroll in the SHL program at all. To be clear, we are not claiming that our findings directly speak of the larger Latinx student body, even given the protocol for enrollment in the Spanish program described earlier. Moreover, because of the nature of the available data, we are not taking into consideration factors (institutional and personal) that could affect retention or interruption that are external to SHL courses.

Spanning the years 2005 to 2014, the black and gray bars shown in figure 8.1 below represent one- and two-year retention rates for students in the College of Liberal Arts and Sciences who self-identify as Hispanic/Latinx. As can be seen, and despite variation from year to year, one-year retention rates are systematically and considerably higher than two-year retention rates. This is not only logical, but it is to be expected and consistent with data from other higher education institutions. For one-year retention rates, the highest value was observed in 2012 (83.8 percent), and the lowest value was observed in 2007 (76.8 percent). For two-year retention rates, the highest value was observed in 2005 (72.8 percent), and the lowest value was observed in 2010 (65.8 percent). For comparison purposes, the average retention rates for Latinx students who took at least one class in the SHL program stands at 95.6 percent, from a total *N* size of approximately 1,800 undergraduates who identified as Hispanic/Latinx in the College of Arts and Sciences from 2014 to 2017.

As can be seen, our data reveal noticeable differences between the two groups of students. Although we do not have conclusive evidence to be able to attribute these differences solely to the effect of the SHL courses on the students, we believe this difference is neither accidental nor fortuitous. Even though this

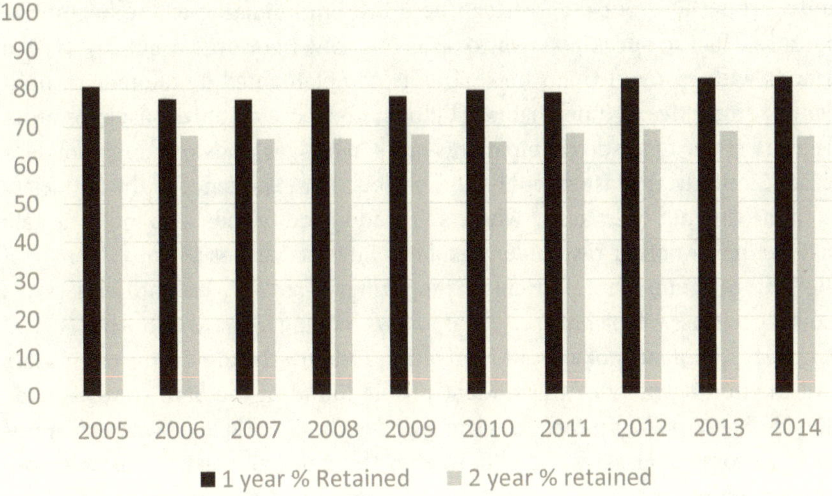


**FIGURE 8.1.** One- and two-year retention rates from 2005 to 2014 for students of Latinx origin. More recent college-level data were unavailable at the time of writing.

relationship cannot be said to be causal, we take these trends to indicate that SHL programs may serve as a supportive and powerful means to provide a solid and inclusive educational experience for Latinx students. This experience may aid not only in reinforcing their sense of belonging on campus, which in turn may yield positive outcomes in terms of academic success, but also in bolstering the institution's advancement toward a more diverse student body.

To further explore these assumptions, we turn to the data obtained from ethnographic interviews conducted with eight Latinx students enrolled in the SHL program. These interviews were conducted individually, lasted around 33 minutes (with the longest one being 39 minutes long and the shortest one 27). Four respondents identified as male and four as female, with ages ranging from nineteen to twenty-six. All participants volunteered to be interviewed as part of a broader action research project; interviews evolved around their experiences as undergraduate students in general but had an emphasis on the effects of attending an SHL course. After transcription, multiple references and statements related to retention and intentions to graduate in connection to the SHL program were identified. These have been thematically grouped into three categories: (1) Building a network I can relate to (4 codes); (2) Spanish as a skill (7 codes); and (3) A home away from home (6 codes).

*Building a network* refers to the interpersonal opportunities attending an SHL program/course affords. One respondent explained, "I talk to people in this class so much more than in other classes. . . . There's a lot of discussions and working in groups, and it can be a little intimidating at the beginning, because I had to speak Spanish to strangers, but I got over it quickly.... I'm friends with many of them now." This is complemented by another respondent's perspective: "Nunca había estado en una clase de puros hispanos antes de este y sí que tengo dos compañeras que son amigas y nos vemos afuera de la clase." Similarly, the last respondent described her experience in the SHL class as "a melting pot of Latinxs," where she made good friends who look and talk just like her. Another respondent explains how the classes she took as part of the SHL program were particularly engaging: "I really liked both classes.... Coming to class wasn't hard.... I was always looking forward to the next class." A male respondent spoke about motivation and how the topics covered in class and the homogeneity of the student profile found in the SHL context made him "happy to wake up early and show up for class." He said, "I was very motivated to come to class.... You know, after three or four weeks I normally lose interest and start missing class, but I was very motivated to finish this class, and the one I took last semester." Taken together, these quotes illustrate how attending an SHL class may stimulate a sense of belonging, and the development of connections with other students from a similar background, both of which are referred to in the literature as being important for minority student retention.

The second category, *Spanish as skill*, might seem disconnected from the notion of retention. However, seven codes within this category were explicitly connected with students' understanding of academic success (as it applied to them) as linked to developing their Spanish skills. For example, one respondent spoke about a "need" to focus on developing her "professional Spanish," as she wanted to become a nurse and feeling comfortable using Spanish in new situations was important. She finished her statement by saying, "I will continue to take Spanish until I graduate, every semester, maybe even in the summer. I'm going to do the Spanish major." Another respondent explained how he did not like the idea of taking Spanish (as a requirement) given that his major was in technology, but things changed thanks to the SHL program. He stated, "I really didn't like studying Spanish; it was so boring in high school ... but this is a very different class. I thought this was going to be a waste of time and money, honestly ... but it wasn't. I'm thinking about doing a minor ... like, I speak Spanish but I need to get my writing to the next level if I want to use it in hospitals when I graduate." Finally, another respondent explained how in one given semester, she found her SHL class to be the only one that "kept her going"; more specifically, she said, "it's been a bad semester.... Things have been tough at home and two of my professors didn't really care ... but I really enjoyed practicing Spanish in this class, and I feel that I've really improved, and I wanna get better in Spanish. It kept me going." This second category illustrates how the pursuit of Spanish as a skill engages and motivates some students to the point that it keeps them on track toward graduation. However, this will to learn (about) and practice Spanish appears to be reinforced in the SHL context. This encouragement is explored and illustrated in the next (and last) category.

The third category, *A home away from home*, refers to how the SHL classroom provides a welcoming environment to Latinx students where they can talk about their own personal experiences, examine them, and connect them to the experiences of others. In this environment, as one of the respondents explained, "Me puedo sentir más vulnerable que en otras clases. . . . Los otros estudiantes tienen el mismo background que yo." She continues, "Casi que podrían ser mis hermanas o mis primas. . . . Y eso es muy diferente a cuando era estudiante en el high school, que éramos apenas dos hispanos en la clase." Similarly, another respondent explained how "it [the SHL class] is like a home away from home]. Y'all [instructors, program director, coordinator] really care . . . like . . . it's more personal. . . . I don't have to always be white . . . and Texas Tech is pretty white . . . [*laughs*]." Another participant talks about the feeling of seeing other Latinx students' professional development and how it makes him want to report home. He explained, "You know, some people don't have expectations for us, you know, Hispanics . . . coming to college is like . . . people look at you like 'OK, you'll drop out by Thanksgiving. So, it's nice to like, call my parents and be like, hay una clase apenas con puros hispanos y todos estudian ingeniería, y leyes, y maestras, you know . . . I take pride on that and I like, want to report home you know. I want to be part of it . . . like, a successful story." This participant finished his interview by explaining how he has become very good friends with two classmates: "We sit together every day; they're nice guys, you know [name 1] and [name 2]; they don't come from money, they're hardworking people. We're like family now, we go to [local bar] a lot!"

We take statements falling within this category to illustrate how the environment characterizing this SHL program creates a space where the histories of Latinx students are reflected and recognized, and where meaningful relationships can be developed, beyond the merely academic.

Having provided an overview of the data used in this report, we now turn to discussing them and deriving implications for practice, with a focus on the programmatic administrative aspect.

## Discussion

As we have mentioned, our main goal for this manuscript is to evaluate the effects of SHL teaching and learning on bilingual Latinx students' academic success, herein conceptualized as higher retention rates. SHL teaching core principles and focus on community building, linguistic awareness, identity formation, and cross-cultural sensitivity are factors that have been found to affect students' sense of inclusion and belonging and can lead to positive changes that go beyond mere linguistic gains (Carreira 2007). Specifically, we predicted that SHL students would reap important personal benefits and greater academic success. Our findings, though not conclusive considering the limitations stated above, seem to support this prediction: bilingual Latinx students who have taken at least one SHL course seem to display higher rates of persistence toward degree completion than those who have not. Within their limitations, these positive results respond to more than simply "being enrolled in an SHL program"; they may be taken as evidence of the opportunities for growth afforded by the (inter)personal and social focus exerted by these programs and courses. Multiple publications have explored different aspects of the (inter)personal dimension of SHL programs (e.g., Leeman, Rabin and Román-Mendoza 2011; Parra 2016), producing a combined narrative that underscores notions of belonging and positive identification. While the qualitative data we report here provide insight into this issue, we can establish a meaningful connection between the present study and Diego Pascual y Cabo, Josh Prada, and Kelly Lowther Pereira (2017). In that study, the authors investigated a group of students enrolled in the SHL program reported on in this chapter, emphasizing that the positive effects participants reported for the service-learning component of the program should be considered in relation with the broader program. In other words, while the service-learning program evaluated yielded positive results, as the participants developed positive identities regarding their linguistic profiles and skills, this did not happen in a vacuum but rather in connection to other educational factors and classroom practices characterizing the SHL program (as described earlier). Expanding on our argument in Pascual y Cabo, Prada, and Lowther Pereira (2017), we would like to emphasize that the simultaneous pursuit of multiple foci characterizing SHL courses/programs makes it particularly difficult to ascertain the degree to which individual pedagogical aspects promote particular outcomes. In other words, while literacy activities are certainly tools to develop literacy, it is not so simple to tease apart the compounded effects of reading, discussing, writing critical reflections, engaging with community members through outreach initiatives, researching in the community, coming into contact with other heritage speakers and getting to know their histories, and so on, on social-cognitive aspects, such as positive identity and belonging, both of which are central to retention.

Moreover, an important related issue brought about by our report is how SHL programs and courses contribute to—and, perhaps, expand on—the elements proposed by Braxton et al.'s (2004) and Swail et al.'s (2003) frameworks. For example, Swail and colleagues included a series of institutional aspects to consider in order to support minority students' success in higher education settings. This area refers to "the ability of the institution to provide appropriate support to students during the college years, both academically and socially" and is concerned with "issues related to course availability, content, and instruction affect[ing] a student's ability to persist, as do support mechanisms such as tutoring, mentoring, and career counseling." They continue by describing how these strategies "can be seen as a flexible set of programs or conditions that the college can mold to meet the diverse needs and attributes of individual students" (79). As we see it, at least in the case of the program whose results we are investigating here, SHL programs, and to a lesser degree stand-alone courses, may contribute to this goal. SHL programs following best practices in the field reflect the student population of the area, their specificities, and their particular needs. SHL programs, as we see it, must work with the students they have, not the students they wish they had. This point also brings to the table the limitations of the program under study. At this stage, and as a result of engaging in this evaluation, we wonder, among many other questions, how could we move from courses that promote Spanish as a heritage language to programs that serve the students' needs more holistically? How can we develop partnerships with other nonacademic departments in our institutions or with local agencies to provide financial support for our students? Is the development of courses with an explicit focus on "navigating university and beyond" a possibility for freshman students? These and many other questions that necessarily connect with our overarching goal to facilitate academic success are brought forward not only by our results but by the limitations of our data.

We warn the readers about the likely possibility that not all SHL programs and/or courses will yield the same positive results, particularly if the focus of their particular SHL program is mainly on language or if the instructors do not have a background in the teaching and learning of Spanish as a heritage language. For the reasons that we have given earlier—which include the fact that SHL speakers are often seen as faulty, flawed, and fragmented—we advise newcomers to the field, or faculty in charge of developing these courses and programs, to turn to the existing literature (e.g., Pascual y Cabo 2016; Beaudrie, Ducar, and Potowski 2014; Potowski 2018; chapters of the present volume) and annual meetings, special interest groups, and well-sourced newsletters for guidance. We think that the focus of SHL educational efforts must be on the betterment of the people, as opposed to on language promotion. By exerting a traditional narrow focus on language maintenance, to a large degree, we deprioritize the speaker, and in doing so SHL programs and courses may become perpetuators of the same institutional structures that have kept our students in positions of subordination. While we agree that multilingualism should be understood as a powerful tool in today's society, a neoliberal take on this perspective does not necessarily fortify minority communities; conversely, it often exploits them (see Prada and Turnbull 2018, and Prada 2021 for discussions). It is, therefore, a paramount aspect of any SHL course to pursue a re-focalization that brings individuals and communities to the core of the language teaching/learning enterprise in the US.

## Conclusions and Future Directions

This chapter has examined the potential academic impact that may result from embracing and adopting a model for Spanish heritage language teaching that goes beyond the promotion of language development, maintenance, and revitalization to also include the development of positive perspectives on multilingual and ethnolinguistic minority identities, intercultural sensitivity, and experiential learning. By comparing institutional retention rates, we have shown that Spanish-English bilingual Latinx students who take SHL classes display higher retention rates than Latinx students who have not taken an SHL class. We believe that most higher education institutions, even those with limited resources, could achieve comparable outcomes across the United States. We also believe our findings are a strong indicator of how fertile our field is, not only to aid SHL students but also for administrators to see the extent to which the implementation of an SHL program may contribute to the betterment and to the strengthening of the university's character as a more diverse and inclusive institution. Regrettably, an issue often presented as a reason why SHL courses cannot be implemented is a lack of resources. As we see it, reports such as the one presented here may serve to develop a convincing argument for administrators who might otherwise choose to neglect the presence of bilingual students. As we have illustrated here, a small number of mixed classrooms will often provide a large enough number of students to create at least one stand-alone course. This stand-alone course may be offered every fall or every spring and serve as an opportunity to collect data. These data, together with evidence such as the report we have provided and couched within a narrative of best practices in Spanish language teaching and learning (Pascual y Cabo and Prada 2018), may help lay out the groundwork to support the need for SHL programs during conversations with administrators. Fundamentally, these conversations with administrators (as many of us have experienced) may not be easy topics to tackle.

Often, the impetus for the creation and implementation of SHL courses/programs comes from faculty members, who, out of good intentions, identify the need to cater to the specific needs of heritage speakers in their own classrooms. When this happens, we cannot assume that administrators know exactly whom we are talking about. Possibly, if our administrators have a background in languages or education, they may have heard about heritage speakers at a professional meeting, by reviewing reports released by similar institutions, or through conversations with colleagues. In cases in which the development of SHL courses/programs is faculty member initiated, we must approach our administrators with evidence to support our claim for this need, particularly if we are in institutions where budgets are being cut. We believe that reports, such as the one presented herein, are important tools if you find yourself in this situation. It is important to also consider that these requests to create new courses may come with more expectations than support.

As we mentioned earlier, we hope this report (despite its limitations) will serve to encourage other course/program directors and coordinators to design their own studies into how SHL courses may help their students in particular to move from enrollment to graduation. In the teaching and learning of SHL, the consideration of contextual and student population variables is paramount to achieving ideal results: our efforts must reflect (and adapt to) our student population in the context of our institutional parameters.

## Notes

1. In the state of Texas, where this analysis took place, 38.2 percent of the respective overall state population report being Latinx (US Census Bureau 2014). Additionally, it had the largest increase of Latinxs from 2016 to 2017 (US Census Bureau 2018).
2. It is crucial at this stage to underscore that the field of SHL is yet to extend its scope of activity to more administrative issues, particularly at the higher educational level. Exceptions, for example, are Beaudrie and Ducar (2005), who offered a set of strategies to develop a lower-level program, and Beaudrie, Ducar, and Potowski (2014), who devoted chapter 10 of their book to administrative issues in the creation of heritage language courses. Retention, however, remains a topic typically addressed in the broader field of education.

## References

Alvarez, Stephanie M. 2013. "Evaluating the Role of the Spanish Department in the Education of U.S. Latin@ Students: Un Testimonio." *Journal of Latinos and Education* 12(2): 131–51.

Arbona, Consuelo, and Carolina Jimenez. 2014. "Minority Stress, Ethnic Identity, and Depression among Latino/a College Students." *Journal of Counseling Psychology* 61, no. 1 (January): 162–68.

Astin, Alexander W., and Leticia Oseguera. 2005. "Pre-college and Institutional Influences on Degree Attainment." In *College Student Retention: Formula for Student Success*, edited by Alan Seidman, 245–76. Westport, CT: Praeger Publishers.

Bean, John P. 1983. "The Application of a Model of Turnover in Work Organizations to the Student Attrition Process." *Review of Higher Education* 6(2): 129–48.

Beaudrie, Sara M., and Cynthia Ducar. 2005. "Beginning Level University Heritage Programs: Creating a Space for All Heritage Language Learners." *Heritage Language Journal* 3(1): 1–26.

Beaudrie, Sara M., Cynthia Ducar, and Kim Potowski. 2014. *Heritage Language Teaching: Research and Practice*. New York: McGraw-Hill Education Create.

Beaudrie, Sara, and Marta Fairclough. 2012. *Spanish as a Heritage Language in the US: State of the Science*. Washington, DC: Georgetown University Press.

Berger, Joseph B., and Susan C. Lyon. 2005. "Past to Present: A Historical Look at Retention." In *College Student Retention: Formula for Student Success*, edited by Alan Seidman, 1–29. Westport, CT: Praeger Publishers.

Berkner, Lutz, Shirley He, Marcinda Mason, and Sara Wheeless. 2007. "Persistence and Attainment of 2003–04 Beginning Postsecondary Students: After Three Years. First Look. NCES 2007-169." *National Center for Education Statistics*.

Braxton, John M., Amy S. Hirschy, and Shederick A. McClendon. 2004. "Understanding and Reducing College Student Departure." *ASHE-ERIC Higher Education Report* 30, no. 3 (April): 1–105.

Carreira, Maria M. 2007. "Spanish-For-Native-Speaker Matters: Narrowing the Latino Achievement Gap through Spanish Language Instruction." *Heritage Language Journal* 5, no. 1 (Summer): 147–71.

Carreira, Maria. M., and Tom Beeman. 2014. *Voces: Latino Students on Life in the United States*. Santa Barbara, CA: ABC-CLIO.

Cronin, Tracey J., Shana Levin, Nyla R. Branscombe, Colette van Laar, and Linda R. Tropp. 2012. "Ethnic Identification in Response to Perceived Discrimination Protects Well-Being and Promotes Activism: A Longitudinal Study of Latino College Students." *Group Processes and Intergroup Relations* 15, no. 3 (May): 393–407.

Fairclough, Marta. 2012. "A Working Model for Assessing Spanish Heritage Language Learners' Language Proficiency through a Placement Exam." *Heritage Language Journal* 9(1): 121–38.

Flink, Patrick J. 2018. "Latinos and Higher Education: A Literature Review." *Journal of Hispanic Higher Education* 17, no. 4 (October): 402–14.

Fry, Richard. 2002. "Latinos in Higher Education: Many Enroll, Too Few Graduate." *Pew Hispanic Center*, September 5, 2002. https://www.doleta.gov/reports/papers/Latinos_in_Higher_Education.pdf.

Gramlich, John. 2017. "Hispanic Dropout Rate Hits New Low, College Enrollment at New High." *Pew Research Center*, September, 29, 2017. http://www.pewresearch.org/facttank/2017/09/29/hispanic-dropout-rate-hits-new-low-college-enrollment-at-new-high/.

Leeman, Jennifer. 2015. "Heritage Language Education and Identity in the United States." *Annual Review of Applied Linguistics* 35: 100–119.

Leeman, Jennifer, Lisa Rabin, and Esperanza Román-Mendoza. 2011. "Identity and Activism in Heritage Language Education." *Modern Language Journal* 95, no. 4 (Winter): 481–95.

Leeman, Jennifer, and Ellen J. Serafini. 2016. "Sociolinguistics and Heritage Language Education: A Model for Promoting Critical Translingual Competence." In *Innovative Strategies for Heritage Language Teaching*, edited by Marta Ana Fairclough and Sara M. Beaudrie, 56–79. Washington, DC: Georgetown University Press.

Medina, Christina A., and Carlos E. Posadas. 2012. "Hispanic Student Experiences at a Hispanic-Serving Institution: Strong Voices, Key Message." *Journal of Latinos and Education* 11, no. 3 (June): 182–88.

Nichols, Vanessa. 2017. "Latinos Rising to the Challenge: Political Responses to Threat and Opportunity Messages." PhD diss., University of Michigan, 2017.

Olivas, Michael A. 1997. "Research on Latino College Students: A Theoretical Framework and Inquiry." In *Latinos and Education: A Critical Reader*, edited by A. Darder, R. D. Torres, and H. Gutierrez, 468–86. New York: Routledge.

Oseguera, Leticia, Angela M. Locks, and Irene I. Vega. 2009. "Increasing Latina/o Students' Baccalaureate Attainment: A Focus on Retention." *Journal of Hispanic Higher Education* 8, no. 1 (January): 23–53.

Parra, María Luisa. 2016. "Understanding Identity among Spanish Heritage Learners." In *Advances in Spanish as a Heritage Language*, edited by Diego Pascual y Cabo, 177–204. Studies in Bilingualism 49. Amsterdam: John Benjamins.

———. 2017. "Resources for Teaching Spanish as a Heritage Language." *Informes del Observatorio*, 032-06.

Pascual y Cabo, Diego, ed. 2016. *Advances in Spanish as a Heritage Language*. Studies in Bilingualism 49. Amsterdam: John Benjamins.

Pascual y Cabo, Diego, and Josh Prada. 2018. "Redefining Spanish Teaching and Learning in the United States." *Foreign Language Annals* 51(3): 533–47.

Pascual y Cabo, Diego, Josh Prada, and Kelly Lowther Pereira. 2017. "Effects of Community Service-Learning on Heritage Language Learners' Attitudes toward Their Language and Culture." *Foreign Language Annals* 50(1): 71–83.

Potowski, Kim. 2018. "Spanish as a Heritage/Minority Language: A Multifaceted Look at Ten Nations." *The Routledge Handbook of Spanish as a Heritage Language*, edited by Kim Potowski, 1–14. New York: Routledge.

Potowski, Kim, Maryann Parada, and Kara Morgan-Short. 2012. "Developing an Online Placement Exam for Spanish Heritage Speakers and L2 Students." *Heritage Language Journal* 9, no. 1 (January): 51–76.

Prada, Josh, and Blake Turnbull. 2018. "The Role of Translanguaging in the Multilingual Turn: Driving Philosophical and Conceptual Renewal in Language Education." *E-JournALL, EuroAmerican Journal of Applied Linguistics and Languages* 5(2): 8–23.

Prada, Josh. 2021. "Translanguaging thinking y el español como lengua de herencia." In *El Español como Lengua de Herencia–ELH*, edited by Diego Pascual y Cabo and Julio Torres. New York: Routledge.

Rivera, Héctor H., Tiberio Garza, Margarita Huerta, Raul Magdaleno, Elda Rojas, and Dora Torres-Morón. 2017. "Fostering an Environment for Resilience among Latino Youth: Characteristics of a Successful College Readiness Program." *Journal of Latinos and Education* 18, no. 2 (April): 178–85.

Sy, Susan R., and Jessica Romero. 2008. "Family Responsibilities among Latina College Students from Immigrant Families." *Journal of Hispanic Higher Education* 7(3): 212–27.

Samuel, Karissa R., and Joyce A. Scott. 2014. "Promoting Hispanic Student Retention in Two Texas Community Colleges." *Research in Higher Education Journal* 25, no. 1 (September): 1–12.

Sánchez-Muñoz, Ana. 2016. "Heritage Language Healing? Learners' Attitudes and Damage Control in a Heritage Language Classroom." In *Advances in Spanish as a Heritage Language*, edited by Diego Pascual y Cabo, 205–18. Studies in Bilingualism 49. Amsterdam: John Benjamins.

Soto, Lourdes D.; Jocelynn L. Smrekar, and Deanna L. Nekcovei. 1999. "Preserving Home Languages and Cultures in the Classroom: Challenges and Opportunities." *Directions in Language and Education* 13, no. 1 (Spring): 2–10.

Spady, William G. 1970. "Dropouts from Higher Education: An Interdisciplinary Review and Synthesis." *Interchange* 1, no. 1 (April): 64–85.

———. 1971. "Dropouts from Higher Education: Toward an Empirical Model." *Interchange* 2, no. 3 (September): 38–62.

Swail, Watson S., Kenneth E. Redd, and Laura W. Perna. 2003. "Retaining Minority Students in Higher Education: A Framework for Success." *ASHE-ERIC Higher Education Report* 20, no. 2 (February). San Francisco: Wiley Subscription Services.

Texas Tech University Institutional Service. 2017. Texas Tech University Factbook. http://techdata.irs.ttu.edu/Factbook/.

Tinto, Vincent. 1975. "Dropouts from Higher Education: A Theoretical Synthesis of the Recent Literature." *A Review of Educational Research* 45, no. 1 (June): 89–125.

———. 1982. "Limits of Theory and Practice in Student Attrition." *Journal of Higher Education* 53, no. 6 (November): 687–700.

Tovar, Esau. 2015. "The Role of Faculty, Counselors, and Support Programs on Latino/a Community College Students' Success and Intent to Persist." *Community College Review* 43(1): 46–71.

US Census Bureau. 2014. *ACS Demographic and Housing Estimates.* Table DP05. https://data.census.gov/cedsci/table?g=0400000US48&d=ACS%205-Year%20Estimates%20Data%20Profiles&tid=ACSDP5Y2014.DP05.

US Census Bureau. 2018. *Hispanic Heritage Month 2018.* Report No. CB18-FF.07, September 13, 2018. https://www.census.gov/newsroom/facts-for-features/2018/hispanic-heritage-month.html.

Villa, Daniel J. 2002. "The Sanitizing of US Spanish in Academia." *Foreign Language Annals* 35, no. 2 (March): 222–30.

Zalaquett, Carlos P., and Alana D. Lopez. 2006. "Learning from the Stories of Successful Undergraduate Latina/Latino Students: The Importance of Mentoring." *Mentoring and Tutoring: Partnership in Learning* 14(3): 337–53.

NINE

# Heritage and Second Language Learners' Voices and Views on Mixed Classes and Separate Tracks

*Florencia G. Henshaw*
University of Illinois at Urbana-Champaign

Considering the steady growth of the Hispanic population in the US over the last few decades, it is not surprising that increasingly more universities have developed courses and programs tailored to the needs of heritage language (HL) learners. However, due to logistical and administrative constraints, mixed classes of second language (L2) and HL learners prevail as the most common scenario in many institutions (Beaudrie 2012), despite some important differences between the two types of learners (see Carreira and Chik 2018 for a comparison of pedagogical and affective needs of L2 and HL learners). Mixed classes present language educators with the challenge of implementing differentiated instruction strategies to help all students develop their language skills while creating a learning environment where everyone is equally motivated and engaged. However, research comparing the views of L2 and HL learners with respect to working with classmates of similar or different backgrounds has been scarce, and even fewer studies have explored their views on course placement practices. Given that the extent to which learners benefit from various instructional practices may be influenced by affective and social dimensions, research on self- and peer perceptions is necessary to better understand the complex dynamics of mixed classrooms, which will help language educators address the affective needs of all learners and, in turn, improve learning outcomes. Furthermore, no studies to date have explored the potential influence that the experience of having taken HL-tailored courses could have on students' views regarding the need for separate tracks. This study aims to fill these gaps in the literature not only by examining L2 and HL learners' attitudes toward working with peers of similar or different proficiency levels and linguistic backgrounds but also comparing the perceptions of HL learners enrolled in a course designed for heritage speakers with those who were not.

## Literature Review

A number of studies have investigated HL learners' attitudes toward the heritage language, particularly with respect to their motivation and goals (Carreira and Kagan 2011; O'Rourke and Zhou 2018; Torres and Turner 2017). Overall, research has found that even though HL learners have positive attitudes toward the language and culture, they tend to perceive their own varieties of Spanish as less prestigious than other dialects, which results in insecurity with respect to their linguistic abilities. Other studies have explored their perceptions of instructional practices (Beaudrie 2009, 2015; Ducar 2008), revealing, among other things, that HL learners regard corrective feedback and cultural content as important components of their language-learning experiences.

Another strand of research has focused on the effectiveness of peer interaction in mixed classrooms. Robert Blake and Eve Zyzik (2003) found that HL learners helped their L2 peers in 75 percent of the negotiation episodes. Nonetheless, the authors suggested that working with L2 peers could help to reinforce the HL learners' "positive self-image of their superior cultural and linguistic knowledge of Spanish" (541). Melissa Bowles (2011) found that engaging in a collaborative writing task could bring about even benefits for both members of the dyad when they were of similar proficiency: HL learners could receive help from L2 learners with orthography-related issues, and L2 learners could learn new words from their HL partners. Laura Walls (2018), on the other hand, reported that matched dyads (L2-L2, HL-HL) were more prone to collaborate with each other, as opposed to exhibiting dominant-passive or expert-novice interactional patterns, which were more common among mixed dyads (L2-HL). However, since attitudinal data were not collected in any of these three studies, it is difficult to say whether the authors' observations matched the students' perceptions.

Bowles, Rebecca Adams, and Paul Toth (2014) explored L2 and HL learners' self- and peer perceptions through an attitudinal questionnaire completed after students engaged in a collaborative task. Results showed that L2 learners in L2-HL dyads exhibited less confidence in their own abilities in Spanish than the HL learners. Nonetheless, both L2 and HL learners seemed to have an overall positive outlook on the experience. Likewise, Ana Fernández Dobao (2020) found that most HL learners enjoyed working with their L2 partners and embraced their role as experts, though some felt that they were expected to perform better based solely on their background. The results of Florencia

Henshaw (2015) partially echoed those of Bowles, Adams, and Toth (2014) in that the HL learners were more confident in their linguistic abilities than their L2 partners, and both L2 and HL learners found the task to be enjoyable overall. However, in the open-ended comments, some of the HL learners alluded to the fact that they had to mask their abilities because they were uncomfortable using words that were unfamiliar to their partners, and one of the HL participants went as far as declaring: "I hated the fact that I knew more Spanish" (262). As for the L2 learners, although most of them appreciated their partners' help, two of them indicated feeling intimidated or unhelpful.

Research on learners' perceptions in mixed classes also revealed similar trends. Kim Potowski (2002) reported that some of the twenty-five HL learners in her study felt the need to mask their own abilities in order to blend in or possibly avoid intimidating their classmates, and they also expressed feeling uncomfortable with the added pressure of being called on first, presumably reflecting the instructors' higher expectations of them in comparison to the L2 learners. At the same time, they felt at a disadvantage relative to their L2 classmates when it came to the metalinguistic knowledge seemingly required to get good grades on assessments, a trend confirmed by Sara Beaudrie (2009).

Bowles and Silvina Montrul (2014) also examined the perceptions and preferences of students at the same institution as Potowski (2002). Participants were thirty-three Spanish HL learners enrolled in mixed classes and twenty-seven heritage speakers who were not taking Spanish courses at the time of the survey. Unlike the HL learners in Potowski's (2002) study, participants appeared to have a more positive outlook on their Spanish abilities. With respect to course preferences, the majority seemed to consider mixed courses to be adequate, with only 15 students (25 percent) indicating that a course designed for HL learners would better fit their needs. It is important to keep in mind that the courses for heritage speakers described in Potowski's (2002) study had been discontinued a year prior to the survey; therefore, it is unclear whether the participants in Bowles and Montrul's (2014) study had taken classes designed for HL learners, which could have affected their opinions on the need for separate tracks.

Both Potowski (2002) and Bowles and Montrul (2014) focused exclusively on HL learners' perceptions; however, in order to have a complete understanding of the affective dimensions of mixed instructional settings, it is important to take into account L2 learners' perspectives. One of the first studies to include L2 learners' voices was Anne Edstrom (2007), which documented the perceptions of sixteen students in advanced Spanish courses, most of whom were pursuing a career in teaching: four self-described as "non-natives," two as "heritage," and ten as "native speakers." Overall, all learners had positive views of mixed classes, and they felt that everyone contributed to the learning experience. However, a third of the heritage/native speakers supported the idea of having separate sections for L2 learners, and several of them reported frustration with some professors' relatively higher expectations of them in comparison with their L2 peers, who found it challenging at times to understand their native peers and participate in class. Clara Burgo (2016) reported similar findings: most of the twenty-five L2 learners viewed mixed classes favorably, but some students felt embarrassed when speaking in front of their HL classmates, and others had difficulty understanding them. Likewise, Teresa Campanaro (2013) reported that most of the forty-four L2 learners surveyed enjoyed working with HL learners, though half of them acknowledged feeling intimidated and uncomfortable by the HL learners' presence. The majority of the eleven HL learners in Campanaro's (2013) study were in favor of mixed classes and did not have a preference when it came to working in a group with L2 learners or with other heritage speakers.

More recently, Vilma Dones-Herrera (2015) surveyed fifteen HL learners and twenty-nine L2 learners in mixed beginning-level Spanish courses. Most of the HL learners had positive attitudes toward working with an L2 classmate and enjoyed helping them. The L2 learners, on the other hand, did not feel as strongly about the benefits of mixed classes. Whereas half of them liked being in the same class as HL learners because they appreciated their help, the rest expressed some concerns, such as feeling intimidated and speculating that the HL learners' presence influenced their instructors' expectations. With respect to course selection preferences, half of the L2 learners said they would prefer a course exclusively for L2 learners as opposed to a mixed course; likewise, 55 percent of the HL learners indicated they would take a course specifically for HL learners, if it were offered at their institution.

Although the studies reviewed here have revealed some important trends with respect to how students feel about working with classmates of different linguistic backgrounds, the limited sample sizes make the results difficult to extrapolate. Furthermore, the lack of information on the students' prior experiences taking different types of courses raises the question of whether the opportunity to take courses tailored for HL learners would influence HL learners' views on the need for separate tracks. Lastly, studies comparing L2 and HL learners' perspectives have focused on either beginning-level or upper-division content courses (e.g., literature, linguistics), leaving classroom dynamics at the intermediate level largely unexplored. The present investigation aims to fill these gaps in the literature by addressing the following research questions:

RQ 1: What are HL and L2 learners' perceptions of working with peers of similar or different proficiency levels and linguistic backgrounds?

RQ 2: What are HL and L2 learners' attitudes toward mixed versus separate courses? Do the perceptions of HL learners who have taken an HL-tailored course differ from those who have not?

## Methods

### Participants

Participants were 108 L2 learners (76 females, 32 males) and 42 HL learners (34 females, 8 males). All participants were undergraduate students (age range: 18–22) enrolled in fifth-semester Spanish courses, which have a targeted proficiency level of Intermediate-High to Advanced-Low on the ACTFL scale. At the time of this study, both courses were required for all Spanish majors and minors. Student placement in the courses is based on either having taken the required prerequisite or their score on a written placement test.[1] All of the L2 learners and 35 of the HL learners were enrolled in a grammar review course; 18 HL learners were enrolled in a special section of Spanish composition for heritage speakers, which is offered fully online[2] (7 of them had taken the grammar course prior to the composition course; 11 of them were taking it concurrently). Heritage speakers are encouraged but not required to enroll in the HL-tailored section of the composition course, in consultation with the course supervisor.

The vast majority of the L2 learners were monolingually raised native speakers of English, born and schooled in the US, who had started studying Spanish as a foreign language between the ages of 10 and 15 (average age of first exposure: 12) and who used only English to communicate with friends and family members. Twenty of the L2 learners were heritage speakers of other minority languages (Polish, Korean, Arabic, Urdu, Turkish, Tagalog, and Hebrew). Only one L2 learner reported attending a bilingual education program in elementary school. The mean self-rating of their current overall language ability in Spanish for all 108 L2 learners was 3.05 (range: 1–4; SD = 0.5), on a scale from 1 ("understand some but cannot speak") to 5 ("understand and speak fluently like a native speaker").

The 42 HL learners were bilingually raised Spanish/English speakers: 37 of them had at least one parent born in a Spanish-speaking country (Mexico, Colombia, El Salvador, Puerto Rico, Venezuela, Honduras); 5 of them had US-born Spanish-speaking parents. One student was born in Mexico and had immigrated to the US at the age of three; the rest were born in the US. As for language use at home, the majority listed both English and Spanish; eleven of them reported using only Spanish during early childhood and learning English at the age of four. They currently used mostly or only Spanish with parents and grandparents, but mostly or only English with their siblings and friends. Seven

HL learners had not taken any Spanish courses before college, whereas the rest had taken between one and five years of Spanish language courses in middle school and high school, and four had attended a bilingual (Spanish-English) program in elementary school. On a 5-point scale, the mean self-rating of their current overall language ability in Spanish was 3.91 (range: 3–5; SD = 0.73). Because the sample sizes were unequal, an independent samples Welch t-test was performed to compare the mean self-ratings of L2 and HL learners. This showed that HL learners rated themselves significantly more proficient than L2 learners ($p < .0001$, $d = 1.37$).

## Materials

Data for this study come from learners' responses to a questionnaire that was completed online, as part of a larger study.[3] The results presented here focus on the ten questions that inquired about the learners' attitudes and preferences when it came to working with learners of different proficiency levels, their experiences in mixed classes, and their views on having separate courses for HL learners, which appear below. There were seven Likert-scale items; for the first six items, participants were asked to indicate their level of agreement with each of the statements, ranging from 1 (completely disagree) to 4 (completely agree), and to briefly explain their answers to each one; for item 7, the scale ranged from 1 (not at all important) to 4 (very important). Items 8, 9, and 10 were open ended.

1. I feel comfortable working with someone who is better than me at Spanish.
2. I feel comfortable working with anyone, regardless of their level of Spanish.
3. I get intimidated when I work with a classmate who knows more Spanish than I do.
4. I prefer to work with someone who has the same proficiency level as I do.
5. I like working with a partner who doesn't know Spanish as well as I do because I can teach him/her how to say things.
6. I like working with a classmate who knows more Spanish than I do because I can learn from them.
7. How important is the proficiency level of your partner (how well they speak Spanish) in determining the effectiveness of pair work, when you do activities in Spanish class?
8. In current or previous Spanish courses, how often have you worked with a classmate who seemed to have grown up speaking Spanish at home?

9. If you've had the opportunity to work with a classmate who seemed to have grown up speaking Spanish at home, how would you describe those experiences?
10. Do you think students who grew up with Spanish (or Spanish & English) at home should be in the same courses as students who learned Spanish as a foreign language later in life, or should they be in separate courses?

## Results

### Learners' Views on Peer Proficiency

The first research question, which inquired about learners' perceptions of working with peers of different proficiency levels and backgrounds, was approached from two angles: more generally, based on their responses to the Likert-scale items and, more concretely, based on the information they shared regarding prior experiences working with HL learners in the classroom (open-ended items 8 and 9). Results from the Likert-scale items plus the open-ended comments explaining their ratings are presented in this section. The next section focuses on the results of items 8 and 9 about the participants' experiences working with HL learners.

With respect to their preferences on working with peers of different proficiency levels, mean ratings and their corresponding standard deviations for the first six Likert-scale items are summarized in table 9.1.

**TABLE 9.1.** Likert-Scale Item Ratings, Indicating Level of Agreement (1 = completely disagree; 4 = completely agree) by Learner Type

| | L2 learners | | HL learners | |
|---|---|---|---|---|
| | Mean | SD | Mean | SD |
| *I feel comfortable working with someone who is better than me at Spanish.* | 2.99 | 1.07 | 3.36 | 0.85 |
| *I feel comfortable working with anyone, regardless of their level of Spanish.* | 2.96 | 0.94 | 3.07 | 1.05 |
| *I get intimidated when I work with a classmate who knows more Spanish than I do.* | 2.57 | 1.24 | 1.71 | 0.83 |
| *I prefer to work with someone who has the same proficiency level as I do.* | 3.12 | 1.11 | 3.45 | 0.63 |
| *I like working with a partner who doesn't know Spanish as well as I do because I can teach him/her how to say things.* | 2.36 | 1.03 | 2.07 | 0.97 |
| *I like working with a classmate who knows more Spanish than I do because I can learn from them.* | 2.85 | 0.93 | 2.90 | 0.98 |

Independent samples Welch t-tests revealed significant differences between the L2 and HL learners' level of agreement with two items: "I feel comfortable working with someone who is better than me at Spanish" ($p = 0.03$, $d = -.38$), and "I get intimidated when I work with a classmate who knows more Spanish than I do" ($p < .001$, $d = .815$). HL learners indicated a higher level of agreement with the first statement and stronger disagreement with the second statement than the L2 learners. With respect to item 7, both L2 and HL learners expressed a statistically similar level of agreement regarding the importance of their partner's proficiency level in determining the effectiveness of pair work: the mean rating was 3.43 among the L2 learners, and 3.22 among the HL learners.

Even though there was no statistically significant difference between the L2 and HL learners' mean ratings for the item "I like working with a partner who doesn't know Spanish as well as I do because I can teach him/her how to say things," the comments participants provided to explain their ratings revealed some discrepancies with respect to working with classmates who are at a lower proficiency level than they are. Half of the HL learners mentioned drawbacks of being paired with someone of lower proficiency, whereas only four of the L2 learners included similar comments. In fact, twenty of the open-ended responses by the L2 learners pointed out benefits of being paired with a classmate whose level of Spanish was lower than their own, both in terms of increased comfort and confidence, as well as the learning opportunities afforded by "teaching" their peers.

Unlike the L2 learners, none of the HL learners' comments indicated a preference for working with a classmate of lower proficiency. Out of the forty-two responses, only two hinted at potential benefits of helping their peers. One of them viewed it as a way to "gain a deeper understanding of the material" while the other was not as enthusiastic: "I don't mind sharing my knowledge, in fact, I find it cool to see people interested in learning Spanish, but I enjoy speaking Spanish with people who speak it better or at the same level as me." The rest of the HL learners' comments mentioned negative aspects of working with a peer of lower proficiency. Many alluded to one-sided benefits, with comments such as "I prefer improving my own Spanish rather than helping a non-native speaker. I should feel like a student in class rather than an extra-helper"; "I don't like to seem like the know-it-all when working with others or have to constantly correct the other person"; and "I feel as if I'm doing all the work." Other concerns included communication difficulties (e.g., "Working with someone that is at a lower proficiency level can get a bit tedious because they have trouble understanding what I say"), and insecurity with respect to their own abilities (e.g., "I don't think I would be able to fully explain certain concepts in Spanish in case they have any doubts; also because a lot of times I, myself, still get very confused by some questions in Spanish"). One of the HL learners' comments reflected the extent to which their linguistic insecurities affect all of their interactions in class: "As a native Spanish speaker, I feel like I should know a lot of what we are learning. However, that is not the case, and when I am paired with someone who knows more than I do, I feel like I am failing in Spanish. But if I am placed with someone who knows less than I do, I do not feel comfortable enough to help him/her out."

## Learners' Views of Working with HL Peers

Open-ended items 8 and 9 focused on linguistic background and inquired about learners' experiences and perceptions of working with HL learners. Most of the L2 learners (76 percent) had worked with an HL peer at some point in a Spanish class. The open-ended comments of those L2 learners revealed mixed feelings. On the one hand, several participants indicated specific aspects of working with HL learners that were particularly helpful. Eighteen responses hinted at the fact that the HL learners' superior oral communication skills were an incentive to improve their own abilities. For example, one of them said: "I pushed myself to keep the conversation going." A total of sixteen comments described the HL learners' overall stronger command of the language, and their wider lexical repertoire in particular, as a valuable resource to either understand or complete assignments. One of the L2 students wrote: "I sat next to a native speaker last semester and she would always answer my questions and help me with in class activities, homework, etc. She even edited my study abroad Spanish essay!"

On the other hand, thirty-six of the L2 learners' responses mentioned some of the negative aspects of mixed classes. Fifteen participants indicated feeling "intimidated," "self-conscious," "inferior," and even "judged" when working with HL learners, which they felt affected their performance in class, as they were "more reluctant to speak" or "made more mistakes." One of them explained: "It always makes me feel like they would notice when I messed up while speaking without quite the understanding that my instructors have." Another drawback of working with HL classmates, according to seventeen of the L2 learners' responses, was the difficulty they experienced in understanding them.

Only five of the HL learners (12 percent) had never worked with an HL peer. The responses from the thirty-seven HL learners who had worked with another HL learner revealed overall positive experiences, with one HL learner going as far as saying: "I would consider those experiences my best experiences, although rare. It was great to be able to speak with someone who had that type of grasp of the language similar to myself. I wish I could have that opportunity more often than not." Only six comments specifically alluded to negative aspects of being paired with another HL learner. Three of them mentioned feeling intimidated by what they perceived as their classmates' superior skills; for example, one of the HL learners wrote: "I felt like I did not know as much as they did even though I did learn Spanish since birth." The other three negative comments referred to specific classmates perceived as unhelpful or arrogant. The rest of the responses included positive aspects of working with other HL learners. Most of them cited the efficiency with which they could complete tasks given that they "understood each other at a faster pace," or were "on the same level of understanding." Others viewed it as beneficial for their own language development; for example, one learner commented: "I found it helpful because they could correct me if I needed it and it was more rewarding to keep up with them." A few alluded to the fact that they found comfort in working with a classmate who had "a lot of cultural similarities," or who "shared the same experiences, having known Spanish since birth but not know the grammatically correct way of writing and speaking it." Three of the HL learners admitted that even though they found it easier to complete speaking tasks, they "would often disagree on grammar rules," "had some difficulty with the grammar exercises," or "struggled with the concept of grammar."

## Learners' Views on Mixed versus Separate Classes

To answer the second research question, which focused on students' opinions about L2 and HL learners enrolling in the same or different courses, responses to item 10 were examined. As shown in table 9.2 below, most of the L2 learners were in favor of mixed classes, whereas approximately 28 percent said they preferred separate courses, and five of them did not indicate a preference (e.g., "I have no strong opinion") or felt it depended on the focus of the course (e.g., "if the course is grammatically based the students should be placed together, but if it is a conversational course there should be a separate section for native speakers"). Among the forty-two HL learners, 52.4 percent said that everyone should be in the same classes, close to 30.9 percent felt it was better for the two types of learners to be in separate courses, and seven of them did not state a clear preference (e.g., "I am in the middle. There are both pros and cons in both cases") or felt that it depended on personal factors (e.g., "It really depends on the comfort level of the person"), as well as the focus of the course (e.g., "They

**TABLE 9.2.** Summary of All Participants' Responses to the Question, "Should L2 and HL learners be in the same or separate courses?"

| | L2 learners | HL learners |
|---|---|---|
| Same courses | 73 (67.6%) | 22 (52.4%) |
| Separate courses | 30 (27.8%) | 13 (30.9%) |
| No opinion / It depends | 5 (4.6%) | 7 (16.7%) |

**TABLE 9.3.** Summary of HL Learners' Responses to the Question, "Should L2 and HL learners be in the same or separate courses?"

| | HL learners in tailored online section | HL learners in mixed classes only |
|---|---|---|
| Same courses | 5 (27.8%) | 17 (70.8%) |
| Separate courses | 10 (55.6%) | 3 (12.5%) |
| No opinion / It depends | 3 (16.7%) | 4 (16.7%) |

should be in the same writing and reading courses, but not the same listening and speaking courses").

To find out whether the experience of taking an HL-tailored course affected the learners' views on the need for separate tracks, responses from HL learners who were enrolled in the online section of Spanish composition for heritage speakers were compared to the responses from those who were not. As summarized in table 9.3, almost 71 percent of the HL learners who had not taken any college courses designed for heritage speakers viewed mixed classes favorably, and only three (12.5 percent) said that there should be separate classes. In contrast, the majority of the HL learners in the special section (55.5 percent) were in favor of separate courses, and only 27.8 percent thought everyone should be in the same classes. Since some cells had a frequency of less than 5, a 2x3 Fisher's exact test was run to determine whether there was a significant association between the HL learners' opinions and their enrollment in the tailored course, and results showed that indeed there was ($p = 0.006$).

### *Reasons in Favor of Separate Courses*

Many of the L2 learners who supported having separate courses cited affective reasons, particularly in relation to self-perceptions, with comments such as "it makes me feel like I don't know anything at all," "it feels like if you don't speak Spanish as well as them you are being judged," "it has always made me undermine myself and my abilities," and "I almost feel bad for not growing up with Spanish like they did." A few of the L2 learners explicitly mentioned how the HL learners' presence impacted their own performance. For instance, one of them explained, "as a student that is competing with these students for good grades, I am at an obvious disadvantage. It is also intimidating when I realize how much better these students are at speaking the language." Two of the L2 learners alluded to more general drawbacks of having HL learners in the L2 classroom: one said, "It defeats the purpose of 'learning the language' since they already know it," and the other described the HL learners' presence as "a bother." Only a handful of L2 learners made references to having different learning needs (e.g., "While they need to focus mostly on grammar, our focus should be on communication and understanding").

On the other hand, the HL learners' comments regarding the need for separate courses revolved mainly around different pedagogical needs, in terms of content (e.g., "Many things that are taught in class are things we already know"), goals (e.g., "Native-speakers and non-native speakers have different ways of learning and different things that they want to get out of a Spanish class"), and pace of instruction (e.g., "Those who already know Spanish, like myself, do not need to be taken step by step for some things. Growing up with Spanish we already have a sense of what's going on and can do most of the activities on our own"). One of the HL learners in the heritage section explained:

> I had to take classes with people who were just taking the class as a language class requirement and it wasn't the same passion for the language. Along with this, someone who did not have the same background with Spanish as myself would not be struggling with the same things. This course has been the most beneficial Spanish course I have taken thus far at the University because it focuses on what my struggles would be and it's important to acknowledge that it's different.

Last, one of the HL learners in favor of separate courses brought to light potential issues with respect to how course placement decisions are made:

> In my high school the first two levels of Spanish were separated by students who grew up with Spanish at home. I believe this is a good approach; however, this was done according to last name which I feel is biased because I don't have a Hispanic last name yet my mother is from a Spanish-speaking country and I heard it frequently as a child. I had an understanding of basic words through interaction with family members while growing up, but I was placed in the regular class.

### *Reasons in Favor of Mixed Courses*

The L2 learners' comments in favor of mixed classes stemmed primarily from perceiving the HL learners as a "valuable resource to the non-native speakers." For instance, some of the responses included comments such as "it gives others a chance to learn how to understand people with different accents," "it gives the beginning students experience with interacting with native speakers," and "they provide the class with first-hand knowledge of the culture." Some of the L2 learners who saw mixed classes as beneficial also added some caveats: "as long as the students who grew up speaking Spanish aren't bored," "as long as they have similar abilities in Spanish," and "provided that the courses aren't curved."

About a third of the responses included comments about similar needs between the L2 and HL learners, particularly when it came to explicit knowledge of grammar rules. For example, one of the L2 learners remarked that despite the HL learners' advantage when it came to oral communication skills, "they probably struggle with the grammar and writing like the majority of the class." Some of the comments also alluded to differences between "the Spanish they use at home and the Spanish we learn in class." On a similar note, some of the L2 learners who were heritage speakers of other languages made references to their own struggles and experiences learning and using a minority language; for instance, one learner wrote: "Even if they grew up in a Spanish speaking home, they might not get it all. For example, while I know Tagalog where I can be placed in the Philippines and live a normal life speaking Tagalog, I don't know the grammar at all; I just learned it naturally."

The majority of HL learners who felt that everyone should be in the same classes also mentioned the shared need to learn "the grammar rules or the formalities." For instance, one HL learner said that "the Spanish that is taught at home is incredibly different than the one taught in the classroom, so it's sometimes like learning a new language." One of the HL learners who had taken lower-level mixed classes at the same institution wrote: "I personally did not learn the proper way of writing in Spanish, or any of the rules of Spanish, and I have been learning a lot of new things in these intro classes that I had not previously known."

## Discussion

The first research question aimed to shed light on the HL and L2 learners' perceptions of working with peers of similar or different proficiency levels and backgrounds. The results of the Likert-scale items, which focused on proficiency, as well as two open-ended items, which focused on their experiences working with HL peers, revealed important differences between the L2 and HL learners' responses with respect to feelings of intimidation and the expert role, which will be explored in further detail.

Results showed that the HL learners felt more comfortable and less intimidated when paired with a classmate of higher proficiency than themselves, whereas the opposite was true for the L2 learners. The HL learners in this study rated their own skills higher than the L2 learners, which could have contributed to this disparity in terms of their level of comfort when working with someone with a stronger command of Spanish. Although some of the L2 learners appreciated the challenge of working with a classmate of higher proficiency as an opportunity to improve their skills, others were explicit about the impact of feeling intimidated on their own performance in class. The same trend emerged when students shared their experiences working with HL learners: some of the L2 learners welcomed their HL peers' assistance, whereas for others it brought up feelings of intimidation and inferiority. Very few of the HL learners, on the other hand, expressed feeling that way when working with another HL learner.

These findings suggest that the affective needs of both L2 and HL learners might be better met by offering separate courses. Feelings of intimidation on the part of L2 learners not only affect their own performance but also have implications for HL learners in mixed classes: being paired with a student who feels uncomfortable and inhibited would likely not bring about any benefits for the HL partner and, in fact, it may be detrimental to their language development in the sense that they might feel more compelled to mask their abilities. However, the reality in many institutions is that having separate courses is not always viable due to various logistical and administrative constraints. One way in which instructors of mixed classes can help to meet the L2 and HL learners' affective needs is by surveying their students and taking into account their self-confidence and preferences with respect to working with classmates of higher and lower proficiency when forming groups or assigning tasks. Other pedagogical implications for mixed classrooms are discussed in the next section.

Another important difference between the HL and L2 learners' peer perceptions was reflected in the fact that the L2 learners seemed much more amenable to the idea of working with a peer of lower proficiency than themselves, whereas the HL learners' comments reflected some resistance toward assuming the role of "expert," which aligns with the findings of Henshaw (2015).[4] The majority of HL learners in this study did not appear to find those interactions as beneficial, not only due to the perceived lack of learning opportunities for themselves but also because the pressure of teaching someone else heightened their own linguistic insecurities. These results appear to stand in contrast with Dones-Herrera (2015), who reported that the opportunity to help their classmates was one of the reasons why most HL learners in her study were in favor of mixed classes. A possible explanation for this discrepancy could lie in the level and focus of the courses. HL learners in Dones-Herrera's (2015) study were in beginning-level Spanish classes, whereas participants in this study were in upper-level grammar and composition courses, which could have made the HL learners unsure about explaining concepts that are much more complex than those covered in introductory classes (e.g., aspectual distinctions, characteristics of an effective introduction to an essay, etc.), and thus they may have been more interested in receiving help themselves. Even though the questions did not inquire specifically about their current experiences, but rather their general perceptions and preferences, it is indeed likely that the students' views may have been influenced by the course they were currently enrolled in.

The second research question inquired about the HL and L2 learners' attitudes toward mixed versus separate courses. The findings reported here align with previous studies in the sense that, overall, most L2 and HL learners viewed mixed classes in a positive way, despite some of the concerns they expressed about working with peers of different proficiency levels and backgrounds. Among the benefits of mixed classes, the L2 learners cited the opportunity to expand their vocabulary, be exposed to different dialects, and receive help with assignments, echoing the findings of Campanaro (2013), Burgo (2016), and Edstrom (2007). At the same time, many of the L2 learners acknowledged that the presence of HL learners made them more aware of shortcomings in their own communicative abilities, which for some served as motivation to improve their skills, while others viewed it as detrimental to their own learning, given that it curtailed their confidence and willingness to participate in class activities.

With respect to the HL learners' perceptions regarding mixed and separate classes, the results of this study are consistent with those of Campanaro (2013), as well as Bowles and Montrul (2014), with less than a third of the HL participants expressing the preference for separate classes. However, when HL learners' responses were separated according to whether or not they were enrolled in the heritage speaker course, there was a distinct contrast between the two groups. The vast majority of learners who had not taken any college courses designed for heritage speakers found mixed classes to be adequate, whereas a little over half of the students in the heritage section felt that L2 and HL learners should be in separate classes. These findings suggest that the experience of taking classes designed for HL learners could influence their opinions on the need for separate tracks. In other words, it is possible that the lukewarm level of interest in separate tracks reported in previous studies (e.g., Campanaro 2013; Bowles and Montrul 2014; Pino and Pino 2000), as well as among the HL learners in the present study who had only taken mixed classes, might be attributed to a lack of understanding of what heritage classes would entail. It is important to bear in mind that only one HL learner explicitly mentioned the heritage section when explaining why she felt that L2 and HL learners should be in separate courses. Although the current study revealed a relationship between the experience of taking HL courses and their views on course placement, further research is needed to explore and confirm it.

## Pedagogical Implications

Given that this study focused on student perceptions of certain pedagogical and curricular practices, there are several implications for the classroom that can be drawn from the data. The results underscore the need for language educators to be cognizant of students' perceptions, experiences, and preconceived notions, not necessarily to base all pedagogical decisions on their preferences, but rather to address potential discrepancies in expectations, and perhaps more important, avoid situations in which affective aspects impact their learning in a negative way. Understanding how peer perceptions, as well as experiences in and outside of the classroom might influence the learning environment is paramount in all courses, but even more so in mixed classes.

The results of this study revealed feelings of insecurity on the part of both L2 and HL learners in mixed classes, which instructors should not only be aware of but also help their students overcome. As the present study and previous research suggest, L2 learners might feel intimidated and reticent, and HL learners might experience conflicting messages and emotions: on the one hand, they feel pressured to excel as "experts," while at the same time, they do not view their own Spanish as "correct" and even doubt their abilities to help a peer of lower proficiency. One way in which instructors could help to curb these negative feelings is by focusing on building everyone's confidence. In the case of L2 learners, affording them opportunities to interact with native speakers from different Spanish-speaking countries via video chat (through services like TalkAbroad) could help them realize what they are indeed capable of accomplishing and make them feel more comfortable about interacting with someone of higher proficiency. With respect to increasing the HL learners' confidence, instructors should focus on cultivating "positive attitudes towards both the heritage language and various dialects of the language," which Sara Beaudrie, Cynthia Ducar, and Kim Potowski (2014, 59) list as one of the main goals of HL instruction. On a related note, educators should not assume that helping a fellow L2 classmate will necessarily contribute to boosting the HL learners' self-confidence because in reality it may have the opposite effect. Instead, all students might be better served by gaining an appreciation for dialectal variation, including linguistic phenomena associated with US Spanish, as other scholars have suggested (Pascual y Cabo and Prada 2018; Potowski 2002).

Another pedagogical implication derives from the finding that both L2 and HL learners have concerns about instructors' expectations in mixed classes, which is in line with previous research (Potowski 2002; Dones-Herrera 2015; Edstrom 2007). On the one hand, L2 learners assume their instructors expect them to have the same skills as their HL classmates, which makes them feel at a disadvantage, while HL learners feel like they are being held to a higher standard than their L2 peers. Whether or not students' perceptions match actual practices, the issue of fairness should be explicitly addressed in mixed classes. Instructors should reflect on ways in which they may be inadvertently failing to recognize and appreciate everyone's bilingualism on its own merits and ensure that each learner has the support needed to succeed in the course by implementing differentiated teaching strategies, such as those suggested by Maria Carreira and Claire Chik (2018). Course objectives and expectations should not only be clear and consistent, but also crafted with both L2 and HL learners in mind. If mixed classes continue to be geared primarily toward L2 learners, many of the issues revealed in this and previous studies will prevail. In other words, the first step toward ameliorating attitudinal issues in mixed classes is to move away from thinking of them as L2-tailored courses where HL learners are also enrolled. Meeting the affective needs of all students can only be accomplished if their pedagogical needs are also met, which goes beyond classroom techniques and grouping strategies and actually requires an overhaul of course content and goals.

With respect to student views on mixed versus separate courses, the fact that the majority of learners seemed to be in favor of mixed classes should not be interpreted as evidence that separate courses are unnecessary. First, the L2 learners' reasons behind their preference for mixed classes suggested one-sided benefits for themselves, and it would be imprudent to justify having mixed classes for the benefit of only one group. Second, the HL learners' justification for finding L2 courses adequate reflected internalized stigmatization of the Spanish spoken at home (i.e., "correct" Spanish is learned in L2 classrooms), which should be addressed, as suggested above. Furthermore, results showed that most students in the section of Spanish composition for heritage speakers voiced their support for separate courses. Taken together, these findings point toward the need for educators to help students understand curricular decisions and inform them not only about course offerings but also about the pedagogical benefits that taking tailored classes entails for HL learners. One way to educate students could be through testimonials similar to what some of the participants enrolled in the course for heritage speakers shared in the survey presented here.

## Limitations and Future Research

This study contributed to expanding our understanding of L2 and HL learners' self- and peer perceptions in mixed classes, as well as their views regarding the need for HL-tailored courses. Considering the heterogeneity of HL learners, caution should be exercised when extrapolating the results, as they only reflect the views of a group of students in one institution. A larger sample size of HL learners taking tailored and mixed courses at institutions nationwide would give a clearer picture of whether these trends occur more broadly. Another limitation that should be kept in mind is the fact that data were obtained only through a ten-item written questionnaire, which may have limited the depth of information shared by some of the participants. Future research should include follow-up interviews so that many of the trends uncovered here could be explored in more detail. Furthermore, even though the current study did not focus on comparing two particular courses, it is possible that the perceptions of the HL learners in the heritage section may have been influenced by the fact that the course was fully online. Future work should explore whether students' attitudes in mixed classes vary according to delivery format (e.g., in-person, online, hybrid), as well as pedagogical approach (e.g., multiliteracies, content-based, grammar-focused, etc.), and targeted proficiency level of the course. On a related note, L2 and HL learners' experiences in K–12 settings, which some of the participants mentioned in their responses, should also be examined in greater detail, as they would help higher education language professionals understand their students' perceptions in a more holistic way.

## Notes

1. The placement test was developed in-house and consists of multiple-choice questions on vocabulary, grammar, and reading comprehension. Students need to receive a score of at least 46 (out of 57) to place into the level of the grammar or the composition course where participants were enrolled. The placement test is optional; students are also able to self-place into the courses they consider adequate for their needs, in consultation with their advisor.
2. Since the population of HL learners is smaller than that of L2 learners in the Spanish program where the study took place, the only feasible way to offer an HL-tailored section without creating scheduling conflicts for the students was to have the course be fully online.
3. Participants completed the questionnaire from home and received extra credit in exchange for their voluntary participation.
4. An anonymous reviewer pointed out that in some L2-HL interaction studies, HL learners appear to resist giving up the role of expert, which may appear contrary to the observation made here. Although several interaction studies have shown that HL learners assist their L2 peers more often than the other way around, we cannot assume it is an indication that HL learners necessarily enjoy that role. In Henshaw (2015), for instance, HL learners assumed and maintained the role of experts, and yet some of them expressed negative feelings toward that experience.

## References

Beaudrie, Sara. 2009. "Receptive Bilinguals' Language Development in the Classroom: The Differential Effects of Heritage versus Foreign Language Curriculum." In *Español en Estados Unidos y otros contextos de contacto*, edited by Manel Lacorte, 325–45. Madrid: Iberoamericana Vervuert.

———. 2012. "Research on University-Based Spanish Heritage Language Programs in the United States: The Current State of Affairs." *Spanish as a Heritage Language in the United States: State of the Field*, edited by Sara Beaudrie and Marta Fairclough, 203–21. Washington, DC: Georgetown University Press.

———. 2015. "Instructional Effectiveness in the SHL Classroom: Comparing Teacher and Student Perceptions." *Journal of Hispanic Higher Education* 14(3): 274–97.

Beaudrie, Sara, Cynthia Ducar, and Kim Potowski. 2014. *Heritage Language Teaching: Research and Practice*. New York: McGraw-Hill.

Blake, Robert, and Eve Zyzik. 2003. "Who's Helping Whom?: Learner/Heritage-Speakers' Networked Discussions." *Applied Linguistics* 24(4): 519–44.

Bowles, Melissa. 2011. "Exploring the Role of Modality: L2-Heritage Learner Interactions in the Spanish Language Classroom." *Heritage Language Journal* 8(1): 30–65.

Bowles, Melissa, and Silvina Montrul. 2014. "Heritage Spanish Speakers in University Language Courses: A Decade of Difference." *ADFL Bulletin* 4(1): 112–22.

Bowles, Melissa, Rebecca Adams, and Paul Toth. 2014. "A Comparison of L2-L2 and L2-HL Interactions in Spanish Language Classrooms." *Modern Language Journal* 98(2): 497–517.

Burgo, Clara. 2016. "Perceptions of L2 Spanish Learners in the Mixed Classroom." *Revista Nebrija de Lingüística Aplicada* 20:1–8.

Campanaro, Teresa. 2013. "Spanish Heritage Speakers and Second Language Learners in Mixed Classrooms: Perceptions of Students and Instructors." MA thesis, University of Alberta, Edmonton.

Carreira, Maria, and Claire Chik. 2018. "Differentiated Teaching: A Primer for Heritage and Mixed Classes." In *The Routledge Handbook of Spanish as a Heritage/Minority Language*, edited by Kim Potowski, 359–74. New York: Routledge.

Carreira, Maria, and Olga Kagan. 2011. "The Results of the National Heritage Language Survey: Implications for Teaching, Curriculum Design, and Professional Development." *Foreign Language Annals* 44(1): 40–64.

Dones-Herrera, Vilma. 2015. "Heritage vs. Non-heritage Language Learner Attitudes in a Beginning-Level Mixed Spanish Language Class." MA thesis, Arizona State University.

Ducar, Cynthia. 2008. "Student Voices: The Missing Link in the Spanish Heritage Language Debate." *Foreign Language Annals* 41(3): 415–33.

Edstrom, Anne. 2007. "The Mixing of Non-native, Heritage, and Native Speakers in Upper-Level Spanish Courses: A Sampling of Student Opinion." *Hispania* 90(4): 755–68.

Fernández Dobao, Ana. 2020. "Exploring Interaction between Heritage and Second Language Learners in the Spanish Language Classroom: Opportunities for Collaborative Dialogue and Learning." In *Languaging in Language Learning and Teaching: A Collection of Empirical Studies*, edited by Wataru Suzuki and Neomy Storch, 92–110. Amsterdam: John Benjamins.

Henshaw, Florencia. 2015. "Learning Outcomes of L2–Heritage Learner Interaction: The Proof Is In the Posttests." *Heritage Language Journal* 12(3): 245–70.

O'Rourke, Polly, and Qian Zhou. 2018. "Heritage and Second Language Learners: Different Perspectives on Language Learning." *International Journal of Bilingual Education and Bilingualism* 21(8): 994–1003.

Pascual y Cabo, Diego, and Josh Prada. 2018. "Redefining Spanish Teaching and Learning in the United States." *Foreign Language Annals* 51(3): 533–47.

Pino, Barbara, and Frank Pino. 2000. "Serving the Heritage Speaker across a Five-Year Program." *ADFL Bulletin* 32(1): 27–35.

Potowski, Kim. 2002. "Experiences of Spanish Heritage Speakers in University Foreign Language Courses and Implications for Teacher Training." *ADFL Bulletin* 33(3): 35–42.

Torres, Kelly, and Jeannine Turner. 2017. "Heritage Language Learners' Perceptions of Acquiring and Maintaining the Spanish Language." *International Journal of Bilingual Education and Bilingualism* 20(7): 837–53.

Walls, Laura. 2018. "The Effect of Dyad Type on Collaboration: Interactions among Heritage and Second Language Learners." *Foreign Language Annals* 51(3): 638–57.

## AFTERWORD

# Studying Outcomes to Bridge the Gap between Teaching and Learning

*Maria M. Carreira*
National Heritage Language Resource Center,
UCLA, California State University, Long Beach

As Melissa Bowles points out in her introduction, though the field of heritage languages has racked up an impressive array of accomplishments in the areas of research, teaching, and institutionalization, the study of outcomes—that is, the effectiveness of specific instructional approaches and practices—remains underdeveloped. This volume is a much-needed contribution to this important topic, one that will hopefully be a launching pad for the field of instructed heritage language acquisition and encourage deeper thinking about how to support the development of Spanish as a Heritage Learner (SHL) learners along a wide number of parameters.

The research literature identifies three pedagogically significant ways in which heritage language (HL) learners differ from second language (L2) learners: namely, with respect to their skills in the target language, their socioaffective needs vis-à-vis the target language and culture, and their receptivity to instruction (Carreira 2016). The studies in this volume address each of these areas, as well as the highly significant, though largely unexplored, topic of how HL education can support the general academic development and broader well-being of US Latinos. In this afterword, I will weigh in on the implications of these studies, individually, as well as clustered by themes, and propose recommendations with three stakeholder populations in mind, namely, HL researchers, educators, and learners. Following the organization of the volume, I will discuss the studies in part I first, and then those in part II.

## Part I: Morphosyntactic Outcomes

The discussion of morphosyntactic outcomes that follows is organized around three themes: the difference between narrow and broad-based proficiency; the relationship between proficiency, instruction, and assessment; and the place of implicit and explicit instruction.

### Narrow and Broad-Based Proficiency Outcomes

Examining the development of morphosyntactic features, the contributions in part I assume a narrow definition of proficiency, that is, one focused on grammatical competence or mental representations of language. From this perspective, successful outcomes are those that conform to or approximate native speaker forms. Effective instructional approaches are those that prove fruitful in advancing those outcomes.

Contrasting with the above, a broad-based definition of proficiency is centered on communication or functional language abilities (Zyzik 2016). Representing this view, the ACTFL Proficiency Guidelines describe learner outcomes in terms of parameters such as global tasks, topics and text-types (e.g., persuasive writing), and communicative strategies employed by speakers to maintain communication in real-world contexts (American Council on the Teaching of Foreign Languages 2012). In addition, the ACTFL framework distinguishes between proficiency and performance, with the former being defined as "the ability to use language in real world situations in a spontaneous interaction and non-rehearsed context and in a manner acceptable and appropriate to native speakers of the language" (American Council on the Teaching of Foreign Languages 2015, 4). Performance, on the other hand, is "the ability to use language that has been learned and practiced in an instructional setting. Coached by an instructor, whether in a classroom or online, or guided by instructional materials, performance refers to language ability that has been practiced and is within familiar contexts and content areas" (American Council on the Teaching of Foreign Languages 2015, 4).

With a narrow view of proficiency, research on heritage linguistics has greatly expanded our understanding of the factors that shape the development of HL learners' grammatical competence and shed light on particular structures that often deviate from monolingual native speaker forms (Polinsky 2018). This research undergirds a tenet of HL pedagogy, which is that grammar instruction should be targeted (i.e., focused on the susceptible structures or knowledge gaps), rather than all inclusive or comprehensive, as typically happens with L2 instruction. The studies in part I of this volume identify instructional approaches that advance the learning of key elements of heritage grammars.

For its part, research on HL learners' broad-based proficiency informs another tenet of HL teaching: that instruction should expand learners' bilingual range and build their multiliteracy skills (see Sara Beaudrie and Bonnie Holmes, chapter 2 in this volume). In a foundational study, Elvira Swender et al. (2014) used the ACTFL Oral Proficiency Interview (OPI) to assess the strengths and weaknesses of Spanish and Russian HL speakers at various proficiency levels. Bearing in mind that scoring at a particular level entails meeting all criteria for that level with the expected degree of accuracy, the researchers sought to understand the particular deficiencies that kept HL speakers from qualifying for the next higher level on the proficiency scale. The Spanish HL learners in their sample that scored at the Advanced level fell short of the Superior level due to difficulties organizing and producing extended discourse, using communicative strategies for dealing with a topic abstractly, producing well-organized messages, and using precise vocabulary. In the area of grammar, they lacked level-appropriate control of the past subjunctive and other complex structures associated with hypothesizing. For their part, the Intermediate-level HL learners in their sample fell short of the Advanced level due to their inability to maintain a conversation in topics beyond their immediate experience and produce paragraph-length discourse, as their speech lacked connectors and internal organization. On the other hand, they excelled at past narration and "were more successful in using past-tense verb forms, aspect, and irregular structures than what is typically expected of L2 learners at this level" (Swender et al. 2014, 433).

From the above, we can see that grammar enters into the determination of broad-based proficiency, but it is one of many criteria. Furthermore, as illustrated below in the ACTFL Proficiency Guidelines for writing, each proficiency level has benchmark grammatical criteria and vocabulary, as well as an expected degree of accuracy. Crucially, though accuracy increases with proficiency, native levels of accuracy are not required, even at the Distinguished level.

## ACTFL Proficiency Guidelines for Writing

| | |
|---|---|
| Novice-Mid | Writers exhibit a high degree of accuracy when writing on well-practiced, familiar topics using limited formulaic language. With less familiar topics, there is a marked decrease in accuracy. |
| Intermediate | Writers use basic vocabulary and structures to express meaning that is comprehensible to those accustomed to the writing of nonnatives. |

| | |
|---|---|
| Advanced | Writers show good control of the most frequently used structures and generic vocabulary, allowing them to be understood by those unaccustomed to the writing of nonnatives. |
| Superior | Writers demonstrate no pattern of error; however, occasional errors may occur, particularly in low-frequency structures. |
| Distinguished | Writers demonstrate no pattern of error; however, occasional errors may occur, particularly in low-frequency structures. When present, these errors do not interfere with comprehension, and they rarely distract the native reader. |

The bulk of the research on instructional approaches and practices that support the development of broad-based proficiency has been conducted on dual-language immersion programs. This extensive body of work indicates that Latino children in such programs become more proficient in Spanish (as well as in English) than their counterparts in English-medium programs (Lindholm-Leary 2014; Potowski 2016). To my knowledge, only two studies have examined the development of both types of proficiency, namely, Adrián Bello-Uriarte, chapter 3 in this volume (to be discussed later) and Bowles and Bello-Uriarte (2019). The latter study found that HL speakers in a genre-based writing course improved their writing fluency and syntactic complexity over the course of a semester, though not their accuracy, lexical diversity, and lexical density. Anticipating an upcoming discussion, these results point to the slow, piecemeal, and skill-specific nature of proficiency development.

Recommendations:

1. Moving forward, more studies along the lines of Bowles and Bello-Uriarte (2019) and Bello-Uriarte's contribution, chapter 3 in this volume, are needed to understand the development of broad-based proficiency, alongside the development of narrow-based proficiency. Ideally, such studies should test the efficacy of HL-specific instructional approaches and strategies. Along these lines, it would be important to study the relative efficacy of macro-based (top-down) instructional approaches such as project-based learning as compared to micro-based (bottom-up) approaches. Macro-based approaches are characterized by the use of real-world language at the onset of instruction, with grammar taking a supporting role as needed to engage with authentic language. On the other hand, micro-based approaches put their initial focus on grammar and vocabulary and progress toward the use of authentic materials to provide practice with the focus structures and vocabulary (Carreira 2016). Notably, both approaches are compatible with explicit as well as implicit grammar instruction. The difference

between them resides on when that instruction takes place, as well as what drives the selection of instructional points. The advantage of macro-based approaches over micro-based ones has been argued to be that the former are more engaging to HL learners and more effective at preparing them to make real-world language use. This claim should be subjected to rigorous testing.

Another clear avenue for future research is community-based learning and, more generally, experiential learning. These approaches have been shown to support outcomes associated with the development of broad-based proficiency, including the use of strategies that facilitate communication across language boundaries and in the community context (DuBord and Kimball 2016; Lowther Pereira 2016; MacGregor-Mendoza and Moreno 2016), enhanced awareness of what constitutes socially appropriate communication, and an increased familiarity with the formal registers (Martínez and Schwartz 2012; Thompson 2013). Future research should elucidate the development of the features of narrow-based proficiency in community-based learning, for example, grammatical accuracy with different structures, as well as vocabulary.

2. For teachers and learners, the present discussion serves as a reminder that (a) achieving native levels of grammatical control is not a realistic or necessary requirement for effective communication, even at the highest levels of proficiency, and (b) many skills and areas of knowledge factor into developing proficiency for real-world language use. Effective HL teaching and learning attends to all of these skills and areas of knowledge.

## Instruction, Proficiency, and Assessment

Calibrating instruction to students' proficiency level is key to designing instruction that is within students' Zone of Proximal Development (ZPD). The ZPD is "the distance between the actual developmental level as determined by independent problem solving and the level of potential development as determined through problem-solving under adult guidance, or in collaboration with more capable peers" (Vygotsky 1978, 86). Put differently, the ZPD refers to knowledge that a learner is close to mastering with targeted assistance. Knowledge that is beyond the learners' ZPD will not be grasped and will likely prove frustrating to students. In terms of ACTFL's conceptual framework, learners' actual development level connects to the notion of proficiency, while their level of potential development connects to performance, which is one or more sublevels above proficiency.

At the low end of the proficiency scale, the students in Beaudrie and Holmes's study (chapter 2) are described as receptive bilinguals, that is, HL learners with the "ability to understand their heritage language when spoken to but comparative difficulty speaking, reading, and writing it" (Beaudrie and Holmes, 42). Fittingly, the structure of focus of this study was fairly basic, namely, the morphological markers of the preterit and imperfect, rather than the considerably more challenging semantic/syntactic distinctions between these two forms. Associated with the Advanced level, the latter would likely be outside the ZPD of receptive bilinguals, particularly where writing—a weak skill for HL learners—is concerned.

Also associated with the Advanced level is the present subjunctive (Gudmestad 2018; National Council of State Supervisors for Language–American Council on the Teaching of Foreign Languages n.d.). This is the structural focus of Julio Torres's study (chapter 1). Torres describes his students as being at the Intermediate level (citing an average score of 32.5 in a modified version of the Diploma de Español como Lengua Extranjera [DELE] exam), which suggests that present subjunctive is within their ZPD; that is to say, it is accessible with instructional assistance. Torres's findings bear this out, as the students made considerable gains in both oral and written production. However, the effect for oral production was greater than for written production, especially in the posttests. Torres posits that this difference may relate to the fact that HL learners have an advantage for oral production. This is another way of saying that HL learners' oral proficiency is usually higher than their written proficiency. Now, since structural accuracy increases with proficiency, it follows that with HL learners the oral domain may be more primed for accuracy gains than the written domain.

But it may be more complicated than that, as the oral modality includes both listening and speaking and the written modality, reading and writing. Typically with HL learners, listening is stronger than speaking and reading is stronger than writing. Taking this into consideration, it is possible that HL learners' reading gains—for example, their ability to interpret the subjunctive in written texts—may outpace their ability to use this structure when writing. Thus, the skills within a modality may show different accuracy gains. It is also possible for differences to cut across modalities. For example, accuracy gains in reading may outpace those in speaking, particularly with formal language. Crucially for future research, it may be that skill-specific proficiency offers a more refined version of the hypothesis that modality mediates outcomes.

Bello-Uriarte (chapter 3) references his subjects' proficiency level both in terms of self-ratings and the course they are enrolled in, the first of a two-course sequence for Spanish bilinguals with an emphasis on writing. Predictably, learners rated writing in Spanish as their weakest skill (1.79 out of 4), followed by writing in English, which was notably higher at 3.55 out of 4. Although the main focus of the course was building on the learners' preexisting knowledge and speaking ability to develop academic writing skill, there were periodic lessons on grammatical structures that pose difficulty for SHL learners, including periphrasis with 'a' and the distinction between gerunds and infinitives, particularly in subject position. With respect to broad-based proficiency, results showed notable gains in fluency, complexity, and lexical sophistication over the course of the semester, suggesting that writing became quicker through practice and that participants used more sophisticated vocabulary, likely as a result of extensive reading and models they were exposed to. They also began to integrate more complex, rather than compound, sentences into their writing. Regarding the specific grammatical targets, learners were significantly more accurate after the course with verbal periphrasis, suggesting that this was within students' ZPD because it was part of their internal grammar. For gerunds and infinitives, trends could not be verified through statistical analyses because there were not enough students using the forms across both of their essays to enable such comparisons. This is a drawback of the open-ended essay prompt task used in the study because it gives writers flexibility to use any number of structures, rather than forcing or prompting them to use particular ones. Nevertheless, since the task was embedded in the normal course activities, it was also more germane than having a separate controlled production task that elicited gerunds and infinitives. The open-ended essay was also more in line with a broad-based view of proficiency.

Finally, the studies by Celia Chomón Zamora (chapter 4) and Sara Fernández Cuenca and Melissa A. Bowles (chapter 5) focus on structures associated with the Advanced-High and especially the Superior level, namely, contrary-to-fact conditional sentences using the imperfect and pluperfect subjunctive and the imperfect subjunctive in adjectival clauses. Despite this commonality, the studies differ in their description of their subjects' proficiency. Specifically, while both studies reference proficiency self-ratings in the four skills, they use a different rating scale. In addition, Chomón Zamora references her subjects' DELE scores, but Fernández and Bowles do not. The lack of a common framework for describing proficiency makes it difficult to compare the two studies. This drawback is not limited to these studies, but speaks to a more pervasive problem with the research on instructed heritage language acquisition.

With an average DELE score of 33.21, Chomón Zamora's students are quite similar to Torres's students, who averaged 32.5 on the same test. This similarity raises the question of whether the selected structures—contrary-to-fact conditional sentences—were within the grasp of this population. Chomón Zamora's description of these structures speaks to its inherent complexity and low frequency, which are features associated with the structures at the ACTFL Superior level.

> These types of conditional sentences are considered to be highly complex and problematic structures for both native speakers and L2 learners of Spanish (e.g., Collentine 2003; López Ornat 1994). They are not very widely used in Spanish and are usually not taught in the first couple of years of language study (Rosa and Leow 2004). Moreover, the subjunctive morphemes are not as salient as other structures, and learners find that native speakers are able to comprehend them despite not producing the subjunctive correctly. (87)

The think-alouds indicate that both HL and L2 learners experienced some stress and frustration with the target structures, and in one case an HL learner was driven to criticize their own Spanish. This is not surprising given the intrinsic difficulty of the material. What is surprising about the think-alouds and of great value to teachers is what they reveal in terms of strategies employed by learners to access material that is well beyond their ZPD. Notably, for HL learners, intuition and background knowledge prove useful for tackling challenging points of grammar and lead to deeper processing and more durable learning gains.

The topic of knowledge sources used by HL learners also comes up in Bowles and Fernández Cuenca's chapter, though this is not its main focus. In reference to this topic, the authors raise the possibility that HL learners tap into different sources of knowledge, depending on the task before them and the response modality. One student's comment in the explicit instruction group is telling in this regard: "I used the rule for the written part, and more intuition for speaking" (117). Why does this matter? Because it once again underscores the role of modality (and perhaps the four skills) in mediating instructed acquisition. Specifically, it suggests that this student's command of the target structure is closer to being part of their grammatical system (and hence accessible through intuition) in the oral language than in the written language.

The actual focus of Bowles and Fernández Cuenca's study—the relative merits of explicit and implicit instruction—is discussed following the recommendations for this section.

Recommendations:

1. Given the central role of modality in the findings of the above studies, future research should reference students' proficiency level in both modalities—and perhaps even in each of the four skills (listening, speaking, reading, and writing)—rather than giving a unitary measure of overall proficiency. Furthermore, researchers should adopt a common framework for describing proficiency, as this would facilitate comparisons across studies as well as render it easier to discern the role that

proficiency plays in the attainment of grammatical accuracy as well as the development of broad-based proficiency.

2. For educators, an important take-home lesson is that with HL learners, accuracy gains are likely to be more pronounced and longer lasting in the oral language than in the written language. Teachers should adjust their expectations and assessment practices accordingly. Furthermore, as Julio Torres explains, more instructional time and effort should be allocated to writing, as compared to speaking, and HL learners should be assessed orally, as well as in writing. It should be noted, however, that in large language classes, conducting oral assessment may prove impractical.

   The From-to Principles of language teaching (table A.1) can be helpful for designing scaffolding activities for the written modality. Put forward by Olga Kagan (2011) and further elaborated in Maria Carreira (2016) and Carreira and Claire Hitchins Chik (2018), the From-to Principles are designed to leverage HL learners' strengths to address their knowledge gaps. The five principles are represented in table A.1, with HL learners' strengths on the left and their areas of need on the right. Connecting the language modalities and skills, the first principle suggests tapping into HL students' listening skills to develop reading skills. Similarly, the second principle calls for using speaking abilities as a springboard for developing writing skills (see Chevalier 2004; Jegerski and Ponti 2014).

3. A second take-home lesson for teachers is that accuracy gains will likely be more robust with the kind of early-acquired structures that HL learners know best, as compared to the late-acquired structures that are vulnerable to attrition or incomplete acquisition. A continuum of difficulty emerges with early-acquired structures in oral tasks that use informal language being most primed for accuracy gains. At the other end of the continuum, late-acquired structures in the written modality using formal language will be least primed for accuracy gains. In terms of the four skills, it is likely that early-acquired structures in listening tasks that use informal language will be most primed for accuracy gains,

**TABLE A.1.** From-To Principles of Language Teaching

| | From | | To |
|---|---|---|---|
| 1. | Aural | → | Reading |
| 2. | Spoken | → | Written |
| 3. | Home-based register | → | General/academic registers |
| 4. | Everyday "real-life" activities | → | In-class activities |
| 5. | Motivation and identity | → | Content |

while late-acquired structures in formal, written language will be the least primed. Future research should test the validity of this proposal.

4. A particularly important lesson for both teachers and HL learners is that intuitions and background knowledge are a valuable resource when it comes to supporting learning, engagement, and self-correction. As seen in Chomón Zamora's chapter, tutorial questions such as "How does this sound to you?" or "Does this remind you of anything that you have heard before?" can help students to tap into these resources. Also relevant in this regard are From-to Principles 3, 4, and 5, which call for designing activities that build on HL learners' home-based register, life experiences and practices, and motivations. Such activities are likely to encourage learners to tap into their background knowledge to access the material being taught. Ultimately, to maximize outcomes, HL learners should learn to make strategic use of all knowledge sources available to them, metalinguistic as well as nonmetalinguistic, as needed for different tasks.
5. The use of tutorial questions connects to the concept of dynamic assessment (DA). This interactive approach to testing is designed to determine how much support or instruction a learner will need to acquire a particular skill. Rooted in Lev Vygotsky's sociocultural theory, DA provides information on the learner's ZPD, or potential for growth. Accordingly, learners are assessed with a view toward determining whether they need minimal, moderate, or maximum support, where each of these classifications is associated with different instructional strategies (Lidz 1991). In contrast with DA, the studies in this volume all employ static assessment, in that they hold constant the type and amount of instruction offered to all learners. Both approaches have their place in research, as well as in teaching, but given the range of proficiency profiles typically represented in an HL classroom, DA stands to be particularly useful for placement purposes, by virtue of its ability to group together students with similar ZPDs, or learning potential. In this regard, it is important to note that two learners who perform poorly with respect to a grammatical structure in a static assessment may actually have very different learning potentials—for one such learner, a limited amount of instruction may suffice to improve accuracy, while for the other extensive instruction and practice may be required. Accordingly, as Marta Antón (2009) argues, "Dynamic assessment allows for a deeper and richer description of learners' actual and emergent abilities, which enables programs to devise individualized instructional plans attuned to learners' needs" (579).

## The Place of Explicit and Implicit Instruction in HL Teaching and Learning

Two studies in part I compared the effectiveness of explicit and implicit instruction of grammar, namely, Beaudrie and Holmes (chapter 2) and Bowles and Fernández Cuenca (chapter 5). In both cases, explicit instruction proved superior in terms of supporting greater and longer-lasting accuracy gains. These findings indicate that explicit grammar instruction has an important role to play in HL teaching and learning. However, as both studies point out, this does not mean that grammar should be the primary focus of instruction but rather that "it should be included in small doses, where needed" (Bowles and Fernández Cuenca, chapter 5, 118).

The findings of these two studies should also not be taken to mean implicit instruction has no place in the HL classroom. Indeed, Bowles and Fernández Cuenca's study indicates that input flood is beneficial for learning grammatical forms, though the gains are not as long lasting as those from explicit instruction. Furthermore, from the point of view of developing broad-based proficiency, it stands to reason that students need input flood in the form of extensive exposure to authentic input where the target structures support real-life functions and are embedded in extended discourse. Taking contrary-to-fact conditional sentences by way of example, using these structures in the real world requires learning the organizational properties of particular text-types as well as their attendant discourse strategies, phrases, vocabulary, and so forth. Educators and learners would be well advised to remember the sheer amount of time and effort associated with this task and, more generally, with progressing to the higher proficiency levels.

Typically, the ACTFL Advanced-low level is associated with undergraduate language majors, and it is the minimum level recommended for K–12 teacher licensure. Heritage speakers with extensive contact with the target language can function at the Advanced-mid level, while learners with graduate degrees in a language and extensive educational experience in the target environment reach the Advanced-high level. For its part, the Superior level is associated with "educated native speakers and educated language learners with extended professional and/or educational experience in the target language environment" (American Council on the Teaching of Foreign Languages n.d.). University language professors, court interpreters, and foreign area officers operate at this level of proficiency (American Council on the Teaching of Foreign Languages n.d.).

While classroom-based learning alone is not likely to get students to the highest levels of proficiency, effective instructional practices can support the development of particular competencies associated with such levels. To this end, Beaudrie and Holmes's study indicates that Computer Assisted Language Learning (CALL) technology can be an effective tool for developing grammatical accuracy. As the authors point out, when used as the online piece in a hybrid course, CALL can free up class time to focus on higher-order tasks, such as writing. This aligns with a previously discussed recommendation by Torres: allocating more instructional time to writing. CALL can also play an important role in the classroom. For example, it can provide meaningful work to some students while the instructor meets with other students. This use of technology speaks to what is arguably its most important contribution to HL teaching: its potential to differentiate instruction.

## Recommendations

1. Research is needed on the relative effectiveness of explicit and implicit instruction for different components of broad-based proficiency as well as for different proficiency levels. It is conceivable, for example, that the ability to write a research paper and make a class presentation in advanced content courses (e.g., literature, linguistics, culture) is best developed through extensive exposure to authentic models of each of these products and focused attention on certain features. On the other hand, for structures that are "already part of students' grammatical system," implicit instruction may suffice.
2. Explicit instruction (e.g., through focus on form techniques like the ones in part I) can serve to prime students so that the extensive naturalistic input they receive outside of class in their homes and communities is processed differently. For instance, they might learn about a form in class and subsequently notice it in conversation, which could reinforce what they learned in the classroom and help them create new connections in the real world. In light of this process, fostering learner attitudes and practices that maximize exposure to Spanish and training students to apply that exposure to their learning advantage should be a priority of HL pedagogy. In connection with this idea, teachers and learners would do well to remember the sheer amount of time and extent of exposure needed to reach the higher levels of proficiency. While some instructional practices will undoubtedly prove more useful than others in this regard, progress will likely take a significant amount of time and exposure. Furthermore, as Bowles and Bello-Uriarte's study (chapter 3) suggests, the skills associated with a given level of proficiency are likely to develop in a piecemeal fashion, rather than all at once. Future research should elucidate the stages of acquisition of such skills.

## Part II: Social and Educational Outcomes

> By exerting a traditional narrow focus on language maintenance, to a large degree, we deprioritize the speaker, and in doing so SHL programs and courses may become perpetuators of the same institutional structures that have kept our students in positions of subordination. (Josh Prada and Diego Pascual y Cabo, 183)

Inherent in the above remark is one of the main arguments for studying social and educational outcomes, namely, that HL instruction should be, above all, about serving the needs of students. To this end, it is important to put the speaker—or more precisely, as I see it, the *learner*—at the center of the teaching and learning enterprise. My preference for the term "learner" over "speaker," is intended to spotlight the importance of attending to instructional outcomes that go beyond those strictly associated with speaking Spanish and that connect to the broader goal of supporting Latinos' personal and academic development.

Chapter 6, by Damián Vergara Wilson, explores the linguistic experiences and attitudes of receptive bilinguals in the classroom context and, to a lesser extent, in naturalistic settings. Finding that most of these students had studied Spanish previously (on average, 2.27 years), Vergara Wilson asks why they placed into the beginning level of the SHL program at his university. As a point of reference, two years of high school Spanish typically places second language learners at the Novice-high level (American Council on the Teaching of Foreign Languages n.d.). Given that the students in this study had some degree of proficiency at the onset of instruction, it stands to reason that they should have achieved this level, at the very minimum. So why didn't they? It appears that the students' previous Spanish classes had much to do with this. Emphasizing mechanical activities and rote memorization, these classes did not capitalize on the considerable funds of knowledge of the receptive bilinguals.

As Vergara Wilson explains, capitalizing on this knowledge requires putting the focus on active learning, that is, speaking and engaging with the culture and practices of HL communities. However, using language in authentic settings can prove daunting for receptive bilinguals. This difficulty may explain an intriguing finding of this study, specifically, that a large number of students embraced mechanical learning and memorization. According to Vergara Wilson, this tendency may be due to the fact that mechanical learning is perceived to be less intimidating than active learning. The take-home lesson for teachers is that active learning requires careful attention to issues of affect—self-doubt, anxiety, shyness, and so on—particularly where receptive bilinguals are involved. Adding to the prior discussion on the importance of calibrating grammatical instruction to proficiency level, Vergara Wilson's study shines a light on the importance of also calibrating instruction to students' affective susceptibilities.

Florencia Henshaw's study (chapter 9) focuses on HL and L2 learners' attitudes about working with L2 or HL peers and about their preference for being enrolled in a mixed or heritage-tailored course. Results from a Likert-scale questionnaire reveal that proficiency is again an emerging issue for these students. Whereas L2 learners overall are pleased to work with a peer of lower proficiency (most commonly, another L2 learner) and take an expert or teaching role, HL learners indicate discomfort, preferring to work with a peer of similar proficiency to them, or even a peer of higher proficiency (most commonly, an HL learner). These findings further problematize mixed classrooms, particularly as it pertains to addressing the needs of both populations of learners and providing opportunities for collaborative learning between both learner types.

With this in mind, Carreira (2016) offers an instructional protocol that makes use of two grouping strategies: homogeneous groups (i.e., HL-learner only and L2-learner only groups) to attend to the needs of each population, and mixed groups for collaborative learning. Among other functions, homogeneous groups provide HL learners the opportunity to discuss issues of relevance, for example, those involving their lived experiences with their home language and culture. For L2 learners, this grouping configuration can help prepare them for activities where they tend to feel at a disadvantage relative to HL learners, such as participating in class discussions. Mixed groups engage learners in activities that leverage the complementary strengths and needs of both types of learners (see Henshaw 2015 and Carreira 2016). The findings of the studies in part I point to additional uses for homogenous groups, for example, to give HL learners extra practice using particular structures when writing and, with L2 learners, to provide practice using the same structures when speaking.

Another important finding of Henshaw's study is that HL learners' preferences for a mixed or a heritage-tailored course are strongly affected by their past experiences. HL learners who have had the opportunity to be in a heritage-tailored course have a significant preference for that environment, whereas HL learners who have only been in mixed classes do not show such a preference. Crucially, although HL learners reap benefits from being in tailored courses, they are content in mixed courses if it is all they have known. These findings offer a cautionary tale for departments on the use of students' preferences for deciding on whether to offer HL-tailored classes and other high-stakes curricular decisions.

## Recommendations

1. As noted in the literature, there is a need to train teachers on the principles and practices of HL teaching (Beaudrie, Ducar, and Potowski 2014). In this regard, the above studies identify receptive bilinguals and the mixed classroom context as areas of high priority. Formative assessment, which gives teachers information on students' needs and learning trajectories, as well as differentiated instruction, particularly strategies that support flexible grouping, also emerge as important areas of training. Hand in hand with improving teacher preparation is the critical need for pedagogical materials specialized for receptive bilinguals, as well as for the mixed context. Without such materials, it is doubtful that significant improvements in teaching will ensue.
2. To date, most research on institutional practices has focused on documenting the availability of HL classes (see Beaudrie 2012; Carreira 2017). Moving forward, more studies along the lines of Vergara Wilson and Henshaw as well as classroom-based observational studies, are needed to take stock of actual instructional and assessment practices at all levels of instruction and identify areas where improvement is needed.
4. Vergara Wilson's question about his students' apparent lack of progress in earlier courses points to the need for research on SHL learners' learning gains as a function of instructional time. In effect, this is what Bello-Uriarte's study (chapter 3) does for writing and Claudia Holguín Mendoza's study (discussed next) does for the development of critical language awareness. This line of research is the foundation for curricula and assessments based on realistic expectations.
5. Concerning receptive bilinguals, future studies of instructional outcomes should pay particular attention to the modes of communication: (1) the interpretive mode, which involves understanding spoken or written language; (2) the interpersonal mode, which involves interacting with an interlocutor orally or in writing; and (3) the presentational mode, which involves the one-way presentation of information to listeners or readers. A reasonable hypothesis is that receptive bilinguals' learning gains in the interpretive mode may outpace those of the other two modes.

## Preparing Students to Navigate the Real World

The studies by Holguín Mendoza (chapter 7) and Parada and Pascual y Cabo (chapter 8) focus on how instruction prepares SHL learners to navigate the real world. In Holguín Mendoza's case, the goal of such preparation is to "offer students access to every possible strategy that better equips them to make their own, well-informed decisions in their professional and personal lives" (163).

Drawing on critical pedagogies, the protocol outlined by Holguín Mendoza involves increasing students' awareness of their HL community's language use and the power structures contributing to linguistic hierarchies. This approach proved fruitful at changing students' attitudes for the better and developing their abilities to tap into their sociolinguistic resources. However, this change did not materialize overnight, or even over the course of ten weeks. Attitudes, especially deeply ingrained ones, take a long time to change.

Interestingly, Holguín Mendoza does note a number of small changes in the students by the end of the first quarter of instruction. Specifically, some students were able to better evaluate and articulate their abilities and were more positive about their bilingualism. This change raises the possibility that there might be stages in the development of critical language awareness akin to those proposed by Agnes He (2006) for identity. Future research along these lines is needed to elucidate this point. Also needed is research on teachers' own development of critical language awareness. Like learners, they are likely to need extensive training in this area before they can change their attitudes and practices for the better.

A particularly noteworthy aspect of this study was its inclusion of English pronunciations associated with US Latino communities (e.g., "picsa" and "pecsi") in the training and subsequent assessment of the participants. For educators and researchers, this variation serves as a reminder that HL learners navigate two languages and cultures in their daily lives. To make well-informed decisions surrounding their use of language, Latino students need critical language awareness of English, as well as of Spanish.

Finally, turning to Josh Prada and Diego Pascual y Cabo, this study, asks how postsecondary SHL education can contribute to improving educational outcomes. The authors observe that SHL education is particularly well suited to this task by virtue of its emphasis on developing students' linguistic and cultural self-esteem and responding to their socioaffective needs, among other areas of emphasis. Supporting this proposition, the authors found that the retention rates of Latino students who took at least one SHL class exceeded those of the Latino population in the College of Liberal Arts at their university. Delving further into this issue through student interviews, three features of SHL classes emerged as being particularly important in this regard: (1) the opportunities afforded to connect with other Latinos with similar experiences and needs, (2) the opportunity to advance career goals by developing professional-level Spanish, and (3) having a place where Latino experiences are "reflected and recognized" (181). Revisiting an earlier discussion, these findings bring to light another strength of community-based learning: its potential to contribute to higher Latino retention and graduation rates by providing opportunities to advance career goals and connect with other HL speakers in culturally relevant settings.

The significance of research on academic outcomes of SHL instruction cannot be overstated. For one, it sends a message to Latino students and families, as well as society at large, that the Spanish language and Latino cultures are vectors for success. For another, it puts the work of Spanish departments at the center of one of the most important tasks facing the American education system: improving Latino educational outcomes and their labor-force preparation. Spanish departments in Hispanic Serving Institutions, in particular, should take note of what this means in terms of raising their profile in their institutions of learning, as well as in the way of funding opportunities from the US Department of Education to increase and improve their course offerings.

Despite these and other potential benefits of SHL learning, the research literature rarely, if ever, makes explicit mention of Latinos' broader educational needs, let alone considers how to address these needs. In large part, this situation stems from the fact that SHL practitioners typically see their role as being first and foremost about advancing Spanish language learning, rather than advancing the general academic well-being of Latino students. While understandable, this situation leads to a significant opportunity cost for Latino students and Spanish departments.

Returning to the words by Prada and Pascual y Cabo about the importance of prioritizing the speaker (or learner), for this final set of recommendations I will draw on my own experiences as an SHL learner.

## Recommendations

Like many Latino students, I struggled with feelings of insecurity about my English throughout most of my years in school. In large part, this is because I arrived in the United States at age twelve, which meant that I had a steep learning curve to acquire academic English. Having teachers that despite being well intentioned were not prepared to help students like me didn't help either, and neither did the diminishing effects of comparing myself and being compared to my English-speaking peers.

This experience as well as my nearly thirty years teaching SHL learners has alerted me to the importance of addressing my students' linguistic and affective needs with respect to English. Accordingly, in my teaching I draw frequent comparisons between English and Spanish. For example, when I teach a transitional term such as "sin embargo," I also review its English equivalent and provide practice with both terms. I also provide opportunities for my students to discuss their English-learning experiences and attendant feelings, as well as how they can compensate for gaps in their knowledge. All of these elements are part of an overarching effort to expand my students' total linguistic repertoire and to attend to them as bilingual and bicultural individuals, and not just as Spanish speakers.

Another childhood experience that informs my teaching relates to my parents' inability to help me with school matters. This was not because they were uncaring or uneducated but because they had little understanding of the practices of the American system of education and also because they were overwhelmed by the experience of being in a new land. Thus, from filling out school forms, to preparing class presentations, to writing college application essays, I was on my own. This is a common experience of many Latino students, which results in missed opportunities. Accordingly, in Carreira (2007), I argue that a central goal of SHL education should be to help students navigate the American school system. At the high school level, for example, this might involve having students work on their college application letters in Spanish, as a way to prepare them for the actual task in English. In my own teaching at the college level, I engage students in writing a professional profile and curriculum vitae in Spanish. In so doing, they reflect on their linguistic strengths and needs vis-à-vis their life goals and also consider how to best present themselves to potential employers.

This type of guidance, targeted to my status as an immigrant and a Spanish speaker, would have greatly facilitated my academic trajectory and personal development during my formative years. Although this guidance could have come from any number of sources, my preference would have been for it to come from my Spanish instructors by virtue of the cultural connection that I felt with them and their specialized knowledge of my linguistic background.

## Final Thoughts

Reflecting on the notion of outcomes, I have been struck—if not overwhelmed at times—by its sheer complexity, in particular, its relationship to proficiency; and to modality, assessment, and different types of instruction and knowledge (implicit and explicit); as well as to nonlinguistic factors. In due time, the emerging field of instructed heritage language acquisition will surely unravel these and other complexities, with highly positive consequences for teaching and learning. The studies in this volume provide a strong foundation toward this end.

For now, what does this all mean for teaching? Below are my five big takeaways from the studies in this volume:

1. *Proficiency level puts a ceiling on performance.* To be within students' reach, the topics of instruction have to be just the right level of challenging. Topics that are at students' actual level of proficiency will not be challenging enough to maximize learning, while those that are too far above their proficiency level will prove too challenging. However, this predisposition does not mean that teachers should refrain from exposing lower proficiency students to material associated with the higher proficiency levels but rather that they should adjust their expectations

as to learners' performance (i.e., what they expect learners to do with the material). In addition, they should pay careful attention to affective issues, especially when presenting difficult material.

2. *Proficiency is a multifaceted construct.* As a general rule, learners' proficiency level—that is, what they can do spontaneously with language—varies by modality (oral vs. written language), the four skills (listening, speaking, reading, and writing), and the three modes of communication (interpretive, interpersonal, presentational). Because HL learners' oral proficiency typically exceeds their written proficiency, it follows they will perform better (i.e., be more accurate) in oral tasks than in written ones. Although not investigated by the studies in this volume, proficiency in the four skills (listening, speaking, reading, and writing) and the three modes of communication (interpretive, interpersonal, and presentational) is likely to have a similar effect on performance.
3. *Students' intuitions and life experiences can support grammatical learning.* Curricula that reflect HL learners' life experiences have long been understood to be essential to promoting engagement and addressing learners' socioaffective needs. What has not been fully appreciated until this volume is that learners' intuitions and background experiences can also support deeper processing and more durable learning gains in the area of grammar. Explicit instruction can further support these sources of knowledge as well as compensate for knowledge gaps where intuition may fail HL learners.
4. *Attitudes, practices, and proficiency are slow to develop.* This tendency makes it all the more important for Spanish departments to retain HL learners for as long as possible—at minimum, beyond one course. Offering courses that are engaging, meaningful, and valuable for HL learners, and that are calibrated to their proficiency level, is essential in this regard. It is also important to remember that implicit learning takes longer than explicit learning.
5. *It's not just about seat time; past experiences in Spanish courses matter.* Language departments often rely on students' course history for placement decisions as well as for curriculum design. However, formal instruction does not always result in proficiency gains, especially when it consists of rote learning and memorization. Accordingly, student questionnaires aimed at gathering background information that bears on proficiency should inquire as to the methods and activities of prior courses. This information, combined with the use of DA, should inform HL instruction, placement, and syllabus design.
6. *Above all, the learner matters.* Taken together, the studies in this volume underscore the importance of listening to learners' voices. From enhancing HL learners' grammatical learning, to equipping them to

make well-informed linguistic decisions, to supporting their academic and personal development, these voices prove essential to designing effective instructional approaches.

To conclude, calling on SHL specialists to direct their attention to the relationship between teaching and learning, the studies in this volume provide essential starting points for creating the conceptual framework for such explorations.

## References

American Council on the Teaching of Foreign Languages. n.d. "Oral Proficiency Levels in the Workplace." Accessed June 17, 2021. https://www.actfl.org/sites/default/files/pdfs/TLE_pdf/OralProficiencyWorkplacePoster.pdf.

———. 2012. "ACTFL Proficiency Guidelines 2012." https://www.actfl.org/publications/guidelines-and-manuals/actfl-proficiency-guidelines-2012.

Antón, Marta. 2009. "Dynamic Assessment of Advanced Second Language Learners." *Foreign Language Annals* 42(3): 576–98.

Beaudrie, Sara. 2012. "Research on University-Based Spanish Heritage Language Programs in the United States: The Current State of Affairs." In *Spanish as a Heritage Language in the United States: The State of the Field*, edited by Sara Beaudrie and Marta Fairclough, 203–21. Washington, DC: Georgetown University Press.

Beaudrie, Sara, Cynthia Ducar, and Kim Potowski. 2014. *Heritage Language Teaching: Research and Practice*. New York: McGraw-Hill Education.

Bowles, Melissa A., and Adrián Bello-Uriarte. 2019. "What Impact Does Heritage Language Instruction Have on Spanish Heritage Learners' Writing?" In *Evidence-Based Second Language Pedagogy: A Collection of Instructed Second Language Acquisition Studies*, edited by Masatoshi Sato and Shawn Loewen, 219–39. New York: Routledge.

Carreira, Maria. 2007. "Spanish-For-Native-Speaker Matters: Narrowing the Latino Achievement Gap through Spanish Language Instruction." *Heritage Language Journal* 5, no. 1 (Summer): 147–71.

———. 2016. "Approaches and Strategies for Teaching Heritage Language Learners: Focus on Mixed Classes." In *Advances in Spanish as a Heritage Language*, edited by Diego Pascual y Cabo, 159–76. Amsterdam: John Benjamins.

———. 2017. "The State of Institutionalization of Heritage Languages in Postsecondary Language Departments in the United States." In *The Routledge Handbook of Heritage Language Education: From Innovation to Program Building*, edited by Olga E. Kagan, Maria M. Carreira, and Claire Hitchins Chik, 347–62. New York: Routledge.

Carreira, Maria, and Claire Hitchins Chik. 2018. "Making the Case for Heritage Language Instruction: A Guide to Meeting the Needs of Learners in the Classroom and Beyond." In *Connecting across Languages and Cultures: A Heritage Language Festschrift in Honor of Olga E. Kagan*, edited by Susan Bauckus and Susan Kresin, n.p. Bloomington, IN: Slavica.

Chevalier, Joan F. 2004. "Heritage Language Literacy: Theory and Practice." *Heritage Language Journal* 2, no. 1 (Fall): 1–19.

DuBord, Elise, and Elizabeth Kimball. 2016. "Cross-Language Community Engagement: Assessing the Strengths of Heritage Learners." *Heritage Language Journal* 13, no. 3 (December): 298–330.

Gudmestad, Aarnes. 2018. "Advanced-Level Mood Distinction." In *The Handbook of Advanced Proficiency in Second Language Acquisition*, edited by Paul A. Malovrh and Alessandro G. Benati, 341–60. New York: Wiley Blackwell.

He, Agnes. 2006. "Toward an Identity Theory of the Development of Chinese as a Heritage Language." *Heritage Language Journal* 4, no. 1 (Fall): 1–28.

Henshaw, Florencia G. 2015. "Learning Outcomes of L2-Heritage Learner Interaction: The Proof Is in the Posttests." *Heritage Language Journal* 12(3): 245–70.

Jegerski, Jill, and Estefanía Ponti. 2014. "Peer Review among Students of Spanish as a Heritage Language: The Effectiveness of a Metalinguistic Literacy Task." *Linguistics and Education* 26 (June): 70–82.

Kagan, Olga. 2011. "Teaching Heritage Language Learners." Paper presented at the 2011 STARTALK/NHLRC Teacher Workshop, Los Angeles, July 18, 2011.

Lidz, Carol S. 1991. *Practitioner's Guide to Dynamic Assessment*. New York: Guilford Press.

Lindholm-Leary, Kathryn. 2014. "Bilingual and Biliteracy Skills in Young Spanish-Speaking Low-SES Children: Impact of Instructional Language and Primary Language Proficiency." *International Journal of Bilingual Education and Bilingualism* 17(2): 144–59.

Lowther Pereira, Kelly. 2016. "New Directions in Heritage Language Pedagogy: Community Service-Learning for Spanish Heritage Speakers." In *Advances in Spanish as a Heritage Language*, edited by Diego Pascual y Cabo, 237–58. Amsterdam: John Benjamins.

MacGregor-Mendoza, Patricia, and Gabriela Moreno. 2016. "Connecting Spanish Heritage Language Students with the Community through Service-Learning." *Heritage Language Journal* 13, no. 3 (December): 405–33.

Martínez, Glenn, and Adam Schwartz. 2012. "Elevating 'Low' Language for High Stakes: A Case for Critical, Community-Based Learning in a Medical Spanish for Heritage Learners Program." *Heritage Language Journal* 9, no. 2 (Summer): 37–49.

National Council of State Supervisors for Language–American Council on the Teaching of Foreign Languages. n.d. "Can Do Statements." Accessed June 17, 2021. https://www.actfl.org/publications/guidelines-and-manuals/ncssfl-actfl-can-do-statements.

Polinsky, Maria. 2018. *Heritage Languages and Their Speakers*. Cambridge, UK: Cambridge University Press.

Potowski, Kim. 2016. "Current Issues in Heritage Language Education." In *Advances in Spanish as a Heritage Language*, edited by Diego Pascual y Cabo, 127–42. Amsterdam: John Benjamins.

Swender, Elvira, Cynthia L. Martin, Mildred Rivera-Martinez, and Olga E. Kagan. 2014. "Exploring Oral Proficiency Profiles of Heritage Speakers of Russian and Spanish." *Foreign Language Annals* 47(3): 423–46.

Thompson, Gregory. 2013. *Intersection of Service and Learning: Research and Practice in the Second Language Classroom*. Charlotte, NC: Information Age Publishing.

Vygotsky, Lev S. 1978. *Mind in Society: The Development of Higher Psychological Processes*. Cambridge, MA: Harvard University Press.

Zyzik, Eve. 2016. "Toward a Prototype Model of the Heritage Language Learner: Understanding Strengths and Needs." In *Innovative Strategies for Heritage Language Teaching: A Practical Guide for the Classroom*, edited by Marta Fairclough and Sara Beaudrie, 19–38. Washington, DC: Georgetown University Press.

# Contributors

**Sara M. Beaudrie** is an associate professor of Spanish linguistics at Arizona State University, where she directs the Spanish Heritage Program. Her research interests include classroom instruction, language program development, critical approaches to heritage pedagogy, and heritage language assessment and literacy development. She is the coeditor of *Spanish as a Heritage Language in the United States: The State of the Field* and *Innovative Strategies for Heritage Language Teaching: A Practical Guide for the Classroom*, published by Georgetown University Press in 2012 and 2016, respectively. She is coauthor of *Heritage Language Pedagogy: Research and Practice* with McGraw-Hill (2014). Her latest book is *Heritage Language Teaching: Critical Language Awareness Perspectives for Research and Pedagogy*, a coedited book with Routledge.

**Adrián Bello-Uriarte** is a lecturer in Spanish at Butler University. He earned his PhD in Spanish linguistics from the University of Illinois at Urbana-Champaign, with a graduate minor in Latina/Latino studies and a concentration in Second Language Acquisition and Teacher Education (SLATE). Prior to coming to Butler University, he taught English as a foreign language in Mexico for more than ten years and Spanish at the University of Illinois at Urbana-Champaign for seven years. His research focuses on how instruction affects heritage and second language learners of Spanish, both in terms of their linguistic knowledge and abilities and in terms of their motivation and self-confidence.

**Melissa A. Bowles** is a professor of Spanish, Linguistics, Second Language Acquisition and Teacher Education (SLATE), and educational psychology at the University of Illinois at Urbana-Champaign. She is also Interim codirector of the National Heritage Language Resource Center. Her research focuses on language testing/assessment, research methods, and instructed second and heritage language acquisition, particularly the ways that instruction differentially affects the two populations.

**Maria M. Carreira** is an Emerita professor of Spanish at California State University, Long Beach, and the cofounder and Emerita codirector of the National Heritage Language Resource Center at UCLA. She is a coauthor of six Spanish language textbooks and of *Voces: Latino Students on Life in the United States*

(Praeger, 2014) in addition to being coeditor of *The Routledge Handbook of Heritage Language Education: From Innovation to Program Building* (Routledge, 2017). She also serves as a board member of ACTFL and associate editor of *Hispania.*

**Celia Chomón Zamora** was born in Venezuela and raised in Miami, Florida. She has had a passion for languages and heritage speakers since she was young, which is what led her to pursue her doctoral degree in Spanish Applied Linguistics from Georgetown University, where she was awarded the Harold N. Glassman Distinguished Dissertation Award in the social sciences. She taught various languages in the K–20 setting for over a decade and has held multiple leadership roles in the education field. She is now the director of Professional Learning and Certification at ACTFL.

**Sara Fernández Cuenca** is an assistant professor of Spanish in the Departments of Spanish and Italian at Wake Forest University, in North Carolina. She earned her PhD at the University of Illinois at Urbana-Champaign with a graduate concentration in Second Language Acquisition and Teacher Education (SLATE). Her research focuses mainly on instructed and heritage language acquisition—with a special interest in mood acquisition—but she has also conducted research on bilingual sentence processing.

**Florencia G. Henshaw** has a PhD in Spanish with a graduate concentration in Second Language Acquisition and Teacher Education (SLATE) from the University of Illinois, Urbana-Champaign, where she is now the director of advanced Spanish. Her research focuses on the extent to which different pedagogical practices and tools may be beneficial to second language and heritage language learners, in terms of not only linguistic gains but also learners' perceptions and attitudes.

**Claudia Holguín Mendoza** is an assistant professor of Spanish linguistics at the University of California, Riverside. She specializes in the sociolinguistics of race in the Mexican borderlands and Greater Mexico as well as critical pedagogies for the teaching of Spanish as a heritage language. Her publications include contributions to *Identities: Global Studies in Culture and Power,* the *International Journal of Multilingualism,* the *Journal of Hispanic and Lusophone Linguistics,* and the *Journal of Hispanic Higher Education.*

**Bonnie C. Holmes** is an assistant professor of Spanish and applied linguistics at Southern Oregon University (SOU). She received her PhD in second language acquisition and teaching from the University of Arizona. Her research interests include the cognitive underpinnings of receptive bilingualism as well as critical pedagogies in instructed heritage and second language acquisition. At SOU she teaches undergraduate and graduate courses in Spanish language and linguistics, bilingualism, and teacher education in both the World Languages and Master of Arts in Teaching (MAT) programs.

**Diego Pascual y Cabo** is an associate professor of Spanish and linguistics as well as director of the Spanish Heritage Language Program at the University of Florida, where he teaches and researches in the area of heritage speaker bilingualism. Over the past few years, his work on this topic has appeared in several scholarly journals such as *Applied Linguistics, Studies in Second Language Acquisition, Linguistic Approaches to Bilingualism, Heritage Language Journal, Frontiers in Education,* and *Foreign Language Annals* (among others). Diego is the editor-in-chief of the *Journal of Spanish as a Heritage Language.*

**Josh Prada** is an assistant professor of Spanish applied linguistics in the Indiana University School of Liberal Arts at Indiana University-Purdue University Indianapolis (IUPUI). His research is in the field of bilingualism and multilingualism, with particular attention to heritage/community language contexts through critical and interdisciplinary approaches. Josh is an associate editor of the *Journal of Spanish as a Heritage Language* and reviews editor of the *International Journal of Bilingual Education and Bilingualism.*

**Julio Torres** is an associate professor of applied linguistics in the Departments of Spanish and Portuguese and Language Science (courtesy appointment) at the University of California, Irvine. He is also the director of the Spanish Language Program and minor in Spanish/English bilingual education. His research interests include instructed heritage/second language acquisition, bilingualism, cognition, and task-based language learning. He is coeditor of *Aproximaciones al estudio del español como lengua de herencia* with Routledge Press.

**Damián Vergara Wilson** is an associate professor of Hispanic linguistics and directs the Spanish as a Heritage Language program at the University of New Mexico in the Department of Spanish and Portuguese. His research focuses on Spanish/English bilingualism in the US context as analyzed through sociolinguistic, sociological, and usage-based approaches. As such, his work contributes to understanding the population of students taking Spanish as a Heritage Language classes.

# Index

*Figures, notes, and tables are indicated by f, n, and t following the pages.*

www.ingramcontent.com/pod-product-compliance
Lightning Source LLC
LaVergne TN
LVHW050151080826
844660LV00002B/159

*9781647122225*